ARROWS IN THE DARK

Cherry Tree Publishing Co.

ISBN-10: 1508534071
ISBN 13: 978-1508534075

Library of Congress Control Number: 2015902777

Printed in the United States of America

Thanks to:
Greg Gubi, book editor, interior design, & publishing consultant
Rick Barry, final copy editor
Steve Hall Creative, book cover & website designs
Readers of earlier drafts who provided valuable feedback

Special thanks to L. Ron Hubbard for his research into the human mind and spirit, and for his courage to present his findings directly to the populace of a world in which those subjects are largely controlled by vested interests.

ARROWS IN THE DARK

By

Merrell Vannier

CONTENTS

AUTHOR'S NOTE

This is a true story. All the scenes depicted actually happened. The facts and settings are likewise accurate. There are three qualifications to those statements: (1) Some aliases have been used. Those names, and the reason for using them, are indicated in the end notes. Otherwise, all names are real. (2) Dialogue is largely based on memory and may not reflect the exact words spoken. And (3) I have taken literary license to substitute layman's language for Scientology jargon in some places.

At one time I was Scientology's No. 1 spy. My code name was "Ritz." My handler was Scientology spymaster Don Alverzo.

As with any intelligence network, the code of secrecy runs deep. It took the prompting of an editor of my novel *Masters of War*, for which I used the pen name Conrad John, and unrelenting grief over the loss of contact with my daughter, Angie, to convince me to write this story.

The church has a policy of "disconnection," a form of shunning. Members, such as Angie, must cut all ties with anyone who has been declared a "suppressive person" as I was in January 2012, no matter the basis for the declaration, which can be arbitrary. It is Scientology's form of excommunication. After a year without any contact with Angie and her refusal to cash a check sent to her as a Christmas gift, I'd had enough. I decided to publicly condemn the destructive policy.

Speaking out, however, has its own consequences. I expect to be vilified for doing so by the current church leader and persons acting under his direction and control, which may deepen the rift between Angie and me. Therefore, I needed to first tell my story, not about the disconnection, but a far more important one that I'd kept to myself so thoroughly I had begun to discount its significance and historical value. After I began writing it, missing pieces of the tale from an unexpected source fortuitously landed in my e-mail inbox. I knew then I had to publish the story, no matter the consequences. Besides, the situation with Angie couldn't get any worse; she has completely shut me, her mother and her brother out of her life.

The policy of disconnection was initially instituted by L. Ron Hubbard as a common sense expression of a person's right to be rid of someone in their circle who is causing distress or holding them down. In 1968, Hubbard cancelled the policy "as a relief to those suffering family oppression," and announced it to Scientologists in *Ron's Journal 68*, an annual update to staff members throughout the world.

The policy was reinstated in 1982, however. The circumstances surrounding its reinstatement are controversial. Hubbard's name was affixed to the re-established policy at a time when he was still alive (he died in 1986), but isolated from church management. His communication channels into the organization were severely limited, and some of the people around him had hidden agendas and were surreptitiously maneuvering the church into the embattled state it is in now. Whatever the circumstances, Hubbard had it right in 1968: the policy causes family oppression and helps create in the general public a disdain for Scientology. The policy should be forever abolished.

The Church of Scientology will never enter the mainstream of society with its current controlling management style and repressive policies. Such practices do not align with the basic tenets of the religion of Scientology, which teach effective communication, honesty, tolerance and strong family values. Thus, opposing messages are being sent by the church – some attractive, others repugnant.

The church's public position – that disconnection is voluntary, by choice of its members – is a blatant lie. Every

Scientologist knows this. Serious consequences exist for any member who does not completely shun persons who have been *declared*. A member who refuses to do so can then be labeled "a suppressive person" as well and likewise be expelled from the church and shunned. So the decision to disconnect is only voluntary in the sense that a person "voluntarily" decides to hand over his wallet to a man who holds a gun to his head.

We live in the Information Age. When people hear of a product or service, or of a person or a business, or of any organization, one of the first things they do is search the Internet. Secret policies, practices and histories are no longer easily concealed. The best and only viable policy is transparency. The Church of Scientology, in accordance with the tenets of the religion of Scientology, should be in the forefront of a move toward transparency, not lagging behind, attacking anyone who dares to reveal or attempts to reform its policies and practices.

This book is a plea for rational reforms in the organization's structure from one-man rule to a system with multiple checks and balances as called for by its founder, and the reuniting of my family and all the other families torn apart by the oppressive policy of disconnection.

FOREWORD

This is a short primer on the subjects of Scientology and its organizations. It is designed to assist readers who know nothing about them. Some pre-publication readers who knew little or nothing about Scientology did just fine with the book; a couple of others suggested I provide further assistance.

The first thing to know about Scientology is that it started with the book *Dianetics: The Modern Science of Mental Health* by L. Ron Hubbard. Published in 1950, it became an instant best-seller. The word "Dianetics" was derived by Hubbard from the Greek words, *dia* (through) and *nous* (mind), and is described as a science of the mind. One of its two most significant principles was the existence of the "reactive mind." This mind, according to Hubbard, is always conscious – in contrast with Freud's "unconscious mind"– even during periods of unconsciousness when the "analytical mind" is shut down. The information stored in the reactive mind during periods of unconsciousness due to shock, drugs, injury or illness can later be re-stimulated. The reactive mind can then overtake the analytical mind to some degree and cause a person to behave irrationally in response to reactivated information, giving it command authority over the individual who does not recognize the source of this irrational behavior.

The other major revelation was a technique to reach and erase the information stored in the reactive mind that could be learned and applied by ordinary individuals. In one-on-one sessions an "auditor" (one who listens; the Dianetics technician) guides an individual to locate and re-live the moments of pain (or high emotion) and unconsciousness and thereby reduces and eliminates the command authority of this stored information. The goal of these sessions is to restore the individual to complete control over his behavior, increase his IQ, and bolster rationality, well-being and level of happiness.

The book caused a major sensation. Centers for the study and practice of the new mental therapy sprang up across the country. And with successes came scrutiny from the medical and psychiatric establishment, which launched a campaign to destroy Dianetics and discredit its founder. Hubbard, after all, they pointed out, was a science fiction writer who held no degrees or licenses to practice mental health treatment of any kind. Lay practitioners of Dianetics, who were likewise not licensed as mental health therapists, were cited for the unlawful practice of medicine, and in some cases were arrested. Their only choice was to either refrain from using the techniques or do so without charging fees for their services. The organization that had begun to form around the movement collapsed.

Meanwhile, Hubbard continued his research. While auditing subjects using Dianetics techniques he discovered, over and over again, that many of these subjects made contact with moments of unconsciousness and distress that took place prior to their births, in past lives. This led to the isolation of the *spirit*, which is distinct from the mind or body, and to the development of methods to separate the spirit from the body while allowing the subject to retain control of his body. This advanced knowledge and methodology was called "scientology." That word was derived from *Scio* (knowledge) and *-ology* (the study of). Its stated goal was total freedom for the person, a spiritual being, who passed from body to body, life to life.

In *Scientology: The Fundamentals of Thought* (1956), Hubbard wrote, "... as studies have gone forward, it has become more and more apparent that the senior activity of life is that of the *thetan* [spirit], and that in the absence of the *thetan*, no further life exists."

One solution to the organizational problem involving the practice of Dianetics, and perhaps the only viable solution, was to form a religion. In the United States, and in most civilized nations, religious activity is outside the regulatory authority of government agencies. The evolution of Dianetics into Scientology provided the basis for that solution. Because Scientology dealt with the spiritual nature and salvation of mankind it *could* be categorized as a religion. More accurately, it is an applied religious philosophy. *Applied* because it has a methodology rather than a faith; the principles of Scientology are applied in one-on-one counseling sessions to increase an individual's spiritual awareness, increase his ability to communicate and get along with others, to improve his conditions in life.

In 1954, a religious organization was established in Washington, D. C. and named the Founding Church of Scientology. Other churches followed. The Church of Scientology of California was later formed in Los Angeles and designated "The Mother Church," from which all other churches are governed. Missions were created as privately owned and operated centers that provided introductory services and encouraged graduates of those services to seek higher level services from churches.

In 1966, in response to increasing legal and public relations issues, Hubbard formed the Guardian's Office (the G.O.) as an autonomous network to handle external matters. Jane Kember was appointed Guardian for her lifetime. Worldwide headquarters of the G.O. were established in East Grinstead, England, near London. Continental Offices were created in the United Kingdom, United States, Europe, Australia, New Zealand, and Africa. The continental offices were further subdivided into local Guardian's offices in every church of Scientology.

In 1967 Hubbard established the Sea Organization (Sea Org) under his direct command. The name was apt. Hubbard had moved his research and operations headquarters, along with his most trusted aides, aboard three ships that continuously sailed, mainly in the Mediterranean Sea, until it moved its operations to a land base in late 1975. Its responsibility was to assist Hubbard in the development of both the religious and administrative technologies for managing Scientology's organizations, which were expanding rapidly.

It is important to stress the different levels of commitment to Scientology. Critics and persons unfamiliar with Scientology tend to lump them together. There are three levels. Parishioners or "Public Scientologists" are people from all walks of life who buy a book, take a course, or receive auditing. "Contracted staff" members are those persons who sign contracts, usually for either two-and-a-half or five years, to work at a mission or church. Being on staff is like having a job in the sense that these persons receive compensation, provide their own room and board, raise families, and so on. Finally, a person can join the Sea Org, which is a lifetime commitment, somewhat like joining the priesthood. Members sign a billion year contract,[1] are provided room and board, work long hours for a mere stipend, and, although they can marry, cannot have children (pursuant to current rules). Contracted Staff and Sea Org members are entitled to receive Scientology training and auditing at no charge, and are even expected to train in the subjects required for them to do their jobs.

Part 1

RITZ: SCIENTOLOGY SPY

Chapter 1

TURF WAR

Justice is a certain rectitude of mind whereby a man does what he ought to do in the circumstances confronting him.

— Thomas Aquinas

A television satellite truck and a small army of men and women armed with video cameras and microphones were camped in front of the St. Louis Church of Scientology. All the attention was centered on church spokesman Fred Rock, who was dressed in a minister's shirt, black with a white clergyman's collar. I worked at the church and was returning from lunch. Other staff members were gathered around the perimeter of the media event. I moseyed over to check it out.

Rock was speaking. I only heard bits and pieces, but enough to catch his drift. He said the Missouri Institute of Psychiatry was conducting drug experiments on patients without their knowledge or consent. He waved a stack of documents, an inch or two thick, and said they were provided by an anonymous MIP employee and proved the existence of the illicit program. He handed out copies, then fielded questions. Yes, it is an ongoing investigation. Yes, we've turned over all our findings to law enforcement and will continue to do so, he said. We're working with other patients' rights groups to protect the rights of mental patients. And so on.

"Pretty cool, eh?" a voice said into my ear when the news conference wrapped up. I turned to see John Spencer.

"Yeah," I said, then began walking toward the church's front door.

"Got a minute?" he asked, motioning me aside. "You went to law school, I heard." "For three semesters. I'm on a one-year leave of absence." He gave me a puzzled look. "I know, I signed a staff contract for two-and-a-half years. I'll figure it out later."

"How would you like to join the Guardian's Office?" he said. "We could use someone with a legal background."

"What's the Guardian's Office?" I asked, and he explained that it was a separate part of the church that handled its external affairs, things like public relations and legal matters, and said they didn't have anyone in the legal bureau yet but wanted to man it soon. Just as Rock passed by he added, "Fred is in the G.O." Rock turned, smiling at the mention of his name, but didn't stop.

I decided that I would return to law school if I wanted anymore to do with law. "No, not really," I said. "I like what I'm doing."

* * *

"Don't believe what you read in this," I advised my parents about the Sunday edition of the *St. Louis Post-Dispatch*, which contained an article entitled, "Expensive Trip to Spirituality," the first in a five-part series. It was March 3, 1974, my twenty-sixth birthday, and I was visiting, with my wife Fran and our two-year old daughter, Angie. My parents lived just outside Wentzville, a small town forty miles west of St. Louis. My mother was a schoolteacher and my dad was a regional salesman for a livestock feed company. "It's a bunch of crap, a hatchet job. Here, this says it all."

I read a paragraph aloud: "Until its recent campaign against alleged drug experimentation abuses at the troubled Missouri Institute of Psychiatry, Scientology attracted little attention among St. Louis area churches, schools, public and private health agencies and governmental authorities.

"See? It's retaliation for us speaking out against psychiatric abuses at MIP."

I was talking to both parents, but was only concerned about my mother's reaction. She was a little distressed about me leaving law school to work for and study Scientology. She grew up in a devout Methodist family and hoped to pass on her values to me. I was required to attend Sunday school every week and had a perfect attendance record over a ten-year period. There, I learned the basic Christian tenets: love thy neighbor, do unto others as you would have them do unto you, tolerance, and forgiveness. When people in our small town went astray, whether as a result of drunkenness, criminality or broken marriages, my mother would point out that they were not church-going Christians. It was a simple plan to follow and everything seemed to fit. Until one day it came crashing down.

* * *

"We might not ever see each other again," Richard said to me. It was the last day of the 1961-62 school year and we were walking home together. My dad had taken a job in Iowa and was moving our family the following week. Richard added that he would begin his summer job the next day, working sunup to sundown.

"I guess not, then."

That led us to reminiscing about our good times together. The school was about a half-mile from the center of town, where we would split off and go our different ways for another half mile; him to the east, and me to the north. He told me that I was his only white friend. Because of my newspaper route in what almost everyone called "colored town," I had made a number of black friends but none as close as Richard, and I told him so.

He had practically saved my life one day. Some of his neighborhood kids ganged up, intent on beating the crap out of me. The front door to Richard's house flew open in the nick of time. One thing about Richard, he was huge. The high school football coach often checked in on him to tell him how he couldn't wait for him to graduate from elementary. Richard tore into those bullies, cussing and threatening to "kick their black asses all the way to Hannibal" if they so much as ever laid a hand on me. Hannibal was nine miles north, so that would be some ass-kicking, but I believe Richard could've done it. So did those hooligans. They cowered and slinked away, never to bother me again.

He said I made up for it by helping him with his math studies, because math was doing to him what those boys wanted to do to me.

We reached the center of town near the Tastee Freeze when I said, "Hey Richard. I should treat you to a soda for being such a good friend." He screwed his head cockeyed and stared at me like I was from Mars. "What?" I said.

"You know."

"Know what?"

"I can't go in there."

Since he and I liked to cut up in class and had been sent to the principal's office a time or two, my mind took me in that direction. "What'd you do?"

"No. Not that," he said sharply.

"Then what? Stop being so mysterious."

He finally let it out. "Because I'm colored."

"Ah, that's got nothing to do with it. This is a business, Richard. People in business want to make a profit. That's all they care about."

He kept looking at me as though I was from outer space. Then shot back defiantly, "Have you ever seen a colored in there?"

No, he had me on that one, but I hardly ever went inside the place myself. I had better things to spend my money on than sodas, I told him. Food and drinks were free at home, except there were no sodas. I spent my money on baseball cards, camping gear, and such. After thinking through his question, I flipped it on him. "Have you ever gone in there and been turned away?"

He softened just a little. "No," he admitted.

"See there? You've been listening to gossip. You can't go on gossip. Besides, the owner knows me. She's in my church and loves me. She buys everything I ever sell just because it's me. She probably throws half the stuff away."

As a kid, I was a budding entrepreneur, always looking for ways to make money so I could buy the things I wanted. In the summer I trolled the streets on my bicycle looking for lawns that needed mowing, and if one did, I'd knock on the door. In the winter I threw a shovel over my shoulder and searched the streets for people who were snowed in. I sold *Grit* magazine, greeting cards, you name it. I scoured the ads in each issue of *Boy's Life* for new and exciting things to sell.

"Go in there with me as my guest, you'll see." I won him over and we trudged into the joint. I led him to a table beside a window looking onto the street and we sat down.

I should have known trouble was brewing when two men turned in their booth and glared at us. The owner, who was on the other side of the restaurant, did not flash her usual beaming smile. In fact, she looked serious as hell. She walked across the room, her somber attention fixed on me as though Richard didn't exist.

"Merrell, we don't serve coloreds here."

Richard threw up his hands and leapt out of his seat. His face was twisted in sheer agony. "See, I told you," he shouted at me, and bolted out.

My jaw was on the floor. I looked back and forth from the lady to Richard, who was flat-out sprinting down the sidewalk. I sprang out of my chair and sped after him.

I hollered for him to stop but he kept running. After my third plea, he slowed to a trot and then to a walk. When I caught up to him I told him I was sorry. He wasn't in the mood for an apology; he was mad-dog furious, filled with pain, anger, hate, and who knew what else. "You did that on purpose," he said.

"No I didn't. Why would I do that? You're my friend."

"Yes, you did it on purpose. You knew. You had to know."

I swore to him that I'd had no idea and was really sorry I hadn't listened to him. He eventually calmed down some but still wasn't ready to accept my apology.

"How long have you lived here?" he asked testily.

"Nine years."

"And you tell me you didn't know and you expect me to believe that?"

"I swear, Richard. I didn't know. I thought she was a good person. She's a Christian. She goes to church." He snorted. "I swear, Richard. I really didn't know."

I could see him turning it over in his mind, relaxing a bit. Finally, he ventured a smile and stuck out his hand. "Okay, I believe you," he said, and we shook.

"The only thing I don't understand," he said, "is how you can be so damned smart and so damned dumb at the same time." His lips curled a little. He was joking. That was funny, really funny, because it was also true. I started laughing and he laughed with me. I knew things between us were back to normal.

As we walked off I asked him what other places in town denied service to coloreds. He pointed to one of the two liquor stores and to one of the two grocery stores, the IGA. My family shopped there. The owner was a Christian and active in Boy Scouts. He always greeted me and asked how I was doing. I thought he was a good person.

For the first time I could remember I had trouble falling asleep that night. Two things kept rolling over in my mind. One was a question I could not answer no matter how hard I tried: What was it like to be Richard? The puzzle interplayed with the stark reality that not all church-going Christians were good people. The ones who refused service to Richard and other people of color were cruel. They were not following the Christian principles I had been taught. They were hypocrites.

The formula for life was not so simple after all. Something was missing for me.[2]

* * *

"What's really going on," I continued with my parents, "is a turf war between the psychiatric, medical and pharmaceutical industries, and Scientology. We have non-drug, non-medicinal tools to help troubled people, and they think that's their turf. It goes back to the early 1950s. These groups ganged up and sicced regulators and media on us, trying to shut us down." I put a book on the table next to the newspaper, *The Hidden Story of Scientology* by Omar Garrison, a non-Scientologist, investigative journalist. "Read this if you want to know the real story. Or ask me about it."

I told them the American Medical Association (AMA) was really just a powerful trade union that considered any non-professional outsider to be a quack and used its vast influence with the government and media to stomp on anyone who dared trespass into its zone of operation. "The book goes into what they've done to Scientology. They got the FDA[3] to seize our E-meters for being a medical device used to diagnose and treat disease, which is a complete fabrication."

The E-meter is used during Dianetics and Scientology auditing sessions. An individual undergoing counseling holds two metal cans that are connected to the meter by wires. A tiny, imperceptible electrical current runs through the cans and through the subject's body, measuring changes in electrical resistance and skin conductance. Because it detects emotional trauma, and because the part of a person's mind that contains the source of that trauma is out of view to an individual, the meter is highly effective in helping identify moments in a person's life that need to be addressed.

"The evidence is in the book. The AMA and the FDA worked together to stop Scientology. The FDA had an undercover agent enrolled in a Scientology course in the Washington, D.C.

church. Their plan was to gather evidence that the E-meter was being used for medical purposes and therefore shut it down. The FDA is just an enforcer for the AMA and drug companies; it's there to protect the public in name only.

"You know that, dad. Look at how they treat nutrition." My father had a degree in animal husbandry from the University of Missouri. He was fond of saying that the Ag school taught nutrition in order to keep livestock healthy and prevent disease, but the medical school didn't teach nutrition so that doctors could keep people healthy and prevent disease. Instead, the medical industry was geared toward treating sick and injured people. He would bring home vitamins and minerals he sold to farmers for their livestock to give to our family. It sounds weird, but they worked to keep us healthy and out of doctors' offices.

My father nodded. "I sure do."

"Same here," I said. "The FDA raided the Washington church in 1963 and hauled away enough E-meters and Scientology publications to fill two vans. The church had to battle it out in the courts for *six years*. A U. S. court of appeals finally ordered all the material returned and declared that Scientology was a legitimate religion and the E-meter was being used as a religious device."[4]

I tapped the book. "It's all in here. Psychiatrists are members of the AMA. Not only does Scientology threaten their interests, but L. Ron Hubbard publicly denounced some of their practices as being barbaric. Electroshock therapy; prefrontal lobotomies; and mind-numbing drugs that don't cure anything. We keep expanding and digging up their dirt and they hit back with propaganda pieces like this."

My dad totally got it. My mother seemed fairly satisfied as well.

* * *

John Spencer intercepted me outside the St. Louis church. "Someone from Los Angeles wants to meet you." I cocked my head. "About the Post-Dispatch articles," he continued. "Are you interested in talking to him?"

This time I was receptive. I had seen the fallout from the series. One person I ran into even had the gall to laugh and tell me I had fallen under "the spell of a cult." I asked him what he knew about Scientology. Plenty, he said; he'd read the Post-Dispatch articles. Then it was my turn to laugh. I was amazed. Not many people insulted me to my face, but I could tell that the articles had made an impact. I didn't blame the people I ran into. Most people trusted and believed what the news media told them. I used to myself. I blamed the Post-Dispatch. And I wanted to do something about it.

"I have to be back at work at seven," I said.

"I covered that for you," Spencer said. "This is important."

* * *

He led me to a booth in a back corner of a restaurant that was occupied by a friendly-looking guy about our age, mid-twenties. He had curly dark hair and toyed with his moustache. His eyes passed over me, scanning behind and all around us. Not until Spencer slid into the seat across from him, and I took the open spot, did the guy zero in on me.

"Don Alverzo," he said, extending his hand. I was immediately drawn to him.

"John told me you were in law school before coming to St. Louis?" he said.

"Yes, at UMKC, University of Missouri – Kansas City. Three semesters. I took a leave of absence during my fourth and moved to St. Louis to train to be an auditor in Dianetics and Scientology technology."

Alverzo motioned for me to speak more quietly. I nodded as he carried on the conversation without missing a beat. I marveled at his ability to pay attention to our surroundings while engaging me. I was liking this guy more with each passing minute.

I explained how I had gotten interested in Scientology during my third semester and had scarfed up all the books I could find on the topic, and was so engrossed in the subject matter I had little time left to do my homework the following semester. Something had to give.

As I spoke, I watched him closely. He seemed to absorb every word I said with interest, yet his eyes continued to glide all around. I realized he was just as attentive to potential onlookers and eavesdroppers as he was to what I was saying. I had never known anyone who could do that so smoothly.

He inquired about my military background. That meant he either had access to my staff application or had been briefed by Spencer, who may have known about it. I told him I had completed a three-year enlistment in the Navy, where I trained and worked as a fire-control technician, handling the ship's weapons control system – radar, computers, and related equipment.

"How about you?" I asked.

"Vietnam," he told me. "Helicopter pilot."

I asked him what that was like. He answered only briefly, then asked whether I had a security clearance in the Navy. That was my first inkling that he was screening me for something and not just getting to know me. And a masterful job it was, since I'd barely recognized it was going on. I had a Secret security clearance, I told him. A military vet would know that Secret was not very high. As we went into that, Alverzo reached for a pack of Marlboros, pulled one out, fitted it into a filtered cigarette holder, and lit up.

He offered me one but I turned it down. "I quit."

"Good for you. I should do that."

"It's easy," I said. "I've quit dozens of times." They both broke up over that. I didn't bother to credit Mark Twain for the joke.

Spencer didn't smoke, either. In fact, he was clean-cut all around. He had short blond hair, blue eyes, was always friendly and polite, and dressed in a nice shirt and slacks. He looked like he belonged in an early-60s folk music trio.

We ordered drinks and a bite to eat. Alverzo said it was on him, so I opened up a bit and got a sandwich and fries to go with a Coke even though I had already eaten. He bantered with the waitress as she took our orders, which obviously pleased her.

Alverzo asked what I thought about the *St. Louis Post-Dispatch* articles. I told him they were really messed up. "Going to psychiatrists and the heads of other religions for information about Scientology is like asking Nazis about Jews or Baptists about Catholics. And relying on former members who have an axe to grind? Geez. But a lot of people eat it up. It's amazing. Grown people. Educated people."

"They know how gullible the general public is," he said. "They created the effect they wanted to create. Do you know why they attacked us?"

"Yeah, the thing Fred Rock did. Drug experiments at MIP."

He asked if I knew about the PR team that was sent to the newspaper before the series was published. I told him I didn't, and he explained that they went there to help the newspaper get its story straight. "One of the PR people reported back that she overheard one of the writers of the articles, Elaine Viets, holler out to someone who had called for her, 'Not now; I'm trying to save MIP.'"

He added, "The State threatened to cut off funding for MIP after the local Guardian's Office exposed their illegal drug experiments, and the Post-Dispatch was trying to save it by attacking the church."

Spencer leaned in, his face aglow. "That was our operation. We uncovered the MIP scandal and gave the story to Fred Rock in PR to run with. Kate Toftness was the one who overheard the reporter admit that. Viets didn't know we had a PR team there when she blurted it out."

Toftness was the Dissemination Secretary, the head of my division, so I knew her well but didn't know she was part of a PR team sent to the Post-Dispatch. Nor did I fully understand the distinction between PR functions conducted by the Dissemination Division of the church and those run by the G.O.

"So what do you do, John?" I asked.

"I'm in the Information Bureau. So's Don. He's from U.S.G.O., in Los Angeles, which oversees all the local G.O. offices in the United States. We do intelligence."

"Do you know what intelligence is?" Alverzo asked. I shook my head. "We find out what is *really* going on, hopefully before any attacks occur so we can head them off." He said they gathered information overtly and covertly. Overt data collection relied on public sources, like libraries and newspapers. Covert data collection was information gathered from non-public sources, undercover.

Hearing it described that way, of course that's what it meant. I had heard the word before but had never connected it with those specific activities. I was stoked. It was a different approach. These were the kind of thoughts that had been running through my mind lately, and suddenly here was Alverzo, blown in by a west wind.

"That's exactly what I think needs to be done," I said. "A libel lawsuit isn't the answer. The reporters covered their tracks and made their articles appear balanced and authoritative. Someone should go inside the *Post-Dispatch* undercover and find out what's really going on."

Alverzo grinned and turned to Spencer. "We've got a good one, here."

Chapter 2

A Fool's Errand

The man with an idea is a fool, until the idea succeeds.

— Mark Twain

"How would you like to apply for a job there?" Alverzo asked me.

We were in his "safe house," a one-bedroom apartment. Spencer was there, too. The only furniture in the living room was a small table with two metal folding chairs pushed underneath. On the table was a white telephone with a very long cord, a typewriter, a pack of Marlboros, cigarette holders and an ash tray. Boxes of files and papers were scattered about the floor, along with an open box of Ritz crackers.

"They won't hire me."

We were talking about Evans, Hoemeke & Casey, one of two law firms representing the *St. Louis Post-Dispatch*. (The other one was Bryan, Cave, McPheeters & McRoberts.) Alverzo had instructed me to do research about them in a local law library.

That was overt data collection. I used the Martindale-Hubbell lawyer index, a comprehensive list of law firms and attorneys throughout the country, including their educational backgrounds, client lists, contact information, and other public details.

"Why won't they hire you?"

"For one thing, summer interns and law clerk jobs are filled before the spring semester ends. It's too late. Besides, these kind of corporate law firms usually hire law students from prestigious Ivy League schools or students from in-state schools with grades in the top twentieth percentile."

"How high are your grades?"

"Exactly two-point-zero. Just enough to make the cut and stay in school."

"Did you fuck off in school, or what?" Alverzo asked, casting a mischievous glance at Spencer.

"Hey, law school is tougher than learning to fly a helicopter, asshole."

They both laughed, then Alverzo said, "I think we can put together a good enough résumé for you that they might hire you." He added that it would help him if I could just get some intel on the lawyers: what they look like, their emotional makeup and whatever else I might observe. "A layout of the office alone would be worth the effort."

* * *

"What makes you think you're qualified to work for this firm?"

I was being interviewed by Robert Hoemeke in his office on the 14th floor of the Boatmen's Bank Building in downtown St. Louis, a cordial guy with dark hair, black-rimmed glasses, fortyish.

"I think I'd make a good trial lawyer. I have excellent communication skills. I'm personable, presentable, and people respond well to me. Those qualifications don't show up on a law student's résumé, but hopefully you can see that in me. Additionally, I'm a hard worker."

"I'm more interested in research and writing skills in a law clerk," he said.

"I'm good at those, too."

"It isn't reflected in your law school GPA or class ranking."

"Uh, well, sir, I don't believe I listed my GPA and class ranking."

"I know. I figured you would have if they were any good."

He made a very good point. I decided to display my advocacy skills and shift the subject away from a losing argument. "I think you will agree that some of the top students with great GPAs don't make the best lawyers in practice."

"True, but there is a high correlation between the two. The high level of research and writing skills we demand are generally reflected in a student's GPA, class ranking, and participation in law review. I don't see that listed on your résumé, either. I assume from its omission that you were not in UMKC's law review program."

"Yes, sir. That is correct. I'm married with a young child and am self-dependent for my education. I worked part time and didn't have time for law review."

"Were you invited?"

Another excellent question. Only students with at least a 3.0 GPA after their first year in law school were invited to law review. "No, sir. I was not. However, I would appreciate the opportunity to demonstrate my skills. I'm willing to work on a research assignment for you, or even give you a week or more of my time, free of charge. I'm confident I will prove my worthiness for a clerk's position with your firm."

He leaned back in his chair and looked skyward. An amused smile appeared on his face. "Excellent idea, young man. I will take you up on your generous offer."

As he scribbled the assignment on a legal pad I scoped out his office, committing the layout to memory. He tore off the sheet of yellow paper, folded it, and handed it to me as he stood. "Two days, I think, would be a good turnaround time on this."

I took the paper without unfolding it and enthusiastically shook his hand. "Thank you, sir. Thank you very much. I look forward to working on it."

* * *

Alverzo and Spencer were sitting on the floor when I returned to the safe house. Alverzo was puffing a cigarette, his back propped against the wall. Something was wrong with this picture. They were really blasé when they should have been excited in anticipation of my report.

"You didn't get the job," Alverzo announced flatly, flicking his ashes into the tray on the floor beside him. His comment burst my balloon and confused me. I held the research assignment in my hand, and was all prepared to celebrate.

"How do you know?"

"Because a lawyer from the firm called the church about a half hour ago and asked for you by name. The receptionist said she expected you in at 7 p.m. and took a message."

I'd completed the interview about then, which meant that someone, probably Hoemeke, made the call right after I left. I groaned. "You're shitting me."

"Afraid not," Alverzo said, snuffing out his cigarette. "It was our fuck-up. We should have briefed the receptionist." He jumped to his feet. "Whatcha got there?"

My head was still reeling. I handed him a sketch of the law firm suite and office where I was interviewed. I drew it right after I left. Alverzo looked at it, and brightened. "Good job." He handed it to Spencer.

"I thought the interview ended well. He gave me this research assignment." As I handed the folded yellow sheet to Alverzo it hit me like a flash and everything came into focus. "That asshole," I muttered aloud. But it was also funny the more I thought about it. I chuckled. "At least he has a sense of humor."

Alverzo gave me a questioning look as he began to read the assignment out loud: "Write a memo for the editor and reporters of the *St. Louis Post-Dispatch* explaining to them in layman's terms the practical effect of New York Times v. Sullivan."

Hearing it read aloud made it even funnier. I broke out laughing.

"What's it mean?" Alverzo asked with a twinkle in his eye.

"New York Times versus Sullivan is a famous U. S. Supreme Court case that established the requirement for proof of malice in a libel case brought by a public figure. The case is directly on point with the church's libel suit because the church will be considered a public figure. In other words, this is a message to the church that it's going to lose its case against the Post-Dispatch because it's pretty much fair game."

We all laughed, and Alverzo said, "You're right; he does have a sense of humor. I like this guy."

"I told you they wouldn't hire me."

"That's okay. I've got a better idea. There's an opening for a nighttime janitor at the building."

"What? After what just happened?" I was astounded by Alverzo's casual lack of concern. In fact, he seemed entertained by my stunned reaction. "What's that got to do with anything? They won't see you. You'll be working from ten at night to six in the morning."

"Are you kidding me? I'd have to give my name and address. They're the same ones listed on the résumé I gave the law firm."

"Give a different name."

"I only have one Social Security number, and it's in my name."

"Have you got a middle name?"

"Yes," I said, nonplused with the idea of using it. "I hate my middle name."

Alverzo chuckled and turned to Spencer. "I think we found a button we need to flatten." He turned back to me. "What's your middle name?" He was having fun now. I just looked at him. "Huh, what is it?" he repeated with a shit-eating grin.

"George," I finally replied.

"George Vannier. There's nothing wrong with that name. I like it. George. Let me hear you say it again."

"Fuck you."

Alverzo roared, and that got Spencer going. "See how serious he is? We need to loosen him up." He flirtatiously wrapped his arm around my shoulder and put on an affected voice. "Hey there, Georgie Boy." Just as I went to push him away he planted a wet one on my cheek.

"Ick. Get away from me, faggot," I said, wiping off the kiss as the two of them howled.

"Hey, John," Alverzo said. "We found another button."

"Okay, okay, I'll be a janitor."

Chapter 3

JANITOR SPY

Pay no attention to the man behind the curtain – or to the janitor.

– (With apologies to) L. Frank Baum
The Wonderful Wizard of Oz

"Have you ever been a janitor before?" Sam Miller[5] asked me when I reported for work in the nineteen story Boatmen's Bank Building at the corner of Broadway and Olive streets. He was the foreman who handed out our assignments.

"Not really, but I was in the Navy and we had to clean our assigned stations."

"Good. You should know how to handle a mop. I'll put you on the hallway floors." In the Navy we called it a swab, not a mop, but yes, I knew how to handle one. The day I left the Navy I vowed never to touch one again. Oh well, duty called.

Miller divided the crew into two teams, one per floor. Each team was further subdivided into those who cleaned offices and bathrooms and those who cleaned hallway floors. The floor job was straightforward. First we swept the broad, tiled floors with a shop broom. Then we mopped and buffed them. One floor at a time.

Miller trained me on how to operate the buffing machine. "Push down, it goes to the left. Up, it goes to the right." He demonstrated, going side-to-side, smooth as silk. Piece of cake.

21

He stepped aside and had me to try it. The rest of our floor team looked on. That was the first clue that I was being set up, but I missed it. I pressed down and the damn thing took off like a bat out of hell, practically yanking me out of my shoes. I clung to the handles off-balance, which depressed the handle more when it should have been lifted. The buffer accelerated and slammed into the rubber baseboard with a crashing thud that rattled my teeth. The onlookers rolled with laughter, including Miller. I knew that I'd been had, and played a good sport.

By morning I was a buffing machine virtuoso. I owned that sucker and made it glide and sing. At 6 a.m., and not one second later, I was out the door. By then it was daylight and some of the early bird office dwellers were already arriving. I was fearful of running into Robert Hoemeke, although I realized he might not notice me with a mop or broom in my hand, or if I was operating the buff machine. One thing I had already learned was that men in suits don't see janitors. That observation might not apply to Hoemeke, however. He was pretty observant.

The next night I traded off with one of the office cleaners for half the night but made sure to avoid the 14th floor. I wanted to fully acclimate myself to the routines of the crews before I did any snooping. Cleaning offices was easier than doing the hallways, except for the bathroom detail, that is. I hated cleaning bathrooms. For the offices, we only had to vacuum floors, empty trash containers and clean the ashtrays. We were forbidden to touch anything on the desks. I learned an important fact that night. Each office cleaning duo was given a master key for the night.

By the third night I had the job down. And I had possession of a master key.

On my first break, I slipped off to the 14th floor, two floors above the one I was working on. I went to Suite No. 1410, the law offices of Evans, Hoemeke & Casey. I scanned the hallway one last time, and inserted the key. It didn't work. I jiggled it several times to make sure. The blasted thing didn't work.

At the end of my break, and back on my work floor, I persuaded one of the office cleaners to let me stay on his crew a little longer. I wanted to clean offices on the 14th floor so I could learn how to get inside 1410.

When we reached the target suite, my workmate walked right past it to the adjacent office door. "What about this one?" I asked, lagging behind.

"We don't do that office."

"Really? Why not?"

"They use their own cleaners."

"Oh," I said. "Are there any other offices we don't clean?"

"Nope. Just that one."

* * *

"The building has to have a key in case of an emergency," Alverzo said. "Poke around. Be careful, but find out where the key is. Otherwise I'll have to go in and pick the lock, and I prefer not to do that." The three of us were sitting in the safe house. My routine was to drop by each day after I had eaten, debrief, and go over that night's plan. On this day, however, I picked up a burger and fries on the way and ate with the guys.

"You know how to pick a lock?" I asked between bites.

Alverzo instantly froze. His reaction bemused me. Maybe he thought I was probing and was alarmed by it, but I ruled that out since he was the one who had offered that tidbit in the first place. Perhaps he realized he had slipped up by revealing not only that he could pick locks, but that he had done so previously. I discounted that option as well; the slip did not justify the magnitude of his reaction in light of our joint covert activities. He regained his composure almost as quickly as he had lost it, and his normal affable self returned. "I can pick any lock," he said. "It's easy. But keep that here."

This exchange caused me to ponder what else Alverzo and Spencer were up to. I knew that Hoemeke's law firm was not the only target of interest because Alverzo had initially asked me to do overt data collection on the St. Louis Better Business Bureau and the law firms representing the two St. Louis newspapers, the Globe-Democrat and the Post-Dispatch. The Globe-Democrat had run a series of articles critical of the church in January, two months prior to the Post-Dispatch series, but it was a PR fluff piece by comparison. The interest in the Better Business Bureau was based on intel that connected the BBB to both media attacks in some way.

* * *

I warmed up to Miller during our first work break a few nights later. He gave me the perfect opportunity to inquire about an emergency key when he asked me which I liked better, cleaning floors or cleaning offices. "Floors," I said without hesitation. "But I don't mind switching off to break the routine. I cleaned offices part of last week. Hey Sam, why don't we clean that one office on the 14th floor?"

"They're overly security conscious and don't want our people cleaning it."

"Oh yeah. What's with that?"

"I don't know. They just said they needed tighter control over who gets access to their offices and wanted to get their own people in there."

"Oh, so we used to clean their offices?"

"Mm-hmm, up until two or three months ago. As far as I'm concerned that's one less office to clean, so it's no sweat off my brow."

"So the master key doesn't work on that suite?"

"No, they changed the lock."

"Isn't that dangerous? I mean, what if there's an emergency?"

"Murphy has a key." The name threw me. "You haven't met Murphy? He's the guy on the roof. He's with Building Security, a different company. You should go up there and meet him on one of your breaks. He's all by himself and gets lonely. Besides, you should see that monster radio antenna up there, and the view of the Arch and the river from the roof."

"I might just do that."

And I did. At 4:30 a.m., the start of my second break period, I climbed a metal staircase from the 19th floor to the roof. There, I saw a small white shack, perhaps four feet square and eight feet high. A light from inside spilled through plastic window panes on all sides, illuminating the surrounding area. I approached and peered around the front. A split door (top half, window, bottom half, wood) opened to the inside. The place was unattended. A lone stool sat in the center, an arm's-length from a wide, desk-like shelf.

A voice sounded from behind me. "Can I help you?"

I turned. "Hi. You must be Murphy." He was about my size and perhaps five years older. "Sam sent me. He said you needed company."

He chuckled, and stuck out his hand, "Yeah, I'm Murphy. What's your name?"

"George," I said. "This is my second week here and Sam told me about the great view you have."

"Yeah, it is great. Let me show you around."

The radio antenna was truly a monster, rising 574 feet above street level, he told me. "It has a ten kilowatt transmitter feed and sends out 70,000 watts," he said, adding that KXOK and KXOK-FM owned it. "This is the main reason I'm here, to guard the antenna and keep an eye on the system." He walked into his station. "Do you smoke?"

I wanted an excuse to bullshit with him longer, and more often, so I answered "Yes, I'm trying to cut down, but I could use one now if you're offering."

He grabbed a pack of Pall Malls off the shelf. "I hope you don't mind unfiltered." He tapped out two of them as he spoke.

"That works."

Murphy hoisted himself onto the stool and fired up both cancer sticks. "So, how do you like the job so far?"

"Fine. Not much to it. Just a lot of the same thing."

He laughed. "I'm sure. A lot of floors and a lot more offices."

"No shit. Nineteen floors, and I don't know how many offices. Except I just found out we don't do one of them."

"Yeah, I know." He pointed to a spot above his work shelf. My eyes followed his finger. A key on a small chain dangled from a brass hook just above the window pane. "Fourteen-ten," he added. I could barely contain myself. How easy was that? Good ol' Murph, my new smoke buddy.

* * *

The next night I rushed up to the roof on my first break. Murphy was walking back to the shack when we met up. I pulled a fresh pack of Pall Malls out of my shirt pocket. "Hey, I got a pack so I don't have to mooch off you. I'm going to keep it here so I don't smoke so much. Feel free to use them."

"Okay. Just throw it on the desk." As I leaned into the hut and tossed the pack onto the desk, I added, "If I keep them on me, I'll smoke the whole damn pack."

He let out a half-laugh. "I hear ya. Yeah, just come up any time. If I'm making my rounds, you can grab one, but I can't let you in the shack alone when I'm not here. I could lose my job."

"Got it. How often do you make your rounds?"

"Every half hour. Sometimes I have to go to the john on the 19th floor, so if I'm not here or on my rounds, that's where I'm at. Either that or I'm dead and you need to call someone." His comment befuddled me, and for a second I wondered if he was serious, if his job was actually dangerous, but then he started cackling, so I joined in. Gallows humor.

I played it cool with Murphy. I didn't rush things even though Alverzo was getting antsy. I took a few days to adjust. I wanted everything to feel right before I made my move. By the beginning of my third week Alverzo lost his patience. He set a time: 2 a.m. that night. That was the same night I received my first paycheck. I was flush with cash for the first time in months, felt frisky, and was game for a little action.

At 1:55 a.m. I took an early lunch break and went up for a smoke. Murphy wasn't there. I reached inside for a cigarette while my eyes darted in all directions. No sign of the security guard. I dropped the cigarette pack and in the same motion snatched the key off its hook with a flick of my hand. Quick, like a Muhammad Ali left jab. I headed back to the staircase while glancing over my shoulder into the surrounding darkness. I didn't see him and I hoped like hell he didn't see me. My heart was pounding.

I scrambled down the stairs two and three steps at a time. My feet barely touched down. I hit the 19th floor, made a quick scan to ensure it was empty, then hauled ass for the elevator. When the doors opened on the first floor I scampered to a metal side door that opened into the alley and pushed with both hands. The door flew open. Alverzo was calmly standing there. I handed him the key.

"Good job," he said. "I'll copy it and be back precisely at two-twenty."

"Two-twenty," I repeated, still huffing.

Waiting for Alverzo to return was the longest, most nerve-racking twenty minutes of my life. I half-expected Miller, or worse, the police, to burst in on me. Had Murphy seen me? If he had, he would either have alerted Miller, his security company, or the police. I tried to view my actions on the roof from Murphy's point of view. He may not have seen me snatch the key, but might he have seen me leave? Did I leave too hurriedly? Too furtively? What would he think then? I know I'd made a conscious effort to appear casual, but my adrenalin rush might have kicked me in the ass. My stomach was tied in knots. I checked my watch every fifteen seconds. Damned dial seemed to have been dipped in cold molasses, it moved so slowly. I really did need a cigarette now.

Eighteen minutes passed. I headed for the ground floor. I arrived a minute early and heard a light tapping on the exit door. I threw it open and Alverzo shoved Murphy's key at me. I grabbed it and darted off.

I didn't slow down until I hit the metal stairs leading to the roof. I caught my breath on the final flight and did my best to slow my rapid pulse, which shot up all over again at the thought of seeing Murphy. This was the moment of truth. I took deep, slow breaths with each step. As soon as my head cleared the roof I surveyed the area. No security force. No police. No Murphy. Nothing.

I strode toward the security shack. No one visible. I looked all around. Nothing. I reached the split door to the hut and peered inside. Empty. I thought about quickly replacing the key but held back. I wanted more information. Just then I heard the stairwell door to the 19th floor open and close. I figured it was Murphy returning from a restroom break. I hastily replaced the key and grabbed the pack of cigarettes. I was lighting one when Murphy rose from the staircase shadows.

"Oh, there you are," I said, knowing I needed to get back on the job but wanting to gauge his demeanor. I shook loose a cigarette for him and we shared a quick smoke. Murphy was effusive and all smiles. I relaxed.

* * *

The next day I dropped by the safe house bearing a large pizza.

"I'm going to make a test run tonight," Alverzo said. "I want to locate the firm's files on Scientology so I can estimate how long it will take to copy everything I want. Then I'll do the copy run tomorrow night."

"You plan to copy the files in their office?" I said, incredulous.

"Yes," he said.

We never discussed an exact plan before. We had been taking one step at a time. I assumed Alverzo wanted to view the information, and maybe take notes. "You can't copy the files on their machines," I said.

"Why not?"

"That's burglary, a felony. I don't want to be involved in a felony. I'm too young and good looking to go to a penitentiary."

"Who said you were good looking?"

"My mother. She would know." He and Spencer got a kick out of that.

"How can it be a felony?" Alverzo asked. "I'm not stealing anything."

"Yes you are. If you use their copy machines, you're stealing their copy paper."

Alverzo rolled his eyes. "Copy paper? I'll probably be using less than twenty dollars worth of paper. That's not a felony."

"Oh yes it is. An unauthorized entry for the purpose of committing a crime therein is the definition of burglary. It could be an ashtray worth a buck-fifty, but if that's why you entered – to take it, then that's burglary. And that's a felony."

Alverzo looked at Spencer. "I didn't know that. Did you know that?" Spencer shook his head no. Then Alverzo turned to me. "Well, I don't plan for us to get caught."

"I know we won't get caught because we're not going to do it," I said, wondering how he would react to my putting my foot down for the first time.

He lapsed into thought for a second or two, then bounced back to his positive, energetic self. "Well, okay. So much for that plan." To Spencer, he said, "How big is the copy machine at the church?"

"Not big, and it's not dependable. We've had a lot of problems with it lately."

"I don't want to go back to the church, anyway," Alverzo said. He pondered the problem for a half minute or so and then said, "We'll figure out something after I know how big the job is. In the meantime, find a place with two high-speed copy machines as close to the building as possible. Get on that now." Spencer grabbed the St. Louis Yellow Pages directory and began to rifle through it.

"Okay, listen up, Merrell. I'll be there at 2 a.m. Sharp. Let me in the building and point me to the stairway. You take the elevator and make sure the 14th floor is clear. Don't let me on it unless it is. If we have to abort the mission, we'll try it again tomorrow, so let's not take any unnecessary risks. If it's clear, give me a go-ahead sign and point me to 1410, lay back and keep a lookout. Once I'm inside the office, leave. Come back about 2:25 and, if it's clear, double-rap on the door like this." He lightly rapped his knuckles twice in quick succession on the table. "Once I make it back to the stairs, take the elevator to the first floor and prepare to cover my exit."

We went over the plan several times. We also discussed different things that could go wrong and how to handle each of those scenarios.

* * *

I let Alverzo inside at 2 a.m. The plan worked perfectly. He entered Suite 1410 and I left to grab a quick bite to eat. I tapped the office door at 2:25 and headed for the elevator. The first floor was clear so I signaled for Alverzo to exit the stairwell. He calmly scurried down the hallway and slipped out the backdoor. I let out a deep breath. Only then did I notice how tense I had been.

* * *

The next day I was awakened early by a phone call from my father. He had some rather disturbing news, although it seemed less disturbing the longer I considered it. By the time I reached the safe house I viewed it as potentially good news, with a little help from Alverzo that is.

"You're here early," Alverzo said.

"I got a call from my father."

Alverzo's shoulders sagged. I could read his concern. It was *the* big day, the grand finale, and his man in the arena gets his mojo messed up. "What's up?"

"He received a notice from the bank. In addition to the GI Bill benefits I was getting, I took out a couple of student loans through his bank. I have to start making monthly payments on them if I'm not back in school by September. I can't afford to make payments on my staff salary."

"Why don't you go back to school?"

"I have a year and a half left on my contract with the church."

"I want to get you back in school," he said. "I was going to talk to you about that later. I like working with you and you're doing great. We can do some big things together if you get your law degree. I can take care of the contract."

"Really?" I said, enthused.

"If you go back to Kansas City can you stay away from the Kansas City mission and your Scientology friends?" A Scientology mission is similar to a church, except that it offers only low-level Scientology training courses.

"Why?" I asked. "What are you thinking?"

He said he wanted me declared a suppressive person and excommunicated from the church as a pretense. "Will that be a problem for you?"

"I can handle that," I said, my excitement about the prospect of finishing law school growing. I wasn't really being kicked out of the church, and I only had a couple of Scientology friends in Kansas City that I would miss.

Alverzo slapped me on the shoulder. "Great. Let's get a good result tonight. Then I know I'll be able to push that through."

We went over the night's plan again and again. He said he had a lot to copy, enough to keep two copiers humming for hours, so our timing had to be really tight.

* * *

I let Alverzo inside the building at midnight, the start of my first break. He was carrying a large banker box in one hand. He headed for the staircase and I hit the elevator. The 14th floor was clear. I motioned him onto it. "Five minutes," he whispered as he scooted past. After he entered the office I strolled to the other end of the hallway.

A minute went by. Then another. I headed back toward the staircase. Three minutes. Then the elevator doors opened and I jumped out of my skin. It was Miller.

"What the hell are you doing up here, George?"

My heart raced out of control and my mind froze. "I'm on break," I uttered.

"Well, I know that, but what are you doing up here?"

"I didn't know..." I was still in a defensive, reactive mode and was about to say I didn't know I was restricted to any one place during my breaks when I regained my composure mid-sentence and changed the subject. "Why? What do you need?"

"I want to go over the rest of the shift. Steve got sick and we're already down a man. I need my best floor men to double up, cut down the lunch break and maybe even knock out the second break." He started backtracking to the elevator. "Come with me. Let's get this worked out real quick so we don't come up short." He pushed the call button and the door immediately opened.

I didn't want him to return the conversation to what I was doing on the 14th floor so I took control of our descent. "What's wrong with Steve?"

"He has a migraine. He isn't faking it, either. The guy's in real pain, I could see it in his face." I milked the topic all the way to the first floor.

Miller's briefing only took a few minutes. I was told to head to the tenth floor, pronto. Fortunately, because of the ad hoc shift assignments, I had the entire floor to myself. As soon as the elevator doors opened, I high-tailed it to the staircase and flew up the stairs to the 14th floor. I had totally lost track of time. Alverzo was in there at least ten minutes, maybe fifteen. I skidded to a stop at 1410 and double-tapped the door. No response. I double-tapped again. Nothing. He must have sensed something was wrong and let himself out. He either took the files with him or aborted the mission. In any event I couldn't waste another second. I sped back down to the tenth floor and got to work.

I came to accept that Alverzo had somehow managed to smuggle the files outside. My concern then shifted to getting him back inside the building to return the files at 5 a.m. and still do my job. There was only one solution. I turned into Speedy (George) Gonzalez, the world's fastest floor man. It worked. By break time we were completely caught up, and I was back in Miller's good graces.

"Excellent job, George. You kicked ass. Take a break, you deserve it." It was 4:30 a.m., our normal second break time.

"Not now," I said. "I'm on a roll. I'll take a break in another half hour or so, if that's okay with you."

"You got it. Thanks for stepping it up, man." I gave him an A-OK sign.

Shortly before 5 a.m. I shut down and headed to the first floor, hoping that Alverzo was waiting in the alley with the files. I didn't want to go through this another night. The memory of Miller dressing me down for being on the 14th floor still haunted me. For him to catch me there a second time was more than I wanted to experience. Enough of this drama. I wanted to wrap up.

I opened the alley door prepared for anything. Alverzo stood there holding the banker box and an accordion file bursting at the seams. I held the door open and let him pass, then rushed ahead of him and peeked into the hallway. All clear. I signaled him forward and then hustled onto the elevator while he took the stairs. The 14th floor was clear. I made it to the staircase and waited. Alverzo arrived, huffing and puffing. I checked the floor again and motioned him along. He set the box outside the suite and pulled the key out of his pants pocket. Seconds later he was inside, and I ambled away. I gave him two minutes, the amount of time he had asked for in his briefing, and then double-rapped on the door. He emerged, gave me a thumb's up and headed for the stairs. A minute or so later, he was out the door.

I breathed a huge sigh of relief and went up to the roof for an unfiltered smoke with Murphy. I needed a good jolt of nicotine.

* * *

At the safe house the next day, the three of us were high as kites in an April wind. Alverzo gave me a bear hug and we all slapped hands.

"Good stuff?" I asked. Obviously it was. I wanted some details.

Alverzo fanned his face as he let out a sizzle between clenched teeth, then added: "Hot, hot, hot."

"What kind of stuff did you get?" I asked. "Give me an idea."

He repeated both his gesture and the words, "Hot, hot, hot."

"Oh, come on," I said intently. "I almost died of a heart attack last night. You gotta give me something."

Hesitant, Alverzo finally said, "We got more from this intel run than anyone expected. Far more. It goes beyond St. Louis. We even found a nugget of intel we've been searching for since the time when the Old Man was in Phoenix twenty years ago. It was a missing piece of the puzzle to a problem that arose back then." By "Old Man," he meant L. Ron Hubbard, the founder of Scientology.

Alverzo said he had given a summary of the file contents to his people in L.A. and they were going nuts. "They can't wait to see this stuff and analyze it along with everything else. I'm going to fly it out tonight. You're a hero. We all are. Great job." We shared more hugs and hand slaps.

"When are you coming back?" I asked. I needed to know because I hoped we could work out my return to law school. I had told Fran about it and we were getting excited about the move.

"In a few days. While I'm there, I'm also going to plan out your move back to Kansas City. I've already got the green light for it."

I was pumped. The idea of being able to quit my janitorial job also occurred to me. It wasn't the work itself. I didn't mind the work. I felt better for it. More exercise, more activity – and I actually enjoyed my smoke breaks with Murphy, the views of the

Arch and the Riverfront, and working a night job. I was just nervous about being spotted or found out. Alverzo dashed my hope for an early exit. He said he wanted me to work the rest of the week and to keep an eye out for any signs that people know what went down.

"Tonight is the most critical night," He said. "So be extra alert. John knows how to reach me in case something comes up. Get a hold of him right away if needed."

The next night was calm. So were the following ones.

Chapter 4

SLEEPER AGENT

Do the right thing. It will gratify some people and astonish the rest.

– Mark Twain

A mid-size rental car pulled into our driveway. "It's him," I said to Fran.

"Perfect timing. Supper's almost ready," she said. She had fixed a nice meal.

I picked up Angie. "Let's go outside and meet Don." It was mid-April 1975. It had been more than a year and a half since I last saw him. He had called and said he wanted to meet with me and go over a few things, and I was anxious to introduce him to my family. He had never met them.

"Where are you from, Fran?" Alverzo asked during supper. "Sigourney, Iowa," she told him. She grew up on a farm. "Oh, really?" Alverzo said, showing a genuine fascination, and asked her all about farm life, her family and general history. He grinned, laughed, and beamed throughout their conversation.

"So where did you meet this guy?" He gave me a playful nod. "In high school," she told him. He knew I was from Missouri, so I clarified that my parents had moved to Iowa after I finished eighth grade. "Oh, okay. I get it now. So you two were high school sweethearts?"

I let Fran answer. "We didn't date until he got out of the Navy and was in college," she said. "I was a senior in high school. He took me to my senior prom. We got engaged in August and married the next June." She explained how we planned for Angie to be born after my graduation from engineering school and for me to get a job and settle down as a family, but then I decided to go to law school instead.

Alverzo expressed eagerness for more details, like a reader with a good book who couldn't put it down. He asked what led me to change from engineering to law. I told him the seeds were planted by a friend whose father was a lawyer and in whose footsteps he planned to follow. "My friend and I both worked part time jobs in a TV repair shop. We were military vets trained in electronics.

"He talked me into taking the law school entrance exam and to consider law school. I took his advice and did well on the exams, but I didn't apply for admission. The job market is what did it for me. The year I graduated was a down year for electrical engineers. I only had one offer, from General Electric. I went to my job interview in Kansas City and it was like... The parking lot was bigger than my home town. There was this humongous rectangular, red brick building. I think they had five thousand employees, something like that, and they all looked the same: a bunch of white men in white shirts, ties and dress pants. On my way inside I felt like a tiny ant being gobbled up by a gigantic anteater. The only thing I remember about the interview was that I got an offer for $14,000 per year. The rest is blank. When I got in my car to leave, I thought, *I can't take this job,* and then I thought of Fran. She was pregnant, looking forward to a life as a mother and homemaker. I felt horrible. I didn't have the heart to tell her but at the same time I couldn't take the job. That's when I decided I wanted to go to law school."

"How did you take the news?" Alverzo asked Fran.

"When he told me what he wanted to do, and explained why, I told him, 'Okay, you can go to law school.'"

"Even though it meant that she had to keep working," I said to Alverzo.

He shuddered as though struck by goose bumps. "Ooh. "That's love."

Fran and I cracked up. It was clear to me that she had taken to Alverzo as I once had. Now she had an inkling why I enjoyed working with him so much. She didn't know what we did together, only that it had something to do with helping the church, and it was secret.

Alverzo asked about the law school admissions process, and I told him it was a problem for me. I had barely gotten in, due to a sudden spike in applications, not only at the University of Missouri, but at law schools all over the country.

I applied for law school in Columbia, the main campus for the University of Missouri, but only made the waiting list. They accepted one hundred applicants and another fifty went on the waiting list. Many people apply to several law schools. I was told that in a normal year I would have no trouble getting in but that they weren't sure for 1971. I looked for other law schools in Missouri and picked UMKC. I drove to Kansas City with my transcript and Law School Admission Test results in my hand. I filled out an application and asked to see the dean of admissions. I was told it didn't work that way, and I would be contacted. When I persisted, the Dean agreed to see me. I really lucked out. He was an older guy who used to be in the Army Corps of Engineers. He had a lot of strong opinions and I fit into each one. Military veteran, married, father, engineer, all the things that he thought would make a good law student and a good citizen. He didn't mince words. He hated long-haired, free love, anti-war hippies, and there I was in a suit and tie, short hair, clean shaven, humble and respectful.

He asked me what I'd do if he accepted me but Columbia also accepted me. He said a lot of applicants who applied at both schools ended up choosing Columbia. I told him I would turn down Columbia if he accepted me that day, then and there. He said, "Sign that in blood, and you've got a deal." I told him to call in the nurse. He loved that. He broke up and said, "That won't be necessary. I believe you."

Alverzo thanked Fran for the delicious meal and asked "Can I steal your hubby for a private meeting?" She got up to take Angie away. Angie squawked – she wanted to stick by Don and me. He offered to swing her by her arms some more if she'd let us be alone for awhile. She agreed. They played while Fran and I cleared off the table.

When we were alone, Alverzo said, "I like Fran. She's a good catch." I agreed. He asked how things were going. "Great," I told him. I got straight As last semester and am on track to do it again this semester."

He cocked an eye, nodding his approval. "What caused you to go from C's to A's? Was it Study Tech?" He was referring to Scientology training that teaches a person *how* to study and actually *learn* a subject rather that just pass a test, a prerequisite course for auditor training. Study Tech comes in different forms. I took the advanced course, which included many steps, one of which was looking up 10,000 words in a dictionary, many of them small, commonly used words, such as "a," and "the."

"Mostly Study Tech. But I'm also more driven. Before I was coasting a little."

"Aha," he said, "So you were fucking off."

He later asked me if I was keeping my zipper closed. His question startled me. I knew what he meant but it seemed to come from out of the blue and was none of his business. "Don, I don't have time to mess around, even if I was inclined to, and I'm not."

"Good. It's important for you to stay clean." He added that the "Old Man," L. Ron Hubbard, did a study and found that promiscuous conduct was a common denominator for all blown covers of operatives and all failed operations. I told him I found that heartening, if true, because it meant that my cover would never be blown and all my operations would succeed because it was easy for me to remain faithful to Fran. "Good," he said again.

"Have you heard back from the FBI?" On his suggestion I had applied for a job at the FBI and other federal agencies. For no stated purpose. I assumed that he wanted to get me into a position where I could access information vital to the church's interests.

"Not yet, but I expect to be hired."

"Why do you feel that way?"

"Because I didn't just apply; they recruited me. They hired one of my classmates who recommended me. His father is an agent, and also an uncle. They're all Mormons. Did you know there are a lot of Mormons in the FBI?" Alverzo shook his head, no, he didn't know that.

"Well, there are, and they're pretty tight, according to my friend. He pulled some strings and an Agent in the Kansas City office called me in for an interview. My classmate told me the Special Agent in Charge sent my application to FBI headquarters in D.C .with a strong recommendation to hire me. Get this: he rated my interview as *outstanding*. They don't even have an outstanding rating, it only goes from poor to excellent, and I got *outstanding*."

"Do you have a copy of your application?" Alverzo asked. I told him I did. "Let me look at it. Get me all your applications while you're at it." I headed off to retrieve my file. "Have you heard from any of the others?" he said to my back.

I stopped to answer. "I was declined by the Foreign Service, State Department. I haven't heard back from the others. The FBI delay is no big deal, I'm telling you. The application has to go to D.C., is all."

Alverzo opened my file and combed through it. I could tell something was wrong. So I asked what concerned him.

"Two FBI agents went by the St. Louis church and interviewed Doug Weigand."

"Oh no. Not again." I was thinking of the time in St. Louis when someone called the church asking for me right after my interview with lawyer Robert Hoemeke, and the receptionist took a message for me. "I thought you were going to take care of that?"

"We told the receptionist to refer anyone asking about you to the Guardian's Office. But the FBI agents asked for Doug. He was nearby and answered up, and they took him outside."

I groaned. "Thank you, Doug," I said under my breath.

As he thumbed through the application, Alverzo asked if I knew why the agents asked for Doug by name. "Because I listed him as my supervisor at the church," I responded.

"You put the church on your application? Show me."

"It asks for my employment history and residence addresses for the past ten years." I spoke as I searched for the relevant page. "Here. The application has to be signed under penalty of perjury, a five-year felony for false statements. Look at the signature page. The warning is in bold caps right above the signature line."

He looked it over then tossed it aside. "I'm not asking you to commit a felony or to do anything you disagree with. You won't succeed if you do. Something will go wrong. I just don't want you to put this kind of information on an application."

He said he wished I had consulted him so he could have helped me fill it out. I asked him what he would have suggested because I sure didn't see a way around the question. He said he didn't know but would have come up with something. After a pause, he added, "Or I would have told you not to submit the application."

"What about the cover we had for me? I blew my staff contract. I was ex-communicated. So what if they know I was part of the church? I'm not now."

"They asked Doug if you were still a Scientologist and he said you were."

"What? Didn't he see the notice of excommunication?"

"He saw it, but he said he wanted to put things in a good light for Scientology."

"Huh? That doesn't even make sense."

"It did to him. He figured outsiders are always trying to make a big deal out of people who join Scientology and then leave, or something like that. Look, you won't get the FBI job, and even if they offer it to you, I'm not sure I want you to take it now. It's too risky. It could be a setup. If you get an offer, call me before you accept it."

I sighed and slumped in my chair. "So where do we go from here?"

"There may be other uses for you. Just sit tight for now. But don't fill out any more applications without first running them by me, okay?" I agreed. It then occurred to me that I had also submitted my application for membership in the Missouri Bar Association and it contained the same information. I told Alverzo.

He was surprised. "Already? You haven't even graduated."

I told him that all law students submit applications at the beginning of their final year. "I'll be eligible to take the bar exam at the end of July. If I pass, I'll automatically be eligible for admission in September."

Chapter 5

CLEARWATER

The ultimate tragedy is not the oppression and cruelty by the bad people but the silence over that by the good people.

– Martin Luther King, Jr.

"I need you here in Florida," Alverzo said. I was groggy and wasn't sure I heard him right. The house was dark. The window was even darker. It was pitch black outside. I could feel the cold December air through the pane and the cold linoleum floor under my bare feet.

"Florida? For what?"

He asked if I had seen any promotions about Flag establishing a land base in a subtropical resort. Flag referred to the international management organization that sailed the Mediterranean Sea aboard ships, one of which was the flagship *Apollo* that Hubbard and his top aides occupied. A flagship in a Navy fleet is the ship that carries the commanding officer. In the mid-1960s, L. Ron Hubbard formed the Sea Organization and took to sea in order to complete his technical and administrative research without societal distractions.

I told Alverzo I heard about the plan, but not the location, which I had been told was confidential. He said it was still confidential but that he could tell me it was in Clearwater. I told him I had been there before. "Nice place," I said, shivering.

45

"Not for me, it isn't," he said. "All hell has broken loose and I need you down here right away." I tried to clear the sleep from my head and take it all in. Meanwhile, I was freezing my ass off so Florida didn't sound half bad. I asked what he had in mind.

"I need you to be my eyes and ears in the legal community." He said the town was backwoods. None of the lawyers would touch Scientology. They had to go seventy miles south to Sarasota to find an attorney who would represent them.

It was December 1975, eight months after his visit to our house. I was working in a private practice in Raytown, Missouri, a suburb of Kansas City. I had my name on the door, Kirby & Vannier. I had only been licensed three months. My law partner, Russell Kirby, knew I was job hunting and couldn't commit to a long-term arrangement. He didn't care. He was my supervising attorney on the legal practice program I took at UMKC. He liked working with me and was willing to team up on my terms.

"Don, I can't practice law in Florida without a license." He asked what it took to get one. "For starters, I have to apply to take the Florida Bar exam. It's given twice a year and the next one would be at the end of February. I don't know if the deadline for applying has already passed. Results come out in late May. Only then could I get sworn in and be able to practice law there, assuming I pass the exam."

"Find out the deadline and if it's not too late, get started on the application." He paused. "Is this something you're up for, moving your family down here?"

I told him the idea of studying for another state's bar exam, busting my butt for a couple of months preparing for it, did not appeal to me, but that Fran and I both liked the area, "So, yeah, I'm game. I think Fran will be, too."

"Good," he said, thanking me. I could feel relief in his voice. "I'll call tomorrow night, same time," he added.

* * *

Alverzo picked me up in Lakeland after I finished the February bar exam. I had submitted my application to take it just before the deadline. I agreed to visit Clearwater and work with him for a week, then I planned to return to Kansas City and await the test results.

"How did you do?"

I told him I nailed it, but then joked, "Famous last words."

In his car he handed me a list of ten places he wanted me to give my résumé and get inside for an interview while I was in town. I ran my finger down the list. Mostly law firms and a few local agencies. He said they were ranked in order of importance to him, "From the top down."

He said his purpose was different for each office. There were checkmarks next to some of the places. He wanted me to get inside those for an interview but not to work there. "Check them out and meet their personnel." The list was divided into two groups: those with vital intel he wanted me to access, and those that would garner me the most credibility and contacts in the local legal community. "The one at the bottom is one of the oldest and most respected law firms in Clearwater. You'd be able to quickly build a lot of social contacts in a place like that." Phillips, McFarland, Gould & Korones on Missouri Avenue. Nice omen, I thought. Alverzo said he would love to be able to turn to a well-placed lawyer and find out what was really going on in town.

He threw a thumb toward the back seat. I looked over my shoulder at a stack of files and folders. "We're getting bombarded daily by all forms of media – TV, newspapers, radio talk shows. We're front page stuff, lead stories. Every day." He wanted me to review a pack of newspaper clippings when I settled into the bungalow he had rented for me.

"The whole thing smells of one big intel op," he added and then went into detail. Bob Snyder was a local radio host who had a connection to the IRS, which he obviously meant was intelligence related, not merely a connection as a taxpayer. Gabe Cazares was the mayor of Clearwater. He started out as an ally and then suddenly turned against the church. He had an intel background in the Air Force, retired as a Colonel, went to work as a stock broker for Merrill Lynch in Tampa, then suddenly became a political activist. He showed up at a march for the United Farm Workers, walking next to Cesar Chavez at the front of the pack, and then ran for elected office.

"It stinks," he said. "Intel written all over it. He's probably an FBI asset."

Bette Orsini was an investigative reporter for the *St. Petersburg Times*. The editor of the Times was former CIA and had tons of heavy intel connections. "The campaign against us was probably orchestrated by those four, and the rest of the media piled on." He added, "It's turned into a bloodbath. We know it's an intel op, but we don't have enough evidence to connect all the dots."

Alverzo asked me to grab the file folder with the rubber band around it and carefully study the contents when I had time. It was material about the FBI's Counter Intelligence Program, or COINTELPRO, as it was called.

He told me about a group, the Citizens' Commission to Investigate the FBI, that had burglarized an FBI office in Pennsylvania in 1971 and stolen several dossiers. The group exposed COINTELPRO through leaks of the documents. The *New York Times*, Washington, D. C. columnist Jack Anderson, and others published numerous articles detailing domestic spying operations against political and minority groups.

I thumbed through the articles, reading some of the headlines and portions of the articles silently and occasionally out loud. A May 1973 article revealed that the FBI urged a reporter to write about intimate details it had uncovered about Martin Luther King's personal life. An August 1974 article revealed an entire COINTELPRO operation targeting King.

"Notice how they use the media to attack selected targets," Alverzo said. Several unpopular groups had been targeted: the Socialist Worker's Party, the Black Panthers, the KKK and many others. I read from one of the clippings, "FBI Director J. Edgar Hoover issued directives governing COINTELPRO, ordering FBI agents to 'expose, disrupt, misdirect, or otherwise neutralize the activities of these movements and their leaders.'"

"That's what we think is going on against us here in Clearwater," Alverzo said. The articles included FBI statements to the media claiming they discontinued running COINTELPRO against American citizens and groups. One of them was a *Los Angeles Times* editorial in which the FBI stated that it deeply regretted its role in COINTELPRO, but took consolation in a statement from new FBI Director William Webster, who said: "The days when the FBI used derogatory information to combat advocates of unpopular causes have long since passed. We are out of that business forever."

Alverzo said it wasn't true. The FBI had not stopped. In fact, they were doing it right now against the Flag Land Base in Clearwater. But it was still one of those, we-know-it-but-can't-prove-it things. "It's our job to get the intel that proves it." Meanwhile, the G.O.'s PR department was pushing for Congressional investigations into both the FBI's and CIA's domestic intelligence activities and aligning with other like-minded groups.

He said the situation was grave for Scientology. Beginning in the late '60s, the CIA and other elements of the intelligence community, including the State Department, U.S. embassies and foreign intelligence agencies friendly to those agencies, had been waging a campaign of false reports and harassment against the Scientology flagship, *Apollo*. In ports where the ship once had friendly receptions, she suddenly encountered problems. They started in the Greek port of Corfu. The Guardian's Office traced false rumors about the *Apollo* to a British foreign officer. G.O. officials got him fired, and the Greek interior minister wrote Hubbard a letter of apology.

But then the ship ran into a similar problem in Casablanca. The U.S. consul there circulated false reports about the ship and the church, portraying the *Apollo* as a nefarious "mystery ship" in the public's perception. And so it happened in the next port, and the next. The ship and its crew were harassed, even arrested on charges of drug use, forcing them to prove the charges false to gain their release. The G.O. traced all the false reports to U.S.

or British intelligence agencies, both of which knew well that Scientology and Scientologists are staunchly anti-drug. By 1974, the ship was running into similar problems in every Mediterranean seaport. The problems culminated in October 1974 on the Portuguese island of Madeira. The *Apollo* was attacked by an angry mob that believed she was a CIA spy ship. The rioters stormed the wharf and tried to untie the vessel from her moorings. They shoved motorcycles belonging to the ship's crew off the dock and into the sea. They threw rocks and incendiary bombs at the ship, injuring more than a dozen staff members.

Alverzo said it was then that the *Apollo* set sail for the United States. Prior to landing in Charleston, South Carolina, they received a tip that officials from various federal agencies were there to keep watch on the ship because its crew was suspected of smuggling large quantities of narcotics. An ulterior motive for searching and seizing the *Apollo* and its crew was suspected, so the ship headed instead for the Caribbean Sea, but ran into similar problems there. Alverzo concluded his briefing by telling me that it was no longer viable for Hubbard and Scientology international management to operate at sea. They had to come ashore.

"The problem with coming ashore is that then we are a stationary target," he said. "We have to dig in and save the Flag Land Base in order to save Scientology." The base was now located in the historic Fort Harrison Hotel in the heart of downtown Clearwater, which the Church had purchased. Alverzo said he needed someone with my unique abilities and qualifications to help get the job done.

As he dropped me off, he said that our meetings and communications must be infrequent and extremely discrete. He gave me a phone number to reach him in case of emergencies. He told me to call him from a particular pay phone and hang up when it was answered, then call again and hang up again. He would then call me back. Even then, he instructed me not to use my real name, only my code name.

"What's my code name?"

"Ritz." I recalled seeing him with a box of Ritz crackers in the safe house in St. Louis, and wondered if that was when he first assigned me the code name.

* * *

Within a month of my return to Kansas City, Alverzo was calling me almost daily. "I really need you here. Come now." That was his mantra. I told him I wanted to get my bar exam results first. "I need a job for income." He said he would pick up all of our living expenses until I found a job and that Fran could apply for employment without having to wait for my bar results.

He wore me down. We moved to Clearwater the first part of May 1976 and rented a two-bedroom duplex on the east side of town, near the Kapok Tree Inn and Courtney Campbell Causeway. Right away I began pounding the pavement looking for a law position on Alverzo's list, which had grown since March to include a job with *any* law firm or agency located in Clearwater.

"I need to branch out," I said one night at a secret rendezvous. "The Clearwater job market for lawyers is dead and I'm beginning to stick out like a sore thumb."

He turned me loose to find any job that interested me. Litigation, either criminal or civil – and lots of it is what I wanted. I reached out to St. Petersburg, which was thirty-five miles south of Clearwater, and applied for a position with numerous insurance defense firms, the Public Defender's Office and the State Attorney's Office. The latter two offered me interviews as did one of the insurance defense firms.

A job with the insurance defense firm excited me. Two young lawyers had left a big law firm to start one of their own. They had more cases coming in than they could handle and wanted someone who could jump right in and carry his own caseload. The interview went great on both sides. They wanted to meet

Fran and invited us to a fancy restaurant, escargot and all that high-end jazz. Fran and I passed on the snails. The evening was otherwise fantastic. We really liked both couples, and got the idea the feeling was mutual. The next day they extended me a job offer. I promised to get back to them within two days.

A day later the Public Defender's office offered me a position pending admission to the Florida Bar. I had just learned that I'd passed the exam but my admission was being held up because my background checks were incomplete. I called Tallahassee in an effort to speed up the process. The admissions administrator told me that two of the people who had been sent letters of inquiry about me had not returned their responses. I obtained their names and contacted them. I lit a fire under them.

My next job interview was with Myron Mensh, the head of the State Attorney's Office in St. Petersburg. His office was responsible for the criminal prosecution of crimes committed in the southern half of Pinellas County. It was part of the Sixth Judicial Circuit's State Attorney's Office, which was headquartered in Clearwater and run by James T. Russell, the state attorney. A state attorney in Florida is equivalent to a district attorney in many states. Mensh offered me a position pending my admission. He said I could start immediately if I wanted to and get a head start and learn the ropes, although he couldn't pay me until my admission went through. I told him I would get back to him the following day.

I met with Alverzo and updated him on the various offers. I was leaning toward the insurance defense firm. Both Fran and I thought it was a good fit, but wanted to hear what he had to say. Alverzo said it was a dead end job for his purposes. He wanted me to take the State Attorney's Office job. I reminded him it didn't have any intel value either. He told me that before I applied there. Anything related to Scientology was run out of the Clearwater office, he'd said then, based on intel he had from inside that office. He didn't reveal his source and I didn't probe, but I speculated that his agent was either a secretary or a member of the support staff since he wanted me there as a lawyer. The agency topped the ten-name list he gave me in March.

"Yes, but if you take the job in the St. Pete office there's at least a chance you could later transfer to the Clearwater office, which would be ideal."

I told him I wanted to go over it with Fran.

She and I went for a stroll on the beach that night with Angie in tow. "The church needs my help," I said. "I know what they're up against. My only question is whether I would be of any value to the church with whatever job I take. Don thinks something may come of the state attorney job down the road. My best role might just be to live in the area. If that's the case, I want the insurance defense job."

We talked about our individual dreams when we married. She thought she would have two or three children by then and no job, and that I would be an electrical engineer. I told her I was glad I had gone with my instincts and turned down the General Electric job and that she had trusted me. I told her I loved litigation and felt so much more empowered as an individual with my legal education, then added: "No way I would turn back the clock on that one."

"Well, then," she said. "Let's do that."

"Do what?"

"Follow your instincts, and I will trust and follow you."

Chapter 6

SMOKING GUN

We can easily forgive a child who is afraid of the dark; the real tragedy of life is when men are afraid of the light.

– Plato

"Just watch and learn," Myron Mensh said as he assigned me to Assistant State Attorney Joe "Cigar" Ciarciaglino, who was set to try a murder case. Joe Cigar was a big man – rotund, not tall. He carried a gun and showed it off to impress me. He said he had a permit to carry it. "All assistant state attorneys can carry," he said. "You, too." He served in Army Field Artillery in Vietnam and won several medals. He didn't mention the medals. I learned about them later from someone else. Joe Cigar did talk about his skills as a competitive marksman though.

That's all I did for a week. Watch a murder trial. A young African-American man was the defendant. The state's case was not strong. I thought the guy probably did the crime, but the evidence was not clear. I kept waiting for another shoe to drop, but one never fell. Just circumstantial evidence. After Joe rested for the State, the defendant predictably asked the judge to throw out the case due to insufficient evidence for the jury to reach a murder conviction. Just as predictably, the Judge denied the request.

I asked Joe Cigar if he thought the defendant would testify. "If he does, I'll rip him a new asshole," he said.

The defendant took the stand. Joe ripped him many new assholes. His cross-examination was brutal, in-your-face mean. The defendant barely got off an answer and Joe shot back yet another accusatory question, one after another, as though Joe was at the firing range popping off rounds. The defendant wilted. All that told me, however, was that the accused was a lousy witness and Joe was a skilled cross-examiner. Had I been on the jury I would have voted to acquit. Probably guilty is not guilty beyond a reasonable doubt. The jury convicted him, 6-0.

From the start, Joe Cigar kept telling me the defendant was guilty as hell. He didn't exhibit a hint of doubt or reservation. His resolve won the case, I decided. He instilled his confidence of guilt in the jury. Hence, I vowed to prosecute only those cases I really believed in.

The next day Mensh assigned me exclusively to Doug Crow, the youngest and most recently hired assistant state attorney. Crow's desk was overflowing with work. Matters tended to bounce down the chain of command to him. I was his gofer, except he often loaned me out to other assistants who needed help. Crow was a quiet, mild-mannered guy; thin, with a dark mustache. More than once I got bored and had to ask for things to do.

From time to time Mensh plucked me away for a training session. In one instance he had me accompany George Osborne, one of the more seasoned assistant state attorneys, to a case intake session with two St. Petersburg police officers. I sat and observed. George went through a police file and reviewed the reports and relevant evidence. Yes, we'll file on that one, he'd say, and then push the file away. I don't see a case here, he'd say about another one. On one of the turn-downs, the police officers groaned. "We really want you to file on that one," one of the officers said. "This is a bad guy. He keeps coming up in a lot of shit." George held his ground. "Gotta have the evidence," he said, and listed the things he wanted to see. "Get that and we'll file." It was interesting to witness the process. After the officers had left, George said to me, "They see a crime committed. We have to see a conviction."

One day I was parked in front of Crow's desk when he received a phone call. I didn't have my own desk. I had to pull up a chair to his. He hung up and said, "That was something you can handle." The St. Pete Police Department had received a request for information under Florida's Government in the Sunshine Law, the state's equivalent to the federal Freedom of Information Act. "He wants to know if they have to respond. Look up the law and get familiar with it, then call him and take care of it." He scratched the name Sergeant Meinhart and a phone number on a piece of paper.

I loved research assignments because the law library had tables and chairs, which meant I had my own work space. I grabbed a legal pad and got right on it.

Requests for information made to public agencies had to be complied with unless one of multiple, enumerated exemptions applied. A written response was required in which the agency must state whether or not any documents covered by the request exist. If documents did exist, and no exemptions applied, copies had to be turned over. If documents existed but the agency claimed one or more exemptions from disclosure, the agency was required to disclose the existence of the documents, claim the applicable exemptions and state the relevant basis for withholding them. The person requesting the documents was entitled to then challenge the exemptions in court where a judge could view the documents *in camera* (in chambers and outside the view of the requesting party) and rule on the claimed exemptions. I took notes and listed out all of the exemptions that might apply to law enforcement records.

I dialed Sgt. Meinhart's number. Someone answered, "St. Petersburg Police Department Intelligence Division," which surprised me. Crow hadn't mentioned the intel part. I asked for Sgt. Meinhart and introduced myself when he came on the phone. I asked him if he had any documents covered by the request. He told me they did, so I turned to my list of exemptions. "Are they part of an active criminal investigation?" He said they weren't. "Are they part of an active intelligence operation?" No, again. "Does the information involve pending prosecutions or appeals." It didn't.

"Well then, you have to turn over the documents," I said.

"No, we can't," Meinhart fired back.

"What do you mean you can't?"

"The Captain said not to turn them over."

"Then why did you contact us?"

"You're our lawyers. Aren't lawyers supposed to find loopholes?"

I snickered. "Sounds like you've been watching too many movies."

He was silent, and finally broke the ice. "So what can we do?"

"Maybe if you explain the problem I can come up with something." He told me that the office had received a request for information from the Church of Scientology.

I felt the air go out of my lungs. When I recovered, I wondered what the hell kind of documents he could have that pertained to the church. Alverzo had not mentioned anything about the G.O. sending out Sunshine Law requests. Anywhere. Particularly to agencies in St. Petersburg where I was working.

"How did you get the documents?" I asked.

"They were given to us," he said. "We were told to bury them."

My heart started pounding. It crossed my mind that I was being set up. On the other hand, his story and mannerisms rang true. I pondered my next move, weighing the potential risks and rewards. "Perhaps I should come by and take a look at what you've got. Maybe then I can come up with a loophole." He eagerly accepted my offer.

The address he gave me was that of a nondescript building in a different part of the city than its police department headquarters. Meinhart unlocked a heavy wire mesh door and escorted me through it to a large file room. There were hundreds of file folders on many rows of open shelves. He extracted two of them from different shelves on the same row and handed them to me.

"These are the documents responsive to the request you received?" I said.

"That's everything."

Each file was numbered in a large block font, 187 and 264. One was a quarter of an inch thick; the other three times that. "District Six Investigation" was stamped on each one. I asked Meinhart what that meant. He said it was a task force made up of six agencies. He rattled them off: FBI, IRS, BATF (Bureau of Alcohol, Tobacco and Firearms), Florida AG (the attorney-general), FDR (Florida Department of Revenue), and the Sixth Circuit SAO (the State Attorney's Office for Pinellas andPasco Counties).

"Is it possible for me to take the files back to the office so I can study them, or can you make me copies?"

"No. The files can't leave this space. But you can take all the time you need in the viewing area." He motioned toward a work space and desk near the metal door. He said he would be working outside the file room and to holler if I had any questions.

I nodded and he walked out, closing the metal door behind him. I heard it latch. Apparently I was locked in. An odd sensation of being trapped rippled through me, but it soon passed.

I opened the thicker file first. It contained newspaper clippings, most from the *St. Petersburg Times*, some from the *Clearwater Sun*, a couple from *The Tampa Tribune* and one from a Miami newspaper. There were also notes about local radio broadcasts. The articles involved the "mystery" surrounding the purchase of the Fort Harrison Hotel and a bank building in Clearwater by a buyer who paid cash for both buildings and turned out to be a front group for the Church of Scientology.

I noticed a pattern: they were all articles either written by Bette Orsini of the *St. Petersburg Times* or reports containing critical statements made by either Bob Snyder, a radio host and outspoken church critic, or Clearwater Mayor Gabe Cazares. These people were prime movers in the attacks against the church. Common themes were questions about who was really behind the purchases, insinuations that raised the possibility there may have been a Mafia connection, and calls for an official investigation.

The file also contained notes indicating that crew members from the Scientology flagship *Apollo* had set up an office in Miami in October of 1975 prior to the Clearwater property purchases, that L. Ron Hubbard and some of his top aides had gone to Daytona Beach, Florida, and that there was coordination between the two groups for the purpose of locating and purchasing property in Florida. This information appeared to have been supplied to the District 6 Investigation through Michael Lunsford, of the Clearwater FBI satellite office, and Francis Mullen, of the FBI's Tampa Field Office.

This was not an investigation; it was a counter-intelligence operation. The FBI knew who the real purchaser was in advance of the news stories but created a mystery and media firestorm through planted news leaks and informants. No wonder someone wanted to "bury" it; no wonder the captain was adamant that they not be disclosed. These files were never going to see Florida sunshine.

I committed the contents of both files to memory, a skill I learned in college and perfected in law school while cramming for final exams: memorize, take the test, and flush. In this case, instead of a test, I would write a full report when it was safe to do so.

On my way out, I told Meinhart I wanted to go over the situation with Doug Crow and see what we could come up with. "Someone will get back to you tomorrow."

He thanked me.

Back at the office I updated Crow. "Tell them they have to turn them over," he said.

"I did. They don't want to."

"Well, tell them they have to. We're their attorneys and we're telling them they have to."

"Doug, they were told to *bury* the documents. The captain said he doesn't want to turn them over. They want us to find a loophole." Doug grew impatient. I had more to say, but he cut me off. "Well, too bad. The law's the law."

"Someone higher up than me needs to tell them that. I'm not even licensed yet."

"But you're a lawyer and you passed the Florida Bar exam, and besides, you work for me. You work for this office."

"What I mean is, I think someone with more altitude than me needs to tell them that. They won't listen to me. That's been made clear."

He scanned the cluttered desk in front of him and heaved a sigh. "Okay, I'll take care of it. I'll call him when I get a chance."

* * *

After I got home from work I wrote my memorized report and met Don Alverzo in the parking lot of the new Countryside Mall north of Clearwater. I hopped out of my Chevrolet, climbed into his sedan, and we drove off. I was high as a kite, barely able to contain my excitement. I held a manila envelope. Alverzo broke into a huge grin the moment he laid eyes on me. "What?" he said. I put him off. "You have something big, don't you?"

I shrugged. "We'll see."

He started giggling. "Look at you with that shit-eating grin. It's big. Tell me while I'm driving." I refused. I wanted his complete attention. Before long he pulled off the road onto a dirt lane alongside an orange grove. We were somewhere near Safety Harbor. The car hadn't come to a complete stop when Alverzo slammed the gearshift into park, causing it to jerk to a stop. He turned off the engine, swivelled to face me, and reached for the envelope.

I pulled it back. "No. First, remind me what it was you were looking for when you brought me down here."

He tittered. "It's big. I know it's big. Let me see it." He reached again, and I yanked it beyond his reach.

"Now, now. Patience. What was it you said? Oh yeah, I remember. Who's behind the attacks on the Flag Land Base? Something about COIN... what was it again? COINTEL... Oh yeah, COINTELPRO. That's it."

His eyes bulged. "That's big. Let me see it." In his excitement I also saw a hint of disbelief. He didn't fully trust my conclusion but was hopeful, is how I read his reaction. He lunged again for the report.

I pushed his greedy hands away. "Not so fast. I want an acknowledgment first." Alverzo backed off, acquiescing to play along. "So, how long have I been down here?"

He chuckled then said, "Not long."

"I mean, in a job, not counting my setup time. Like maybe three weeks?" I asked. He agreed that was about right. "Okay. Just so we've got that straight." I flipped him my report.

He tore into the envelope and extracted my ten-page report. He read it under the red-filtered lens of a miniature flashlight he held below the height of the car windows. The soft beam danced from left to right down the handwritten pages.

"They got one of our Freedom of Information letters," he exclaimed.

"Well, technically, it's the Sunshine Law. Did you know someone from the church sent St. Petersburg Police a request for information?"

Alverzo turned the page as though he hadn't heard me. "Oh, good," he said. "We scored a hit." I repeated my question and he looked up. "I'm sorry. Legal does that. They send them out to all federal, state and local agencies as standard operating procedure whenever there is a major situation." He turned back to my report. Seconds later he said, without looking up, "I didn't know they had an Intel Department."

"That surprised me, too," I said. "A small city like that."

Alverzo continued poring over the report. "Ha. The captain doesn't want to turn them over." A moment later, Don cracked up. "Loophole." He looked up. "Did he really say that?" I nodded. "Oh, this is funny. They're so fucking corrupt."

"Read on. It gets better."

He soon stopped again, and pointed at the report. "This is good. You handled this perfectly. Ask to see the files. Good for you. Very well done." He went back to the report and resumed reading, mumbling and humming as he traversed each line. "District 6 Investigation..." He trailed off... "FBI, IRS, State Attorney's Office... planted newspaper articles... Bette Orsini... St. Pete Times... FBI running Gabe Cazares, IRS running Bob Snyder... COINTELPRO..." He abruptly sat erect, and said, Yes, this is it! This is how they report COINTELPRO ops."

"The FBI knew all along that the church was behind the purchase of the Fort Harrison," I said. "They leaked selected information and rolled out a story to alarm the public, just like you suspected. It was all an intel operation."

"I know," Alverzo said. "This is dynamite."

"The CIA and Clarence Kelly of the FBI are telling the media and Congress that they stopped all domestic counterintelligence programs."

"I know," he repeated.

"They didn't stop. They're lying. Those documents blow the lid on it."

"I know," Alverzo said. "This is huge. The problem is how to get our hands on the documents. They aren't going to turn them over."

"Well, let's see what happens," I said. He shook his head and repeated that they wouldn't turn them over. I told him this was big enough to justify blowing my cover, in that case, and said I could go to a judge with an affidavit or something to expose it.

Alverzo said that even if I were to testify about the files they would deny their existence or sanitize them. He wanted to get his hands on the documents. I thought of our operation in St. Louis and saw what he was thinking. "There's no way you're getting inside that place. The file room has caged doors." He stared blankly at me. I could hear his mental wheels grinding.

"No way, Don. No way. If you even try something they will connect it to me. Please don't even think about it."

* * *

I asked Crow if he had spoken with Meinhart. He lowered his eyes and shifted in his seat as if he had been spooked by a ghost. I got the feeling I was the ghost.

"No. I turned it over to Myron," he squeaked without looking up.

Soon after that odd exchange I saw Mensh speaking with Joe Cigar outside Mensh's office. When he noticed me he muttered something under his breath to Joe, who then peered over his shoulder at me. Both men were cool and distant. Their relationship with me had changed.

Later in the day, Mensh called me into his office. We were alone. He had a long face. "I have to let you go. I have to fill your billet by July or lose it and be a man short. I can't wait any longer for the Florida Bar to finish your admission."

I recalled the term "billet" from my Navy days. It meant a spot on the ship's crew. July 1 began the new fiscal year for most government agencies. The explanation, on its own, sounded plausible, but bringing it up for the first time with only a few days left in June didn't. I wasn't buying it.

Mensh's demeanor, the tone of his voice, and the whole vibe he put out told me that the topic was not open for discussion; that a firm decision had been made. I took a stab anyway and offered to place a final call to Tallahassee to expedite my admission. Mensh shook his head. "I don't want to risk it." He added that he had a qualified candidate ready to start who was already admitted to the Florida Bar.

I nodded my understanding, thanked him for giving me the opportunity, and extended my hand as I rose to leave. He leapt to his feet and threw out his hand. His eagerness to see me out the door was almost comical, which told me that the charade was not easy for him, and that he was grateful I had accepted his pretense.

As I left the building, I nervously watched my back. And my front. And all around. The very real thought of having an "accident" or being murdered and ending up in Tampa Bay stayed with me all the way home.

Chapter 7

CLANDESTINE MANEUVERS

Do not repeat the tactics which have gained you one victory, but let your methods be regulated by the infinite variety of circumstances.

— Sun Tzu, *The Art of War*

"Are you still available?" The question came from Norris Gould, the managing partner of the downtown Clearwater law firm Phillips, McFarland, Gould & Korones. I had met Gould when I applied for a position on my first trip to Clearwater in March after taking the Florida Bar exam. The law firm was on the list Alverzo gave me based on its prominence in the community, not one with vital information he wanted to access. Gould and I had taken to each other then, and he helped me out by giving me the lowdown on local law firms and agencies and even made some calls on my behalf. He invited Fran and me to dinner with him and his wife when we first moved to Clearwater, and continued to assist me. When I lost my job with the St. Pete State Attorney's Office, he was the first person not named Don Alverzo I called. I contacted him again the moment my Florida Bar admission went through and asked him which judge I should ask to swear me in. (Normally, new members are sworn in en masse, but because my application had been delayed, I would have to be sworn in alone.)

I loved Gould's dry sense of humor, and remembered our first meeting when I asked if he had gone to law school at the University of Iowa. He said, "You know, people ask me all the time if I was educated in Iowa, and I tell them all the same thing. I say, 'More or less.'" That cracked me up. I added the joke to my repertoire, although I wasn't sure it would work as well for me. Gould looked like a Marine drill sergeant, with a stocky frame and a close-cropped flattop, a person who might not have a sense of humor, and who might be too proud of his credentials to make light of them.

I told him I was indeed available and he asked me to drop by his office. He quickly added that what he had was only temporary, but it would give me a chance to practice in the community, which might lead to something else. I suited up and was in his office a half-hour later.

"David Korones left us without advance notice," Gould said. "He ran our firm's civil litigation department. He cleaned out his office and took most of the best case files with him. Unfortunately, one of the ones he left goes to trial next week, a jury trial. You said you were a good jury trial lawyer so I thought of you." He stated it with a subtle grin and a gleam in his eye.

I chuckled. More of his sense of humor. He knew I had tried only one jury trial, and that was in a trial practice class I had in law school. The law professor was the judge and high school civics students were the jurors. But it was a real case, with real consequences, and I won a verdict for the defense, and the "judge" told me I had what it took to be a good trial lawyer.

Gould said his firm was searching for a partner-level trial lawyer and needed someone to fill the gap. He offered me a whopping $200 per week. I did a quick mental calculation: $10,400 per year. That was about $4,000 less than I had been offered by General Electric prior to going to law school. The pay was disheartening. But it was a hell of a lot better than zero, which is what I was making. Plus I would get to try a jury case and prove myself locally. I was also happy to return some of the favors Gould had extended to me. I accepted his offer.

There was one additional benefit. Gould ushered me to my new office, which used to belong to David Korones. It was magnificent and plush and as big as my living room. The mahogany desk was huge and sat in front of a monstrous, matching credenza. Those pieces took up only half the space. A large sofa, two easy chairs, and a coffee table took up the other half. Everything was color-coordinated. Gould motioned to the leather, high-backed chair behind the desk. "Have a seat. See if it fits."

It fit alright. I felt like a big shot as I swivelled around to check out my new digs. An empty secretary's space separated my office from the hallway. "What about a secretary?" I asked.

"David took her. We figured any new lawyer will want to hire his own secretary so we won't be filling it." He said I could share his secretary.

* * *

Donald McFarland, one of the partners in the firm, stepped inside my office. "Are you ready to interview witnesses yet?" He represented the business owned by the client whose case was going to trial and agreed to help out on the trial. He wanted me to schedule the key witnesses so we could interview them together. It was Day Two on the job and I was at my desk organizing the jumbled mess of a case file into something I could work with. I couldn't make heads or tails of anything, and had given up trying.

"Not yet," I said.

He looked at my desk. "Are you still organizing the file?" He looked a little perturbed. McFarland was a big man, tall and fit. Like Gould, he had a flattop haircut and looked to be about fifty years old.

"Yes," I replied. "I've created separate folders and put everything in order." I waved a hand over my work. "It takes time up front, but this is going to save us a lot of time prepping and trying the case, and a lot of headaches trying to find things."

McFarland flashed a skeptical look. Clearly, it wasn't the approach he would have taken. Strike One. But I was confident of my plan and unfazed. "I'll be in my office," he said, and I plowed ahead.

The case involved an injury to a twelve-year old boy in an all-terrain motorcycle accident on our client's property while riding his ATM. The injured boy's parents had incurred several thousand dollars in medical expenses and were seeking $20,000 in compensation. Our client's property insurance carrier had denied coverage. To obtain a jury award, the boy and his parents needed to prove negligence on the part of the homeowners. Our defense was that both sets of parents had allowed their kids to play on the three-wheeled motorcycle and therefore had jointly assumed the potential risks.

The trial lasted only two days. I picked the jury, conducted the opening argument and examined all of our witnesses. McFarland cross-examined the injured twelve-year old boy and gave the closing argument. The jury came back with a defense verdict. Zero liability. McFarland shook my hand afterward. "Good job," he said.

I immediately turned my attention to other cases. There were many more files to organize and evaluate, and clients to meet, in addition to preparation for a second jury trial the following month. Gould told me to keep working the files as though the job was mine, and said he would keep me apprised as to the status of their search for a more seasoned trial attorney. "Who knows," he said with a playful expression. "We may have already found our man."

Meanwhile, with Alverzo's coaching, I spread my professional and social wings into the community. I joined the Jaycees, managed and played on its softball team, and met as many business leaders and attorneys as I could. Fran and I joined the St. Petersburg Opera Club. Not because we liked opera, but because Clearwater Mayor Gabe Cazares belonged to it. Cazares was running for Congress on the Democratic ticket and Fran took a volunteer job in his campaign, answering the phone and making calls to notify supporters of campaign events and fund raisers.

Fran's involvement with the Guardian's Office started in Clearwater. Alverzo asked her if she would mind helping Molly, a woman in his office whom he said was in charge of overt data collection. I knew that Fran had gone to the local library to do research and that she had once gone with Molly to Tallahassee, but I didn't know the specific work they did because of the G.O.'s strict need-to-know policy, which Fran and I honored. Once she joined Gabe's campaign, Fran began doing covert data collection, which was Alverzo's domain. But she remained under Molly's direction.

Alverzo and Molly came to our duplex one night, the first visit for both, and the first joint meeting. They parked several blocks down the street and walked the rest of the way. Alverzo asked us to attend a Cazares fund raiser hosted by Mary Ann Doherty, an activist in liberal causes and friend of the mayor and his wife, Maggie, and the wife of Pat Doherty, a partner in the law firm Gross & Doherty, the law firm that represented the Cazareses in libel suits against the church. Prior to my arrival in Clearwater, the church had sued Mayor Cazares and the City of Clearwater for violation of its civil rights. The mayor and his wife retaliated with their own lawsuit.

Alverzo wanted Fran to introduce me to the mayor and for me to re-connect with Gross & Doherty to establish a continuing intel line with them. I had met Doherty and his partner Ray Gross when I visited Clearwater in March, after I sat for the Florida Bar exam. Their firm was on the original list of ten places Don wanted me to apply for a job, not with the intention of getting hired, but just to interview and maybe gain intel. They were young lawyers who had worked as assistant public defenders out of law school and had recently struck out on their own.

When I dropped off my résumé in March, Doherty looked it over and then hollered out, "Hey, Ray. We just got our first job applicant." Gross appeared from an adjoining office and the two of them busted their guts laughing. I joined in on the laughter. They took the joke further and conducted a mock interview of me that turned into a hilarious bull session. I had a great time. When the timing felt right, I eased them into a conversation about the case against the church. "What are two criminal lawyers doing representing a civil litigant?" I asked. They were doing it as a favor to Gabe and Maggie, Doherty replied, adding: "My wife begged me to do it."

Gross agreed that it was Doherty's fault. They made it clear they were regretting that decision. "We're getting papered to death by the other side," Doherty said, "and now they're trying for a change of venue to Lakeland."

"Great intel," Alverzo said of the report I presented him then.

* * *

Fran introduced me to Gabe Cazares. His wife Maggie stood next to him but was engaged in conversation with someone else. He reacted to me oddly, with fearful and jittery eyes. I tried to behave as though I hadn't noticed. "I work at the Phillips McFarland law firm."

"Oh really?" he said, immediately turning away and grabbing Maggie by the shoulder. "Maggie, this is Fran's husband, Merrell Vannier. He works at Phillips McFarland. You know Lloyd Phillips."

"Oh, yes. Nice to meet you." She said, extending her hand.

Gabe said, "I know Lloyd. He's a Democrat. That's good. Maybe we can talk more some time. Glad to meet you, thanks for coming." As this strange scene unfolded, I realized something. I made a mental note for my report to Alverzo and moved on, greeting and meeting Gabe's supporters. I kept one eye on Gabe as he worked the crowd. He was smooth as silk, a real natural with everyone else, which supported my evaluation.

I also ran into Pat Doherty. I stuck out my hand, "Remember me?"

"How could I forget?" he said, taking my hand. "The firm's first job applicant." We shot the shit for a minute or two, then he said, "Hey, you should come by the office on Friday. Go to lunch with us and throw darts afterward." He explained that they took Friday afternoons off. "It's one of the benefits of being in private practice. We don't make any money, but we sure have a lot of fun." I laughed with him and said I'd take him up on the lunch offer and try to squeeze in a game of darts.

I met Alverzo later that night and turned in a written report. "The sonofabitch knows I'm affiliated with Scientology. He's been briefed." Alverzo told me to slow down. He went over my report and asked some questions. "Listen. My FBI application connects me to Scientology. He was working with the FBI earlier in the year. I stumbled onto the COINTELPRO files they were supposed to bury. St. Pete Intel reports back the security breach. The FBI runs my name. They brief Cazares and tell him to watch his ass. They don't want him to fuck up and blow the COINTELPRO op. That's what I saw in him tonight."

Alverzo took it all in stride then challenged me in an easy manner. "He's a politician. That could explain his jittery eyes."

"It was more than jittery eyes. I'll bet you haven't gotten any good intel on him from Fran." He gave me a noncommittal look, which told me enough. "And you won't get any, either. You watch and see."

He asked my opinion of Maggie Cazares. "She's scattered all over the place," I said. "Nobody home. Dumb as a post. Gabe doesn't let her in on what he's doing and what he knows. He's cagey enough to see where she's at."

Alverzo's nonchalant demeanor triggered a realization for me. He didn't need my report on Maggie. He was just testing my observation and evaluation skills. "Does that fit with other intel you have on her?" I asked.

He nodded, then I asked, "So what do you think about my analysis of Gabe?"

"You're probably right." He said we could factor that into our intel strategy. "He and his FBI handler might know you're a Scientology agent, but we know that they know now. Did you let it show that you're on to him?"

"No, I was cool."

He asked what Gabe would report to his handler if asked about the encounter. I answered, "Just that he ran into me, and probably that it looked like a staged event; that I went out of my way to be there and meet him."

"Good. Then we know something they don't know. That's what intel is all about. I don't care what they know as long as I know it and they don't know that I know it."

* * *

"Okay, I'm done," I said. Pat Doherty and Ray Gross had just demolished me in darts. "Your turn," I said to Michael Stuckey, a lawyer friend of theirs who joined us for lunch. Stuckey had his nose buried in a *Screw* magazine. Pat and Ray pleaded with him to put it down and get his ass up for a game, but he wouldn't budge. He said he was immersed in an intellectual article and wanted to finish it.

Doherty grabbed the magazine and looked at the pages Stuckey had open. "Look at this, Ray. He likes gay stuff." Gross cracked up.

"Like father, like son," Stuckey said. I had no idea what he meant. It must have been an inside joke, because Doherty and Gross roared. Stuckey snatched back the magazine and told me to play one more. Doherty handed me the darts.

"Here. You go first." I turned them down, saying I had to prepare for a trial. "What trial is that?" he asked.

"I've got a civil rape case. I'm defense."

"Civil rape?" Both Doherty and Gross exclaimed. "Why didn't she just file charges?" Gross asked. I told him she had, but the state attorney refused to file; not enough evidence. They demanded to know the facts. Even Stuckey put down his magazine to hear my answer. I gave them a snapshot of the evidence; how my client said their sex was consensual and had rounded up witnesses with stories of their own. "Like what?" Doherty pressed. "Yeah, we want details," Gross said. I told them one of my witnesses got a hand job from the young woman the first day they met, at a public beach standing in waist-deep water. The conversation degenerated from there into raucous locker room laughter.

"Oh, that's an easy defense," Doherty said after he calmed down. "Just keep making proffers." He meant to keep offering evidence of the plaintiff's promiscuity for the record outside the presence of the jury. He shoved the darts at me. "Here, you have time for one more."

I took the darts. "Okay, but this is the last one."

* * *

"They're trying to dump the Cazares case," I told Alverzo. "But none of the lawyers they've spoken to want to take it." He waved my report and asked if I included names. "It's all in there. Every lawyer Cazares has contacted said the case is a loser."

He asked what I thought they would do if they couldn't find a replacement. I told him they could file a motion to withdraw from the case, but that I didn't think they would do that until after the election. "That would embarrass Cazares during his campaign. But if you want to push them, get Legal to work the file. Paper them some more. They hate having to write responses." Alverzo said he might do that.

When he finished reading my report, he said, "Good stuff. Stay on top of this. Spend as much time as you can with them." He wanted to know who Gabe and Maggie planned to hire before it happened so he could research the new lawyers and explore his options.

"Will do," I said.

"How's everything else?" I told him everything was fine. Busy at work. Getting results. People there like me. Having fun. All good."

"Staying away from the ladies?"

"Clean as a whistle."

* * *

Gould buzzed me on the intercom to come to his office the morning after I won my second jury trial. He told me how pleased the partners were with my work. "We decided to stop our search for a trial lawyer. We want to make you the permanent head of our civil litigation department." I started to thank him, but he wasn't done. "We're giving you a raise to $275 per week and a budget for you to hire your own secretary." He said they were prepared to raise my salary even more but needed me to first build up my department and get it generating more income. I thanked him profusely and promised I would ensure my department would generate more income than it ever had.

I celebrated both my promotion and the jury verdict that Friday afternoon with Gross and Doherty. After pizza and beer we threw darts. In the middle of his throw, Doherty stopped and turned to Gross. "Hey, Ray. I just had a brilliant idea."

"What's that?" Gross said.

Doherty looked at me, then back at Ray. "We're looking for a good civil lawyer to replace us, right?"

Gross lit up. My jaw hit the floor. "Oh, no," I said.

"Oh, yes," they said in unison.

"Uh-uh," I replied. "No way. I don't want that piece of shit case."

Doherty shoved his darts at Gross. "I'm going to call Gabe right now." He raced off. I quickly followed him into his office, pleading, "No, don't do that. Please."

"Really," he said. "You're perfect for this case." He found the number and started dialing. I leaned over his desk. "No, I'm not perfect for it. I don't want the case. Please don't call him." I felt like grabbing the phone, but refrained. When he finished dialing he leaned back in his chair with the phone to his ear and a broad, confident smile on his face. I implored him to put the phone down.

"Hello. This is Pat Doherty, Gabe's attorney. May I speak with Gabe."

Exasperated, I began calculating my exit strategy. I settled on telling Gabe that I was neither interested nor suited to take his case; that I was new to the firm and that I was not authorized to take on high profile cases.

"Okay, will you please leave him a message that I called." I breathed a sigh of relief and released the tension in my body. Cazares would call back but I wouldn't be there. I had time to think through my position – and meet with someone.

* * *

"You'll never guess what happened today?" Alverzo shook his head, intrigued. "Doherty wants me to take over Gabe and Maggie's case. He even called Gabe right in front of me. I was freaking out. Thank God, he wasn't in."

There was something wrong with Don's reaction or rather, his non-reaction. I guess I expected his eyes to pop out or somehow share my shock. He finally spoke. "That's a great idea."

"What? Are you fucking kidding me? That's a horrible idea. I can't do that."

He sat behind the wheel of his sedan, eyeing me and playfully twisting the end of his mustache. It reminded me of the time in the St. Louis safe house when he asked me to apply for a job as a janitor. He seemed to view my attitude as another interesting button, like the reaction I had to using my middle name, George. "Why not?" he said.

"Why not? Wow. Where do I start? How about with conflicts of interest. I can't work against a client."

"Who asked you to do that?" His blasé manner caused me a system overload. I felt like I was talking with someone from a different planet. He remained poised, and silent. After a spell, I considered his question. True, he had not asked me to do anything wrong, but he was suggesting that I should take the case. I searched for a legitimate purpose that I may have overlooked. All I saw was calamity.

"Don, are you forgetting our last discussion about Gabe? He knows I'm an agent for the church." He didn't flinch. I shook my head. "Oh, man, I can't believe you don't see how stupid this idea is. We'd be walking into a trap."

He let out a half-laugh. "How's that?"

"Listen, Gabe is not going to retain me in the first place, okay? Even if I wanted to take his case, and I don't, I'd have to clear it through my managing partner and he's not gonna want a horseshit case in the office. He just told me he wants me to build up the civil litigation department because the guy before me took all the good cases when he left. For another thing..." I noticed Don patiently churning one end of his mustache again, grinning, unmoved. "I could go on and on, but I guess you're not listening."

"I'm listening. I want to hear your objections and so far I haven't heard anything that bothers me. I don't want you to harm his case and I'm not worried about the FBI because they'll think like you're thinking and look for you to throw the case, and you won't be doing that. You'll be doing something else."

"What will I be doing?"

He said the church was confronted with a number of major situations, life threatening ones. "If you represent Gabe Cazares it will open doors we can't get into but need to get into." I asked for an example and he told me about an INS (Immigration and Naturalization Service) order to deport all non-U.S. citizens from the Flag Land Base, which covered 75 percent of the staff. The high percentage of foreigners was a result of the crew having been on ships that sailed the Mediterranean Sea who had been recruited internationally without concern for their American citizenship status.

"The Old Man said we'll lose the land base if we lose the INS case, and if we lose the land base, we'll lose Scientology."

"Can't you fight that in the courts?"

"We are," he said. "We lost at the district level and appealed to the regional level in Miami." He was speaking of the administrative process, not a federal court case. "Our lawyers predicted that we'll lose there. We can appeal to D.C., but they say we'll lose there, too. We can then petition the U.S. Supreme

Court, but the lawyers said it was a long shot they'd take the case. Legal is not the solution. Intel has to solve this. If you had the calling card of being Gabe's attorney, I could get you inside the INS."

"How?"

"Government agencies all have it in for Scientology. They'll talk to you if they view you as an enemy of Scientology. Just call them up, show your credentials and they'll give you whatever you want."

I was skeptical. Federal agencies were not supposed to assist private parties. But I didn't entirely dismiss it based on my knowledge about FBI COINTELPRO and what I saw in the St. Petersburg P.D. intel files. "What if they check with the FBI, or the FBI sees what I'm up to and tips them off?"

Alverzo put his hand on my shoulder and smiled confidently. "They won't see you. That's how a magician does his tricks. He gets the audience to watch his left hand while he does the trick with his right hand."

I let that sink in as I observed the unwavering confidence he exuded. The idea was potentially brilliant. It might just work. I nodded thoughtfully.

He slapped my shoulder. "Now you're learning to think like an intelligence officer."

Chapter 8

SPY VS. SPY

When you grow suspicious of a person and begin a system of espionage upon him, your punishment will be that you will find your suspicions true.

– Elbert Hubbard
American writer, artist and philosopher

"The insurance company has an outstanding offer of twenty-five hundred dollars," I said to Sheila Bradford,[6] the young woman sitting on my office sofa next to her live-in boyfriend. I sat in a chair across from them.

"David Korones told me that three months ago, and I turned it down," she said. "I won't accept that."

I didn't see any value in pursuing the case, which is probably why Korones let the file gather dust and left the firm without it. As with all my new clients, though, I wanted to meet her and go over my evaluation to see if we were right for each other. I told her I had spoken to the insurance adjuster and he's dug in. "He refused to increase his offer, but did say he could get another thousand dollars if that would settle the case. Does that interest you?"

"Forget it," she said, adding that her share after the firm deducted its one-third fee, would barely cover her current medical bills. "I don't get it," she continued. "They had water on their floor. No signs. I'm shopping, looking at what they want me to look at, the stuff on their shelves, and they don't even have to pay all my medical bills?"

I explained that a case is broken down into liability and the amount of damage, and what she was talking about was liability. I was confident I could prove the grocery store was negligent. "The problem with this case is that the hospital released you and you've only received minimal treatment from a medical doctor. The rest is chiropractic."

"The chiropractor is the only one who gave me relief," she said, almost breaking down. The boyfriend stepped in. "I can testify to that. There were nights when she was in the bathroom hugging the commode, her headaches got so bad."

"That's true," she said. "I had these terrible migraines that were unbearable. They would come on at work, too, and I had to go lay down. She began to sob.

The boyfriend consoled her. "A friend of ours recommended her to a chiropractor," he said, "and that's when she started getting relief."

"Finally," she said. "For the first time since I fell. Why should I have to go a doctor when they didn't do anything for me?"

The boyfriend asked what I thought of chiropractors. "I have a negative view," I replied. "But it's based on things I have heard, mainly from a friend of mine in law school who worked part-time as an insurance adjuster. I don't have any first-hand knowledge. But I know the sentiments I hold are widespread."

He said the medical establishment had it in for chiropractors, and the insurance companies and everyone else were buying their propaganda. His comments struck a chord with me. It's like the AMA's turf war. Scientology had run up against the same medical combine. "That may be true," I said, "but we have to persuade jurors who have also been exposed to that propaganda."

I asked if she had ever had migraines before she fell, and she said she had not. I thought it over. I believed her. And if she had won me over she could probably win over a jury. That only got us halfway, though. "Ms. Bradford ..." I said. She interrupted and asked me to address her by her first name. "Okay, Sheila. If we file a lawsuit, the insurance company is entitled to an independent medical examination by a medical doctor. He'll have credentials a mile long and tons of experience testifying in court, and he will say nothing is wrong with you. It'll be his word against the chiropractor's. But you will have the burden to prove that the treatment was necessary."

"Isn't that your job?" she asked. A smile followed close behind.

I chuckled. "Actually, it is. And I'm willing to fight for you if I think I can win the case. Let me ask you this: what would you accept in settlement of your case?" I was testing her. I wanted to know her idea of a victory. I had already let go of one client whose idea of the value of the case was completely at odds with mine.

She looked at her boyfriend who drew a blank, then said "I don't know."

"Ten thousand?" I asked, adding that her share after deduction of estimated legal expenses would be roughly $5,500. She turned to her boyfriend. "That's good, isn't it?" He nodded, and she told me she would take that.

"Okay," I said. "Here's what I'm willing to do. If your chiropractor will work with me and explain how his treatment works, and how it is helping you, and if I think I can present his explanation in a way the jury can understand, then I'll file a law suit for you.

* * *

Our living arrangement in Clearwater worked out perfectly for Angie, who turned five in July. The neighborhood was safe and three other girls about her age lived nearby. Mary Ann lived in the adjoining duplex while Holly and Charity lived a few houses away. Angie and Mary Ann became inseparable. Even better, Mary Ann had an older sister, Susie, who was eleven or twelve, and was a good babysitter. We often hired her when we were both at work, wanted a date night, or when duty called us both away.

One day I came home and Angie, Mary Ann and Charity were there. I did a double-take on Charity. Her blonde hair was short, around her ears. It used to be shoulder-length. "Charity," I said. "You got your hair cut." Mary Ann tittered and cupped her mouth. I scanned the room. Angie had a sheepish look on her face and Fran made a guttural sound. "Angie cut her hair," she said, casting her a reproachful look.

"Really?" I said. "Looks pretty good to me."

"Her mother took her to the hair salon," Fran said. "You should have seen it when Angie got done. There were slashes and blotches of different lengths all over."

"We were playing hairdresser," Angie pleaded.

"But you should pretend cut, not real cut," I said. Fran said that Angie knew that now and had promised not to do it again. Angie nodded.

"How did her mother react?" I asked. "I hope you paid for the trim."

"I offered to pay but she refused to accept it. She took it all in stride and said they were just being kids, no big deal."

"I like her attitude," I said.

* * *

Bradford's chiropractor studied an x-ray of my neck on a light box. Free x-rays. This was the path Dr. Ron Woodley chose to enlighten me on chiropractic treatment. "You were injured in an accident," he said.

"I haven't been in an accident."

"Think back," he said. "Six months ago." I did, and said, "Nope, no accident."

"Did you ever play football?" he asked. In high school, I told him, but I was never injured. "You're missing something. Look at your neck here. There's a straightening. It should be curved.

"Look at your back. You have a subluxation here. This vertebra is shifted. You've had a whiplash in your past."

He turned to a chart of the human anatomy showing a skeleton, blood vessels and nerves. "A subluxation causes a neurological imbalance, which can cause visceral (organ) problems. "I bet you have digestive problems."

"Yeah, I do. I recently had an upper GI test but it turned out negative."

"Negative to a medical doctor means that they have no treatment for a disorder. It doesn't justify surgery or drugs, in other words. It doesn't really mean *normal*. A chiropractor can treat that condition, so to us it's not negative – it's an abnormality."

He got me thinking. "Wait a minute. I did have an accident, more than a year ago. I was stopped with my turn signal on when a woman crashed into the rear of my car. I went to a doctor who gave me pain pills but said I only had soft tissue damage which would heal itself. Couldn't move my neck for about a week, but the stiffness and pain gradually went away."

"But you were injured," he said. "You had a whiplash. Both the neck and back were injured, and you're still suffering the effects of it. I can treat that." He told me the first few sessions were on him since he wanted me to experience the treatment process and see some results.

"Have you ever testified in court before?" I asked him. He said he hadn't, but was eager to do so. I pointed to his x-ray light box. "Can you explain all this to a jury?" He said I would need a roentgenologist for that.

"A what?"

"That's the chiropractic equivalent of a radiologist, an expert in evaluating x-rays. I know a good one who has testified in court before."

* * *

As summer turned to fall, Alverzo said he wanted me to attend an upcoming meeting of the opera club Fran and I had joined. "Mayor Cazares will be there. I want you to rub elbows with him. Find out the status of his hunt for a replacement attorney." He didn't say how he knew Cazares would be there.

* * *

The opera meeting was held in a member's upscale home. We signed in at a make-shift registration desk. The hostess greeted us and thanked us for coming. We took champagne glasses from a passing tray and began to roam. I spotted Gabe Cazares across the room. He returned a surprised look and wandered over.

"I didn't know you were interested in opera," he said to me after shaking hands and saying he was glad to see me. Of course he didn't know, how would he? I shrugged, nodding. He went on. "Hey, that's something, Robert Merrill coming to Tampa, eh?"

Robert Merrill was scheduled to perform Verdi's *Rigoletto*. I knew that because I had done my homework. I briefed Fran on the drive there. "Yeah, we can't wait." I glanced at Fran, who nodded agreeably.

"You probably know about the St. Louis Muni Opera, don't you?" The sly dog was probing me. "Sure, the Municipal Opera," I replied.

"I heard it was great," he said.

"Yeah, that's what I hear. Kind of like the Starlight Theatre in Kansas City. Outdoors. Light opera. I went to law school in Kansas City. That's where we lived before moving here."

"I see. So you've never been to St. Louis?"

"We've been there. Just not to the Muni Opera."

"I see. Well, I hope to go there the next time I'm in St. Louis." He stuck out his hand and showed his teeth. "Glad to see you again."

I mulled it over as he walked away. For a moment I doubted my prior evaluation of Cazares but then I saw past the charade.

When he was safely out of earshot, glad-handing other members, I lifted my champagne glass to my lips and said softly to Fran. "What did you think of that?"

She whispered back, "He was pumping you."

Her answer confirmed how obvious he had been. "Perhaps that's what he wanted us to think." Cazares didn't need to pump, but I stopped short of explaining my comment. I had not told Fran what I saw in the St. Pete P.D. intel files or shared with her my confidential conversations with Alverzo about Cazares' connection to the FBI.

We spent another twenty minutes or so mingling. In a quiet moment Fran told me she felt out of place and wanted to leave. I looked around for Cazares but didn't see him. The gathering had spilled into other rooms and outside, though. "Did he leave?" I asked. She said she didn't know. I suggested that we take a final lap around to find him and if not we could split.

Just then Gabe and Maggie entered the room and approached us. He said they were about to take off but wanted to have a word with me first. He peeled me off from Fran, steering me toward a corner of the room. I gestured for her to hang tight.

Gabe spoke quietly. "Pat said you wanted to take our case."

I was thunderstruck. Perhaps Doherty said that or perhaps Gabe got it wrong. I saw it as an attempt to entrap me by putting words in my mouth that I never uttered. I was alone. He had a witness. I shook my head emphatically. "No. That's not true. I didn't say that."

Maggie seemed crushed. She shot a pitiful glance at Gabe. Tellingly, Gabe took it in stride, merely saying, "Oh." I could see his mind churning, though. I looked at him intently, keeping him on the hot spot. He quickly became unsettled. His eyes fluttered. He couldn't maintain eye contact. It was weirdly identical to his reaction at the Doherty fundraiser, and it made me uncomfortable, too, but I was intent upon getting across a message: *Don't ever try to pull one on me, pal.* My message must have gotten through. He turned to Maggie. "I guess I got that wrong."

"So you won't take our case?" she said.

"I didn't say that either." I explained exactly what happened, adding, "They want off the case really badly. You probably know that."

Maggie snorted. "They're threatening to file a motion to withdraw if we don't find someone, and that would hurt Gabe's campaign." I told her I understood.

Gabe said they were feeling boxed in because he was too busy with his campaign and his mayoral duties to find an attorney. "I just thought you might want to take the case," he said.

"That's not my decision to make. I work for Phillips McFarland. The firm would have to approve a high profile case like yours and I wouldn't even recommend it unless you asked me to look into taking the case. Then I would want to see the case file and interview you. It's a process. I don't know whether I would be interested in the case and I don't know if the firm would approve taking it if I were."

They both nodded, indicating they understood.

"You must know and talk to a lot of attorneys," I said to Gabe. "Don't you have any other possibilities?"

Gabe answered straightaway with seeming candor, the most I had seen from him in our two meetings: "I do have someone who really likes the case and is with a good firm. It looks like he will take it."

I suppressed a chuckle along with the thought, *So why talk to me about taking the case?* But it was an opening to dig, so what I said was, "Oh, good. Who's that?"

Gabe's demeanor instantly shifted back to his oily, fretful one. His dancing eyes returned. "I don't want to give out the name of the lawyer or the firm."

"I understand," I said. "Well, good luck with that."

* * *

"That's it for me," I said to Alverzo, who was holding my report. "I'm done talking to him about his legal case." He held up his hand to hold me off until he finished reading. He toyed with his mustache for a minute or so, then said, "Do you believe he really has a lawyer lined up?"

"Who knows. He could be blowing smoke."

"What do you think?" he asked.

"I think he's wearing two hats. When he's wearing his politician hat, he's good with people, confident and at ease. I saw him work the crowd, both here and at the fundraiser. He comes across as caring and sincere, and people eat it up. When he puts on his spy hat, at least in my presence, he's afraid and unsure of himself, except when he's prepared for the encounter, but even then, only to the extent of his preparation. The amazing thing is his ability to switch hats, just like that." I snapped my fingers. "So I think he wants to trick me into soliciting his case but at the same time he wants to put out the PR line that he has an attorney lined up and that everything is under control."

"So his comment about having an attorney is probably not true?"

"Yeah, I'd say that. Gross and Doherty won't file a motion to withdraw in the middle of his congressional campaign. He knows they're leveraging the situation."

I was glad he didn't bring up my decision about not having further contact with Cazares regarding his legal case because I was adamant, and it may have led to a confrontation and tarnished our relationship. That's one thing I liked about Alverzo: he paid attention and was perceptive. He seemed to have learned something about my temperament and knew when there was wiggle room for persuasion and when to let go. Looking at it from his point of view, the idea that I might represent Cazares sprang from out of nowhere, like a gift from the gods, and now it had been snatched away by those same hands.

Let's move on, I was thinking. I could see he had reached the same conclusion.

Chapter 9

ALL IN

Pearls don't lie on the seashore. If you want one, you must dive for it.

– Chinese proverb

"Maggie Cazares is on the line," my secretary said. "She sounds very agitated and says it's an emergency." I was dumbfounded. It was late December and I had not spoken with her or her husband since the opera club get-together three months earlier. Gabe had since lost his congressional bid in the November election. "Do you want to take her call?"

I nodded and motioned her to close the door behind her.

Maggie was distressed. "They turned on us. They're out to destroy us." One would think she was talking about a dangerous prowler outside her window by the tone in her voice. I asked who she was talking about. She must not have heard me. "Why would they do this?" she screamed.

"Do what?"

"They even sent a copy to Scientology?"

"Sent what?" I persisted. But she kept babbling. "Maggie!" I almost yelled. "Calm down." She stopped. "I can't understand you. Please just let me ask some questions and you answer them." She whimpered okay.

"Thank you. Now, who are you talking about?"

"Pat Doherty," she screeched and went off again. This time I picked up something about a motion to withdraw. The last I had heard from Doherty was that they had prepared a motion and sent it to the Cazareses with a threat to file it if the couple didn't find a replacement attorney by such and such date, a deadline that kept moving.

So I assumed they had done something more than that. I thought maybe they had set the motion for a hearing. Rules of procedure require that copies be sent to the attorneys for all parties. She must have meant the copy went to the church's attorneys.

"Maggie," I said sternly. She abruptly shut up. "Please just answer my questions. Did Gross and Doherty file a motion to withdraw?" I eventually pulled the story out of her. Doherty threatened to set a hearing on a motion to withdraw and begin charging hourly fees unless they found another attorney within one week of the letter. The date of the letter was December 16 so they had until the twenty-third, which was only two days away, and two days before Christmas.

Just to make sure we were on the same page, I repeated the facts back to her and asked if I had it right. She said I did, followed by, "Do you still want to take our case?" Oh man, that set me off. Gabe's trick of putting words in my mouth... speaking of whom: "Maggie, is Gabe there? Put him on, please." He got on the line. "Gabe, I thought I made it clear that I was not seeking your case; that was Doherty's idea."

"Maggie's just got that wrong." I did a slow burn, enough to melt the phone lines between us. As I silently let off steam, he added: "I thought you might be interested if we couldn't find someone." I asked what happened to the lawyer he was talking to in September. He named an attorney and a reputable firm, but said they were only going to take the case during the campaign in an emergency. "They don't want it now."

"You can't find anyone else to take it? Have you been looking all this time?" He said he was doing his best but that no one wanted the case. "They're all afraid to take on Scientology," he said. I suppressed a laugh. He left off the part Doherty once told me, that lawyers who had been contacted by Gabe were turning it down because the case was unwinnable so they were demanding to be paid hourly rather than on a percentage basis, which the Cazareses could not afford.

Cazares then said the magic words. "Would you please take the case?"

"As I told you before, I would first have to review the case file. If I'm interested in taking it I will then need to run it by the law firm." He said they had the case file at home and invited me to come by.

I grabbed my suit jacket and took off, telling my secretary that I would be back in an hour or two. I drove to a pay phone and signaled Alverzo to contact me.

He called me back. "What is it, Ritz?"

"We need to meet ASAP."

* * *

"If I do this, I need some things from you," I said to Alverzo after I updated him about the latest development. "Number one: benefits versus risks. This thing could blow sky high and be a PR disaster for the church. Not to mention my personal risks." I told him I had done some quick legal research and wanted to do more. "There's a clear conflict of interest, which is an ethical violation, but nothing criminal that I can come up with so far. "I could lose my law license."

He asked me what the rule said. I gave it to him verbatim; it was fresh in my mind. He quibbled with the wording, saying I did not have an adverse financial interest to Cazares and that I was not a member of the Church of Scientology of California, the corporate name of the Flag Land Base. I told him he was being too cute. "I'm a secret agent for that corporate entity." He said he understood.

"So, benefits. Where do things stand with the INS order to deport Flag staff? He said their lawyers were fighting to slow it down but they still expected to lose. "And you really believe the INS will open its files for me if I'm Gabe's attorney?"

"I know they will," he said.

I told him that was hard for me to grasp. "I'm pretty sure that's illegal. At a minimum, the church could sue the crap out of them for doing that."

"The INS is corrupt. They hate Scientology. All those agencies do." He went on to say that getting me inside the INS would not be the only use for me. He had lots of other ideas on how he could make me into the most important asset the Guardian's Office ever had. I asked for examples. He declined, citing security, but assured me the benefits far outweighed the risks.

I mulled it over, then told him I was willing to stick my neck out and do this on one other condition. "Run this up to the highest level." He tightened up a bit, as though his security alarms had gone off, so I threw in: "You don't have to tell me who gave the green light. I just want your personal assurances that what we plan to do is known and the risks are appreciated by someone who has a broad overview of the whole scene, not just in Clearwater. Make sure they know our agreements, that the handling of the Cazares case is off-limits, and make sure they understand that I'm a better lawyer than Gross and Doherty."

He smiled at the last bit, as though I was teasing which I sometimes would do, but I was dead serious. "It's true," I said. "They only know criminal law. I know civil law. And I know libel law." He knew I handled a couple of libel cases on behalf of the firm's client, the *Clearwater Sun*, the local daily newspaper.

* * *

I handed a memo to Norrie Gould from across his desk. I had the Cazares case file under my arm. He took a quick look. "The mayor's case is a loser," he said. "He's a public figure. Maybe his wife's claim has some value."

"I agree. I said the same thing in the memo."

"I can see how there could be value in taking the cases to get your name out, though," he said. I told him that was my plan. He said he would consider it and asked me to leave him the case file. "If I approve that, I'll want to run it by the partners, too."

Gould got back to me later that day. He wanted me to collect $500 in expenses and let him approve the retainer agreement to make sure the firm was not on the hook for expenses. "Beyond that, the decision whether to take his case is up to you."

* * *

I told Alverzo the news. He assured me he had gone "to the top" and gotten a green light. "Someone who has the whole picture?" I asked. He nodded. "And you reported everything we discussed?" He said he had. Everything.

* * *

I entered my appearance in the Cazares case on Thursday, December 23. A reporter from the *St. Petersburg Times* phoned my office an hour or two later and asked for a statement. I rattled off a comment about my intention to pursue the case.

The following Tuesday I received a call from Cazares. "I don't want you to do anything on our case." I was stunned, thinking, *Why tell me now, and not last week?* He said he didn't want me to do anything that might harm his case during his campaign for re-election. The mayoral election was scheduled for the first week in February, almost six weeks away. I asked what he was afraid might go wrong and he said he didn't want a ruling against him. I told him I had no immediate plans to file any motions that might result in a ruling. "Well, I just don't want you to do anything."

He was wobbly. He'd been talking to someone. I dismissed the idea that it was a campaign adviser. *His FBI handler?* It didn't add up, either. But he was the client. I agreed not to undertake any proactive measures without his further instruction.

As I put down the phone, an uneasy feeling gnawed at me. But then I realized something that entirely changed my outlook. *This was perfect. A calling card and no need to work the case. Thank you, Gabe.*

Chapter 10

INTEL OP: INS

Engage people with what they expect; it is what they are able to discern and confirms their projections. It settles them into predictable patterns of response, occupying their minds while you wait for the extraordinary moment — that which they cannot anticipate.

-- Sun Tzu, *The Art of War*

I gave my name to the Officer in Charge of Tampa Bay INS and told him I represented Clearwater Mayor Gabe Cazares in litigation against the Church of Scientology."

"I know," he said. "I read it in the newspaper." That surprised the hell out of me. Not only had he read the newspaper article but had taken note of and remembered my name over the long Christmas weekend.

"So you probably know we are a small firm up against a litigious international organization. I could use all the help I can get." I had more to say. In fact, I had a whole spiel worked out. I had notes in front of me for all sorts of contingencies that might arise during my conversation. But he broke in.

"I'd be happy to help you any way I can. We have some stuff on them. Not sure how much it will help but you're welcome to come over."

Complete cooperation was the one response, perhaps the only one, I had not anticipated, despite the unflappable confidence Alverzo had tried to instill in me. I was impressed. He'd called it – so far, anyway.

"Gee, thanks," I said. "I really appreciate it."

* * *

I met the INS officer in the federal building on Zack Street in downtown Tampa. He was chummy, asked where I was from, the schools I went to, and what drew me to Clearwater. I didn't detect the slightest sign that he was pumping me. He appeared to regard me as a fraternity brother or, more aptly, a fellow member of a secret society. Or perhaps he intended to implant that impression to instill a false sense of security. I refused to let down my guard. For all I knew his true purpose was to obtain evidence of actual spy activity and blow my cover now that I was the Cazares' attorney of record.

He asked me if I was prepared to battle it out with the church and its high-priced lawyers. I told him I wasn't, which is why I was there. "My strategy is to shortcut the litigation and prepare for trial through investigation and research and not rack up a lot of hours and costs engaged in motions and depositions," I said. The Mayor and his wife had limited resources and my law firm was working on a contingency retainer and didn't want to get bogged down. He said he understood, which is what he figured and why he had offered his help.

He pointed over my shoulder to a cardboard box on top of a small, round conference table. "That's all we have. I had one of the clerks bring it in. You're welcome to look through it, but I can't give you any copies or let the files out of my office." He said he had work to do and would be coming and going while I went through the stuff, but would answer any questions I had, or get them answered. He waved his hand at the table, and said, "Take a seat. Stay as long as you like."

I took a legal pad and pen out of my briefcase and dug into the box. The first file contained internal INS memos with some names given. Alverzo wanted names. Otherwise it seemed like a lot of regulatory agency-speak. There were copies of Orders to Show Cause, the legal papers that kick-start the deportation process. The named individuals were ordered to appear and show why they should not be deported. The church would already have copies of these and other legal filings so they had no intel value. I saw a memo showing the command structure of Scientology and describing its history on ships at sea. It was nothing I didn't already know, but something an attorney in litigation against the church would want to know. So I jotted some notes. As a spy, I wanted to know the source of that information. All I saw was an INS agent's name. His source wasn't revealed. I made a mental note to try and figure it out.

I decided to maintain two sets of notes. One as the attorney for the Cazareses. I would place notes of anything of obvious interest to a lawyer who was engaged in litigation against the church on the top pages of my legal pad, open and visible to anyone who looked. The other set would be hidden on the pad's back pages. Notes in that category would include the names of INS decision makers, INS sources of information on Scientology, third party instigators of the INS legal action, and any evidence of COINTELPRO or counterintelligence activities by agencies such as the FBI, CIA, Interpol, and the State Department.

I raced through the files using this method, keeping in mind that the best intel might be in a file at the back of the box, but not so fast that I missed anything. I planned to go through the box again if I had time – and had not been caught and kicked out.

After about twenty minutes, the officer told me he had to attend a staff meeting. As soon as he closed the door behind him I flipped the pages of my legal pad and scribbled coded notes of the intel I had memorized, then found the documents containing it and filled in the details I had forgotten. I took down the authors and dates of important memos and shorthanded their contents. I fell back on my memorization tricks. Before I put away a document, and moved on, I did a quick scan of my notes to see if I could decipher them. When I stumbled, I returned to the document, found the relevant passage, and figured out why my notes had failed me. I then amended them as necessary.

An hour or so later the doorknob rattled. I stopped and quickly returned to my attorney's notes. The INS officer in charge stopped at my desk and looked down. I removed my arm covering the pad so he could have a clear view of my lawyer notes. "How's it going?" he asked.

I told him there was a lot there but that it was going well. I gestured at my legal pad. "I'm taking notes. I'll study them later. I can tell it's helping, though."

"Good, I'm glad," he said. "Take your time. You can always come back." He patted my shoulder. We were pals. Or so it seemed, at least. I thanked him.

I made it through the entire box in a few hours. The INS officer left and returned several times during that period. There were no intel bombshells in the files, no evidence of counterintelligence activities. The officer said he would stay until five but then would have to kick me out. That gave me another forty-five minutes. I decided to spend it beefing up my memory. I revisited the files containing intel I had flagged. Without referring to my notes, I spotted key words, names or dates, and then covered portions of the document with my hand and tested my memory of what I had just gone over. I sneaked quick peeks at my notes occasionally and associated them with my memory. By the time I finished this exercise, I felt pretty good about my duplication of the intel. I still had fifteen minutes left. I employed another technique from my bag of memory tricks. I went back through the box in random order. By the time the officer asked me if I was ready to wrap up, I had it nailed. I told him I was and packed my gear.

He accompanied me to the lobby. I was parked on the street, so we said our goodbyes there. I was glad he didn't linger to shoot the breeze. Memorization of that much information is like a house of cards. It's all interconnected by keywords and images. Pull out one of the cards and the whole damn thing can collapse.

I hopped into my 68 Chevy Impala and sped off to the Tampa-Hillsborough County Public Library. It was nearby, north two major streets and east five or six more. I raced inside, grabbed the nearest isolated table, threw open my briefcase, pulled out my legal pad and began decoding my notes and dumping my memory into a handwritten report. I left the library with an unburdened mind and a sore writing hand, and hoped my intel was worth something. I had no idea.

* * *

In mid-January of 1977 I received a set of interrogatories from lawyers for the church in the Cazares case. These are questions that have to be answered under oath within thirty days. I groaned. I had almost forgotten about the case and enjoyed working my other files. I scanned through them quickly. The questions were relevant and proper. I grabbed the Dictaphone and instructed my secretary to send Cazares my standard letter telling him to provide his answers within three weeks so I would have time to draft legal responses, after which he would come to the office to review, approve and sign them under oath. The letter also instructed him to indicate any information he preferred not to turn over and to state his reasons to enable me to lodge the proper objections, if any applied. I calendared both due dates.

* * *

"You're the man," Alverzo said a week or so later.
"Why?"

"The INS case was dismissed based on your intelligence." He said they analyzed the intelligence report from my visit to the INS and were able to spot the person who instigated the deportation orders along with the false reports he relied on. "We sent in a PR team to his supervisor and straightened it all out and he dismissed the case."

Concern over my cover being blown curbed the sense of triumph that began to swell in my chest. "Oh, no," I said. "I hope that doesn't get back to the INS guy." He waved off my concern. "We made sure that you were well-hidden as the source of our information. Nobody knows. Not even the PR guys know how we got the information."

Hearing that, I released my pent-up jubilation. Alverzo hugged me and called me a hero. He said I saved the Flag Land Base, and therefore Scientology. "Well, not alone," I said. "You guys did the handling. All I did was report what I saw, and I don't even remember any of that."

As we celebrated, Alverzo said: "See? I told you that being Gabe's lawyer would open doors." We relived the INS Op, how easy it had been for me, and how corrupt government agencies were when it came to Scientology. In that mood, he said he had big plans for me and wanted to use me in a new program the G.O. had created. He called it the Anti-Religion Movement, or ARM. He said an intelligence analysis had been done about the increasing number of cults in America and the ever-increasing number of calls for investigations and government regulation of them. He said they discovered that the intelligence community was behind it all. They wanted to regulate or destroy cults. He said their ultimate target was Scientology. They were freaked out about the technology being widely known and embraced, and were going after bizarre fringe groups while trying to pin the cult label on Scientology and lump us all together.

"The Old Man said the answer was for us to take responsibility for the entire field. "So we're going to get very involved through you as our Number One agent."

The entry point into the Anti-Religion Movement presented itself two weeks later in the form of House Bill 527, a House Concurrent Resolution calling for the creation of a joint religious cult study committee, which was introduced in the Florida Legislature.

Chapter 11

INTEL OP: KILL BILL

The greatest victory is that which requires no battle.

— Sun Tzu, *The Art of War*

"I've heard of that lawsuit, and all the furor over Scientology down there," John Culbreath said. "How's that going?" Culbreath was the state representative of District 36, which covered the area surrounding Brooksville, a small city north of Tampa.

I told him I had just gotten involved in the case and was coming up to speed. "I saw that you introduced House Bill 527. I was calling to volunteer my litigation skills and knowledge about cults."

Culbreath was ecstatic. He said he would love to have my help and asked if we could meet. Before I could answer, he added, "I can meet you in New Port Richey, which is about half-way to my office here in Brooksville from Clearwater." I told him to name the time and place and I would be there.

He was a big man, a cattle rancher, and easy to talk to. Unlike another politician I knew, his friendly demeanor felt genuine. We eventually got around to HB 527. He confessed that he did not have much knowledge or interest in the subject of cults but it meant a lot to one of his constituents, a doctor whose daughter had been in one. Alverzo wanted to know who was pushing the bill so I hoped Culbreath would identify the doctor and spare me the task of pumping him for it. But he didn't. I decided to wait for a fitting opportunity.

I asked how I could help. He said that what really intrigued him about my offer was that I was a trial lawyer. "I would love to have you help me prepare for the hearing."

"Great," I said, suggesting that I meet with his witnesses and discover any baggage they might have so he wouldn't get blindsided at the hearing by Scientology lawyers or representatives. "They have a history of using investigators and playing hardball."

Culbreath reacted as though I had given one of his prized steers a blue ribbon. "That's a perfect idea," he said, throwing up his arms. He added that, as an elected official, he had to think about his next election, and the last thing he needed was a black eye over a bill submitted to please a constituent. He thanked me for my willingness to put forth such an effort. He scribbled down the name and phone number of Dr. James Springer[7] and slid it across the desk.

"Don't call him until you hear from me. I want to grease the line and make sure he knows you're working for me." He said Dr. Springer could provide me the names and contact information of the other two witnesses. "He's the one who brought them to me. They're both former members of cults."

* * *

Back at my office I had to take care of another problem. Cazares had not returned his answers to interrogatories and was not returning my calls. I waited until after he won reelection to start pressing him, but now responses were due within a few days and I was getting miffed. I tried calling him again. Same thing. Not available. I left another message, then dictated a letter to him and asked my secretary to make sure it went out that day. I wasn't done. I called church attorney Clyde Wilson.

It was the first time we had spoken. "Can I have a thirty day extension on those interrogatories?" I asked. I started to lay out an excuse that Gabe had been engaged in his mayoral campaign for reelection, but Wilson said I didn't need an excuse. "Maybe someday I'll need a favor from you," he said. Most lawyers are accommodating like that, at least for the first extension, but some aren't. I was relieved and promised to return the favor.

* * *

I met Dr. Springer at his house, a nice place outside of Brooksville. He was very cordial and thankful that I volunteered my time. He took me to his study and offered me a drink. I settled on lemonade. He said that Culbreath had spoken highly of me, asked him to cooperate fully, and said that I was in charge of hearing preparations. Anything I said went. Man, talk about greasing the line; this line was so buttered I could have slid back to Clearwater.

I asked the doctor what he knew about cults, and took notes. He said it all started when his daughter joined the Children of God, which required total devotion, living in communes and abandoning her family and the rest of modern society. He then started investigating it and hooking up with other parents who had lost their kids to cults. He asked me if I knew George Slaughter. I didn't, but one of my mission targets was to get an introduction to him. Slaughter was from Texas and had started an anti-cult group. Slaughter's daughter had joined the Unification Church of the Rev. Sun Mung Moon, the "Moonies." He managed to extract her from their group and then went all-out against religious cults. Cynthia Slaughter became the star witness at the U.S. Senate's investigative hearings of 1976 chaired by U. S. Senator Bob Dole, R-Kansas.

Springer said, "I don't know how interested you are in this area, but we could use someone like you, a lawyer who is willing to devote his time." I told him my interest was growing the more I learned. That pleased him. "I think you should talk to

George. He's wired into the whole movement. I can introduce you." I told him to do that.

We spent the day talking about cults. The more I listened, the more energized and talkative he became. Some of it bored the hell out of me and I had to force myself to stay awake, especially when he went into his pet project: the function of the brain responsible for people falling under the spell of cults.

He had written articles on the subject and was putting it all into a book. He was not a neurosurgeon or a doctor who specialized in the study of the brain but he was fascinated with the subject and was becoming an expert through his own studies and investigations. He shared some of his theories with me, which really tested my powers of attention, because I thought it was all a bunch of baloney. The whole subject was near and dear to my heart, but in the opposite direction: I thought science took a wrong turn when, in 1879, it began to seek a physiological explanation for behavior, ignoring the existence of the human spirit, the non-physical aspect of a person. This led to a reliance on psychoactive drugs, shock treatment and lobotomies to treat behavioral issues. So it was tough for me to hang in there with Springer, but I soldiered on. I even graciously accepted a copy of his incomplete manuscript to read in my spare time.

Eventually we turned to preparation for the hearing on HB 527. "Dr. Springer, I need to ask you a personal question. Representative Culbreath doesn't want any surprises at the hearing. We need to prepare for anything the opposition may come up with." He said he understood and was willing to confide in me. "Good. I need to know any skeletons in your closet."

Springer blanched, drew a deep breath and then said, "Boy, that's a tough one. I guess that could mean anything."

I nodded, "Yeah, pretty much."

"Well, I did hire Ted Patrick to deprogram my daughter," he said. Patrick was a man from San Diego who would, for a fee, help extract someone from a cult. The practice involved force, coercion, and persuasion. "Some people consider that kidnapping."

""Yes," I said. "Patrick has been arrested and charged with kidnapping. On the civil side it's called false imprisonment, so a person can also be sued for it." He said his daughter was safely out of the Children of God and wouldn't sue him. I asked for the particulars and took notes. After we covered the incident in depth I asked if there was anything else I should know about.

He thought for a few seconds and his face reddened. "Well," he said. "I guess I should also mention ..." he paused. "Is copyright violation a crime?"

"It can be, if it's intentional."

"Well, I guess I better go over it with you." He unloaded his guilty conscience regarding his writings about the brain and cults. He admitted that he had plagiarized another writer's copyrighted material.

* * *

I met Rex Banks in his Tampa apartment. He was a young man, about my age (twenty-eight), and upbeat. He was a former member of the Hare Khrishnas, which is the informal name for the International Society for Krishna Consciousness (ISKON). He said he had been deprogrammed by Ted Patrick and that he had himself attempted to deprogram a few other Hare Krishnas.

I explained my need to delve into the details of his deprogramming activities, and he said he understood, no problem. One didn't work out. In fact, he was worried about being charged with kidnapping or being sued over it. I got all the facts and then asked if there were any other skeletons.

He mentioned a traffic ticket for failure to stop at a stop sign. Forget that, I said. He also had some unpaid parking tickets. "Not really a skeleton," I said. "How many are we talking about?" Two, he said. "Nah," I said. "Best to pay them before the hearing, though. What else? I want anything someone who is investigating you or might find out by talking to people you know or confide in."

"I went to a gay bar, would that count?"

"Possibly," I said. "What's the story on that? Is this a one-time deal, or what?"

"I went to a gay bar." He giggled. "I just went there, okay? To see what it was like. I'm not gay. I just went there."

"Just once?" I said.

He giggled again. "Well, once or twice."

"Which bar?"

"Well, I guess there were two of them," he said. "So yeah, I went more than once." I asked for both names and he gave them to me, and repeated that he was not gay. His whole reaction, the giddiness in relaying the story, the insistence that he was not gay, and the increasing number of visits caught my attention. I'd pushed a button, triggering something he felt embarrassed about and wanted to keep secret. And therefore it was something I wanted to know more about.

"Of course you aren't gay. I get it. So what did you do inside these bars?"

"Well, you know, I talked to guys, let them buy me a beer, you know, that sort of thing, just to see." He said this amid titters.

"Did you dance with any of them?"

"Oh yeah, I guess I did a couple of times. You know, just for kicks. I'm really not gay. You can ask any of my friends. I date girls. You can ask them, too."

"No, no. I get it," I said, and kept digging. Turned out there were three gay bars, and that just covered Tampa. I wrote it all down.

* * *

"She's stood me up twice now." I was talking on the telephone with Dr. Springer about the evasive third witness.

"I know. She called me. She feels really bad about treating you that way, but she gave me permission to explain what's going on." She was no longer a member of the Children of God and is now happily married with two kids. He made the mistake of telling her the purpose of my interview and she got cold feet, not just about meeting me, but also about testifying. She had an abortion when she was in college, before she joined the cult, and she hasn't told her family or her husband and she's afraid it will come out.

"Well, it might," I said. "You get into a fight, the other guy gets to fight back."

Springer said he felt bad about it because he was the one who talked her into being a witness, and now she's stressed out and wants to bail. He said he might still be able to bring her back into the fold if we give her some time. I told him he should let her back out, that I didn't want to talk her into doing something she might regret.

"So now we're down to only two witnesses," he said with heavy words. But moments later he rebounded: "Maybe I can round up some others."

My instinct was to discourage him but knew better. I said, "If you do, let me know."

* * *

When I met Alverzo he said he wanted to kill the bill now. He asked me to set up a meeting with Culbreath, present the evidence and recommend that he kill HB 527.

* * *

"Here's what we've got," I said to Culbreath. "First, we have two witnesses, not three. One flaked out. She might change her mind, but I doubt it. You don't want her anyway. She's hiding a teenage abortion from her family and husband. The other ex-cult member is involved in a kidnapping for hire. He gets paid to forcibly seize a cult member, whisk them away, and hold them against their will while he brainwashes them into no longer being brainwashed by the cult.

"One of his victims got away, so he could be sued or charged with kidnapping at any moment. Plus, he frequents gay bars."

Culbreath rolled his head. "Oh, my God."

"Yeah," I said. "And there's more. Dr. Springer is himself involved in connecting parents to Ted Patrick, who has been sued and criminally tried for kidnapping and the use of coercion to change cult members' religious beliefs and get them to leave their groups. On top of that the doctor confided to me that he has committed copyright infringement in his publications. All these witnesses are toxic.[8] They'll blow up at the hearing and poison anyone connected to them."

Culbreath was shaking his head when I finished. "I had a bad feeling about this bill from the start. Thank God you came along. This thing could have destroyed my political career. To hell with it. I'm going to postpone the hearing and let the bill die in committee."

"I think that's a wise thing to do."

Chapter 12

Intel Op: ARM

I never will, by any word or act, bow to the shrine of intolerance, or admit a right of inquiry into the religious opinions of others.

— Thomas Jefferson

"What do you think of her? You can talk to me in confidence," George Slaughter said to me over the phone. He ran the Committee Engaged in Freeing Minds (CEFM) out of his home in Texas. Springer introduced me to him. He was asking me about Rita Flemming, the head of a Pennsylvania-based group called the Freedom Foundation, for short.[9] Springer had also linked me up with her. CEFM and Freedom Foundation were two of the many groups that had sprung up across the country. Alverzo called them ARM groups, as in Anti-Religion Movement. We viewed their activities to be anti-religious, not anti-cult.

As to Slaughter's question, I didn't like being on the spot. My goal was to win over and maintain trust with both of them so I could continue gathering intel from each one. I could sense some sort of friction between them and I wanted to know what it was. "Give me some context," I said. "What's happening?" I managed to pull it out of him.

* * *

"They're trying to merge all ARM groups in America into one large umbrella organization," I reported to Alverzo. "The only thing preventing it is an agreement on who will be the head honcho, Slaughter or Flemming. Slaughter doesn't want to relinquish control to her. He views himself as the stronger, more capable leader."

Alverzo said he didn't want a merger, which would make the movement stronger. He wanted me to create conflict between them without being suspected as the source of the tension: a third party campaign. He asked if I thought I could pull it off.

"It'll be tricky, but if you coach me, I probably can." He said he wanted to think about it and would get back to me.

"Whatcha got?" he asked about a stack of papers I brought to the meeting.

"More anti-religion stuff. I'm getting it from all over the country now, not just from Slaughter and Flemming." He asked if there was anything good in it and I told him I didn't know and noted that I was already spending two to three hours a night on the phone with ARM stuff and didn't have time to go through everything people were sending me. He laughed and told me to leave it so he could make copies.

* * *

"George," I said to Slaughter over the phone. "I've been thinking over this whole merger thing." I paused and he asked me what I had come up with. "We're speaking off the record, right?" Definitely, he said. "This won't get back to Rita?" Absolutely not. "Good, because, well, I like her on a personal level, I think she means well, but she will just run it into the ground."

"I'm glad to hear you say that," he said.

"So you can't let that happen," I said.

He went on to vent his frustrations working with her while mentioning his proven results on the big stage, namely his role in pressing for the Dole hearings. "She can't see past her nose when it comes to running an organization. It's all about her, and you can't run a national organization that way."

"I couldn't agree more," I said. "Her heart's in the right place, but her head is up her ass in that regard." He laughed hard.

My next call was to Rita Flemming. I told her I was checking in and wanted to know if she had made any progress with the merger. She said she hadn't. She sounded discouraged. She said that Slaughter could really infuriate her at times. I told her I could see that, too, adding, "But, please keep that to yourself." She perked up and said she was really interested in my view of things because there have been times when she was ready to give in to him for the good of the cause, but thought it would be a mistake.

"Rita, can we talk very confidentially here?" Yes, she said. "Listen, I don't think you should give in to him. George can be a hardheaded sonofabitch." She said she knew that. I continued: "I think he's on a power grab. He will trample over everyone else's opinions and cast you aside once he obtains control. That's my prediction."

She let out a huge sigh of relief and thanked me for saying that. She had those same fears and asked me if I would help her behind the scenes to make the merger happen with her in charge of the umbrella group. "As long as we can keep this our secret," I said. She said her lips were sealed; she wouldn't even tell her husband.

* * *

Several weeks later Alverzo asked me about the status of the merger talks. "Ain't happening," I said. "They hate each other. They're barely on speaking terms." I told him the breakdown of their relationship was spreading throughout the entire ARM movement. "People are taking sides. They're growing apathetic about a merger, saying it's impossible to bring people together." He loved hearing that, congratulated me, and told me to keep it up. By this point I was in total command of the third party technique and no longer needed his coaching.

As usual I had plenty of ARM intelligence to hand over. My sources continued to grow and so did the flow of information, which sometimes involved big names: public officials, corporate bigwigs, you name it. U.S. Army General William Westmoreland, who commanded all U.S. military operations in Vietnam from 1964 to 1968, for example. He was working with one of the many ARM groups and was considering whether to hire someone to deprogram his daughter or to begin speaking out publicly against cults himself.

"Anything else?" Alverzo asked.

"Yeah," I said, bursting at the seams. I knew he was going to love this, so I saved it for last. I pulled a piece of paper from my pocket and handed it to him. "There's going to be an ambush deprogramming in Georgia next weekend. Here's all the details. The religious group, the person's name, everything." His face lit up. He took the paper and went over it. He congratulated me, then said "I might have a surprise for them."

I told him that more was on the way. "Slaughter said he wanted me to be in the loop for every planned deprogramming in the country." Alverzo was ecstatic. I added, "He wants me to help him avoid any legal problems, so you can't do anything with his intel that gets him arrested or sued."

That was the last conversation I ever had with Don Alverzo.

* * *

A few nights later I parked at our rendezvous spot expecting to meet him. A man I had never seen before approached my passenger side door. He was my age, about six-foot two, athletic build, and blond hair. "Hi, Ritz," he said. "My name is Tom Ritchie. I'm filling in for Don. He had to leave town to take care of something."

I was staggered. I couldn't imagine having any handler other than Alverzo, and wasn't sure I wanted anyone else. I only came to Florida because of Don. Not only was he good at his craft but he was a fantastic handler. He was perceptive and knew how to work with me. I was walking a high wire with no net and needed his kind of support. I shook my head with a mixture of disbelief and confusion.

Ritchie said he could imagine the shock I must be experiencing but assured me that I was in good hands. He said he worked for Don and was familiar with all the covert ops in Clearwater, including my activities.

"Where did he go?" I asked. Ritchie couldn't say. "When will he be back?" He didn't know. I let out a deep breath, thinking, *Oh shit, here we go with all the security stuff.* I thought I deserved some straight answers.

He said Alverzo told him to apologize to me for having to leave so suddenly, and to assure me that Alverzo had fully briefed him. He added, "I'm ready to step in for Don."

Ritchie wanted us to get acquainted first and began telling me about himself. He was from Hawaii and had been the Executive Director of the Hawaii Church of Scientology before joining the G.O. and coming to Flag. He said his church was large and active, with about two hundred staff members. It was similar in size to the St. Louis church when I was there, which gave me a general idea of his responsibilities and experience. I asked if he surfed. He looked that type. "Totally into surfing," he said. Before long we were joking and carrying on about different things. He won me over on a personal level, although I remained concerned about his skills as an intelligence officer.

I asked if Alverzo had briefed him on our agreements regarding the Cazares case. He said that he had. "The case is off limits," I said, partly as a question. He said he understood. I asked if he was up on all the ARM intelligence. He said he was and, in fact, wanted to go over that with me when I was ready. I told him to go ahead.

He started by praising me for the volume and quality of intelligence I was providing. He told me how they used the intel I gave them about the Georgia deprogramming. "We contacted the religious group leaders and alerted them on what was about to go down and asked if the targeted member was strong enough to withstand being kidnapped. They said she was, so we set up a sting with local law enforcement officers who arrested the deprogrammers."

I loved it. "Poetic justice," I said. We shared a good laugh and congratulated each other. He went on to say that they had devised a standard procedure out of that successful action, which was for me to provide the intel and for them to coordinate with the religious group involved and either set up a sting or have the religious leaders send the targeted persons out of harm's way if they were weak or unstable. The goal was to make deprogramming too dangerous to conduct and thereby eradicate the practice. I was pumped, happy to be part of the plan.

* * *

"I'm here to see the Mayor," I said to the receptionist, and gave her my name. She asked if I had an appointment. "No, but I'm his attorney and it's urgent." The door to Cazares's office was open and I heard him say goodbye to someone and the sound of a phone hanging up. "His line is free, I'll ring him now," she said.

"Never mind," I said, and walked in. Cazares about jumped out of his skin the moment he saw me. "Hi, Gabe. We need to talk." He shifted uneasily in his chair and uttered something about his calendar.

"I would have made an appointment but you didn't return any of my calls or answer my letter, so we have both been inconvenienced."

He motioned for me to have a seat and asked the receptionist, who was standing at the door, to close it. As soon as the latch clicked, I cut to the chase. "Your answers to interrogatories are more than a month late." I didn't mention that I had obtained two thirty day extensions and might not be able to secure another one.

"The Scientologists don't turn over evidence to me, why should I give them anything?" he said. I told him I hadn't sent out any discovery, and reminded him that he had instructed me not to do anything on the case until he gave the word.

No, he meant before my involvement, he said. I told him there were steps his lawyers could have taken to force the church to produce good faith answers. "Just because they didn't do their jobs doesn't justify you disobeying court rules of discovery. You can be sanctioned by the court for that. My firm and I can get sanctioned, too."

"They don't answer questions even when the court orders them to," he said. My jaw dropped. His prior lawyers, Gross & Doherty, had not filed any motions to compel further responses. It struck me that he was talking about his other case, the one in which he was being sued by the church and was being defended by lawyers hired by the city's insurance company.

"Well maybe your attorneys in that case don't know how to compel answers," I said. "I don't know. It's not my case." I was ready to suggest that he have the city attorney side-check their work, when he spoke. "No, they know what they're doing. They said the Scientologists never answer their questions so they didn't know why I should answer theirs."

That floored me. "Are you getting legal advice from them about this case?" His hangdog reaction answered my question. "Who exactly are you talking to?"

"Walter Logan," he finally answered. Walter Logan was a newly admitted lawyer who worked for John T. Allen, the attorney who represented the city's insurance company. I met Logan before when I applied for a job at the Allen firm. It was an intel run. Alverzo wanted me to eyeball Allen and report my observations. But I was only able to meet Logan. He was a mousy guy and virulently anti-Scientology. In fact, I had never run into so much vitriol before, which baffled me, especially when he told me that he had only learned about Scientology when he joined the Allen law firm and began working on defending the church's case against Cazares. He had no prior bad experience that explained his hostility.[10]

A smirk formed on Gabe's lips as I sat in disbelief. I had not seen this look before. I sensed in him a feeling he had the upper hand, which didn't make sense unless it was from a view that I was working with the church trying to force him to answer their interrogatories. I could see how a suspicious mind would think that. He knew I was a spy and the interrogatories were sent by the church soon after I entered my appearance in his case. He may have thought I was in a lose-lose situation, and so it appeared I was.

"I take it you plan to follow their advice regarding your answers, not mine?"

"I don't see why I should answer their questions when they don't answer mine," he said. I told him I would get back to him.

I went straight to Norrie Gould, filled him in on what had transpired and asked him what I should do. I told him I thought the firm should withdraw from the case. He said, if it were him, he would call up Allen and Logan and ask them if they want to take over the case, and if they say no, he would tell them to butt out.

I took his advice, called the office, and asked for John T. Allen. I didn't want to talk with Logan but he was the one who came on the line. "Gabe told me you're giving him legal advice not to answer interrogatories in my case," I said. Logan admitted it and said he didn't think Cazares should answer them because of the way the church was conducting discovery sent to them.

"Why don't you take over the case," I said. "Then you can handle it any way you want." He said they couldn't do that since they only work for insurance companies. "No, not the firm. You. Why don't you take the case on the side?"

He said he wouldn't do that. "Then stop giving him legal advice on my case." He said he wouldn't do that either. Cazares was their client too, and they were going to advise him the way they saw fit. I asked him if he will pay the sanctions we incur for not answering the interrogatories, and his response was a quick no.

Before I had a chance to meet with Gould again, John T. Allen called and tore into me. He said the libel case I was handling was a loser and that he had a summary judgment case, which meant that he could likely win his case by motion and avoid a trial. The church case against Cazares was for violation of constitutional rights. The evidence I uncovered in the files of the St. Petersburg Police Intel files would defeat Allen's case for summary judgment, which is why I once recommended to Alverzo that he blow my cover and use it. So Allen was on the verge of winning his case only because Cazares, possibly with Allen's and Logan's knowledge and assistance, was withholding evidence of his role as an FBI informant in an illegal domestic counterintelligence program. And now they were up in arms about the church not being forthcoming in discovery. That was rich.

"If you do anything in that case," Allen said, "you risk a court ruling that could harm the summary judgment motion I'm preparing to file. So don't do anything. That's what we told Gabe. I'm telling you the same thing."

Now I knew why Cazares instructed me not to do anything. It wasn't because of his reelection campaign. But here I was holding a bag of shit loaded with dynamite and a burning fuse.

I told Allen he had no authority over me and that Cazares either had to cooperate with our law firm in his libel case or the firm had no choice but to withdraw from the case. He told me not to withdraw because it might also harm his legal interests. That was a veiled threat to take some kind of action against me, which told me that Allen knew the bind I was in. He could only have known that if he had been briefed by either Gabe or the FBI, probably the latter, which would insulate Cazares and give Allen attorney-client protection from revealing what he knew.

"So what do you suggest I do?" I asked, "since you're in charge of my case."

"You figure it out," he said.

I told him to go to hell, and hung up. I saw my secretary at the door. "Friend of yours?" she asked, which cracked me up.

The next morning Gould buzzed me to come into his office. "I hear you and John Allen butted heads." I said we had and asked how he knew. Allen had called him, he said. *Geez, what a prick.* Gould then said, "I know what it's like dealing with him. He and I have gone at it before. So don't worry about it. We need to talk about what to do with the Cazares case, though."

"Norrie, I want out. There's a total communication breakdown between me and his attorneys. It's impossible for me to do my job."

He said that he understood and was leaning that way himself. "Let me talk to Lloyd [Phillips] and see how he wants to handle this."

* * *

I met with Ritchie that evening the same way I used to meet with Alverzo. I turned over newly acquired intel, including another planned deprogramming. Before we broke, I told him: "Just to give you a heads up, I think the firm is going to withdraw from the Cazares case."

He was taken aback, and asked why. I told him I didn't like working with Gabe's other attorneys and the case was a distraction. Ritchie looked worried. I reassured him. "Look, it doesn't matter. I only took his case to have a calling card as an anti-Scientologist. I don't need that anymore. I have my own identity."

He asked how my relationship was with my law firm. "I'm working with them on this. Don't worry about it. Everything's under control."

* * *

Lloyd Phillips established his law firm in the mid-1940s. He commanded a lot of respect in the legal community and was the third-longest practicing lawyer in town. He was a large man with an even larger presence. Friendly and fair, but when he made up his mind things went his way. I had never heard him yell or curse. He didn't have to. You knew when his mind was made up so you accepted whatever he had to say. One of the other lawyers in the firm told me he was that way with everybody, even those outside the firm, and related a story to me.

Lloyd had been called as a witness in a case. When the lawyer questioning him said he was done, Lloyd said that he wasn't. The judge corrected him and asked him to step down from the witness stand. Lloyd said, "Judge, I've got more to say and I'm not stepping down until I say it." The judge let him say it.

Lloyd stopped by my office a day or two after I met with Gould and said he had called Mayor Cazares and asked him to bring his wife to the office for a meeting. "I want us all to get together here so we can fix this."

On the day of the appointment, Lloyd ushered Gabe and Maggie into my office. They seemed surprised to see me. I sat in an arm chair across from them on the sofa with the coffee table between us. I wasn't sure what Lloyd had in mind but he took a seat in the chair at the head of the table in neutral ground, so it looked like he intended to act as an arbitrator.

Lloyd started the discussion by asking Gabe and Maggie what they thought about me and the way I was handling their case. Both of them had plenty to say and jumped over each other trying to get it out. He's trying to make us do things we don't want to do; the church doesn't answer discovery; he barged into my office without an appointment or calling first; and on and on. It was not just what they said, but how they said it. They whined as though I had ruined their lives.

Lloyd asked them to slow down and take up one issue at a time. "What is it that Mr. Vannier is trying to get you to do that you don't want to do?" Both of them were speechless for a moment, then Gabe answered, "He told me to answer interrogatories when I told him I didn't want to."

"Mr. Cazares, the rules require you to answer interrogatories."

"But Scientology doesn't give answers to me." Lloyd asked if I had sent out any discovery that the church hasn't answered. I shook my head. Cazares butted in. "But in my other case," he said. Maggie threw down, too, and went into how terribly Scientology has treated them.

Lloyd stuck his hand up in front of Maggie and she went silent. "That doesn't have anything to do with the case Mr. Vannier is handling," Lloyd said. Gabe insisted that it wasn't fair for him to answer when Scientology doesn't have to.

"Mr. Cazares, that's not how our firm litigates. When the church doesn't answer questions in this case, Mr. Vannier will make them answer."

Gabe backed off. Lloyd asked them what else I was doing that they objected to and they again went off at the same time. I couldn't make out what they were saying, only that they were extremely bitter. Lloyd reacted with astonishment. After a bit, he said, "I get the idea that you two don't trust Mr. Vannier. Is that it?"

"Yes," they answered in unison.

Lloyd asked them why. I locked eyes on Gabe and thought: *Yeah, Gabe, spit it out. Tell him you know I'm a Scientologist because your FBI handler told you.* Gabe shrugged and sheepishly said, "I don't know. I just don't trust him." Lloyd said there must be something. Gabe fidgeted, saying nothing.

"Did he promise something and not come through?" Both shook their heads. "Did he lie to you about something?" Same response.

Lloyd shot me a baffled glance. I could tell he was exasperated. As a trial lawyer, I knew that when things were going my way to keep my mouth shut. I applied that rule and simply cast a confused look.

"Sounds to me like you both would like to part ways with Mr. Vannier."

Gabe shot back a quick no, which jolted Lloyd. "Excuse me," he said. "Didn't you two just say you didn't trust him?"

Gabe hemmed and hawed, saying in effect that they trusted the law firm and their only problem was with me and that maybe the law firm could take over the case. "And do what?" Lloyd inquired. "You haven't said anything that he's done other than not allowing you to avoid answering mandatory interrogatories."

Gabe reiterated that he didn't think he should have to answer them and went back into his mantra about the church not giving his attorneys answers. Lloyd cut him off and turned to me. "Merrell, prepare a motion to withdraw."

Gabe blurted out, "No, I don't want him to do that."

"Mr. Cazares, that's not him doing that. It's me. This is my firm. The firm is going to withdraw from your case."

Gabe replied quickly, as if on cue: "Then I want to dismiss the case without prejudice."

A case can be dismissed either with or without prejudice. If done with prejudice, the case is forever over and can never be refiled. Done without prejudice, it can be refiled later. It was obvious that Gabe had been prepped for the meeting and knew what to say if it came to this.

Lloyd and I exchanged confused looks. "Okay, Merrell, prepare a dismissal without prejudice." As Gabe and Maggie got up to go, Gabe asked Lloyd to contact him when it was ready for their signatures. "No," Lloyd said. "We're doing this today. Right now. Wait in the lobby while he prepares the dismissal."

Lloyd hung back. After they were out of earshot he said to me: "They are two of the craziest people I've ever come across. I can't believe I voted for him."

* * *

Ritchie was in a buoyant mood when we met a few days later. "I see that Gabe and Maggie dismissed their case."

I nodded and said, "Everything's under control," and handed him my latest intel.

He said he had some good news for me. The international head of the Guardian's Office issued an award to Flag G.O.'s Information Bureau. He said the special recognition was for having the most intel and best results in the ARM program of all the Guardian Offices in the country – "combined," he added with emphasis. Then he said, "And that's all you. All of our ARM intelligence is from you. You're our only agent working on the program."

Chapter 13

MELTDOWN

*Just as water, which carries a boat from bank to bank, may also
be the means of sinking it, so reliance on spies, while [producing]
great results, is oft-times the cause of utter destruction.*

— Tu Mu, Sun Tzu's *Art of War*

I was listening to my favorite rock music channel on the car
radio when a news bulletin interrupted the program. "Early this
morning, the FBI raided the Los Angeles and Washington, D. C.
offices of the Church of Scientology." I was on my way to the
office from an early morning court appearance on July 8, 1977.

I turned up the volume. According to the news report, more
than one hundred federal agents seized massive quantities of
documents that had allegedly been stolen by covert agents of the
church who had infiltrated offices of the Justice Department,
Internal Revenue Service, and the U.S. Attorney's Office in
Washington, D.C. The very highest level of the church was
involved, according to information in the affidavit supporting
the search warrant. The person who supplied the information
was reported to have been one of the top officials in the church
and was now being protected by U.S. Marshals because of fears
of reprisal. Church spokesmen denied the informant was a
former top Scientology official, and said that the church had

used only lawful means, such as the Freedom of Information Act, to obtain copies of government documents.

The report left me reeling. I didn't trust the church's PR line. Because of the Information Bureau's strict need-to-know policy, PR spokesmen would be as ignorant as I was about covert ops in D. C. They would only know what they were told. And I found it difficult to imagine that the FBI and Justice Department would undertake such a bold, massive seizure of church property without a solid legal basis.

I wondered if any of this related to the activities of Don Alverzo and explained why he left Clearwater so suddenly. I flashed back to our undercover work in St. Louis and his statement that he knew how to pick locks and was ready to break into the office of the law firm for the Post-Dispatch if necessary. A search warrant for a seizure of this magnitude could not be put together overnight. A detailed probable cause affidavit drafted by Department of Justice attorneys was required, which meant that the G.O. likely knew for some time that their operations in D.C. had been compromised.

I was still sorting out my thoughts when I arrived at my law firm's parking lot. I turned off the engine and grabbed my suit jacket. Then another thought struck me: my representation of Cazares. The case was dismissed May 2, barely two months ago. I let out a deep breath of relief. Close call. Glad I got out when I did. I shuddered at the thought of being their attorney after this news broke. My history as a Scientologist could have been leaked to the media by the FBI when I was still the attorney of record.

I began to open the door when I recalled Gabe's bizarre behavior in demanding that I remain on the case even though he didn't trust me to work on it. *Did his FBI handler know this raid was in the works and instruct him to keep me as his attorney until after it occurred?* I fell back into my seat. I flashed on Lloyd Phillips pointedly telling Cazares it was his firm, and that the firm was getting out of the case. "Wow," I said aloud. *Good thing I went to Gould about this, which led to Lloyd stepping in.*

Other thoughts and ideas rolled through my mind. I was in no condition to work. I tossed my jacket aside and started the engine. I stopped at a hamburger stand, ordered food to go, and made a call from a nearby pay phone. I signaled Ritchie to call me at home. Every TV station repeated the story at regular intervals, adding bits and pieces throughout the day. The investigations leading to the raids began when Michael Meisner, the informant, and another Scientologist were caught using forged IRS credentials to enter the U.S. Courthouse in Washington, D.C. in June 1976. That was the same time period in which I was reading the COINTELPRO files in St. Petersburg. That meant the G.O. knew about a potential problem a year ago. I wondered what people knew in December when I first took on the Cazares case.

Finally Ritchie rang me and I rushed to the pay phone we were using at the time. "I can't talk now," he said hurriedly when I picked up. "Let's meet at seven."

* * *

"You heard the news?" Ritchie said at seven that evening. He appeared subdued and preoccupied. I got the sense he had been scrambling all day and had more important things on his mind than handling me.

"How could I miss it? What the fuck's going on?"

He said it was too early to tell. "We're trying to find out ourselves." He added that it was difficult to get any information it was so chaotic in L.A. and D.C. People were doing damage assessments and getting lawyers on board to get the seized documents returned. "How are you doing?" he asked.

"I'm shocked." I asked if it was true that someone got caught with forged IRS credentials last year and had already pleaded guilty to that. He said he didn't know, he only knows what happens in his area. I tried pulling information out of him with various questions and got nowhere.

"How's Franny taking the news?"

"We're both disturbed. Hey, we're Scientologists. The reason we volunteer our help is because we hope the church does well and gets the message out about the benefits of the technology. We hope to contribute to that. So, yeah, this is not the kind of thing we like to see blasted all over the news."

He said he would contact and brief me as soon as he got anything solid. Then he switched gears. "I need to shut you down. No more intelligence activities. Of any kind. Just as a precaution. Until we can determine what all was seized."

"Why would L.A. or D.C. have any documents related to me?"

"We don't know that they had any."

I felt my eyes widen. "What do you mean, you don't know. There shouldn't be anything about me." I knew something was amiss. Ritchie seemed dumbfounded, as though he was surprised by my reaction, which alarmed me even more. "Don't tell me you put things in writing about me and sent them to other places."

"We would never put your name in a document."

"But, *Ritz*? My code name? You put stuff in writing about me using that name? And sent it to either L.A. or D.C.?"

"We might have sent reports to L.A.," he said. "U.S. Guardian's Office is a senior echelon to us."

That was news to me. I knew U.S.G.O. was senior to outer G.O. offices, but I didn't know the command structure applied to Flag G.O. After all, Flag was the land base for international management. "Are you shitting me? I put my law license on the line and you *might have* put things in writing about me and sent them to L.A.?"

Ritchie was speechless. I shook my head in disbelief, then turned and stared out the window, trying to come to grips with the situation, wondering what I missed along the way, examining all my previous assumptions. I recalled Alverzo being pissed off that I had answered truthfully about my past affiliation with the St. Louis Church of Scientology on my FBI and Missouri Bar applications, and later on my Florida Bar application, all of which I filled out without consulting him. I imagined how bad things would be for me now had I not been truthful. I also recalled preventing Alverzo from using the copy machines in the Hoemeke law firm because it would be a felony. That was in the summer of 1974, and now the G.O. was being accused of doing that very thing inside federal offices. *Did Alverzo go to D.C. after St. Louis to oversee the operation there? Is that why he got the hell out of here? He knew shit was about to hit the fan?*

"Like I said," Ritchie said softly. "We don't know what was in U.S.G.O. files or what was seized. You shouldn't get too worked up about it right now."

Good point. The situation was what it was. I swallowed my frustration.

He said he wanted to go over his order to shut down our intel activities and make sure I gave my intel connections a plausible excuse. The only intel op I was working on was ARM. Slaughter and Flemming were no longer speaking with each other. Merger talks were a thing of the past. The third-party campaign had been a complete success. I was just staying in touch and monitoring the situation. I continued receiving tips of planned deprogrammings, which told me no one suspected me. I found that amazing, considering that not one single deprogramming I learned about went down as planned. They all either resulted in arrests of the deprogrammers or the target being absent by the time the deprogramming team arrived. Funny how people accept "shit happens" as a plausible explanation without looking for a source of cause-and-effect.

"That's easy," I said, regarding an excuse to give my ARM connections. "I can tell them I have a jury trial to prepare for."

Ship's berthing compartment, 1967 Med Cruise

Pollensa Bay, Isle of Mallorca, Nov. 1967

Angie (age 17) holding my son John (age 1), Dec. 1988

John & me, same trip to Big Bear Lake, California

Angie & friends, Clearwater, March 1977

Fran, Angie & me, Clearwater, 1977

Mary Ann and Angie cheer me on, May 1977

My extended family, 1977 summer vacation

Part 2

THE RITZ DOCUMENTS

Chapter 14

TRIAL LAWYER

*What I've learned in these eleven years is you just got to stay
focused and believe in yourself and trust your own ability and
judgment.*

– Mark Cuban
American Businessman

"Where are you two on settlement?" Judge B. J. Driver asked
me and the insurance lawyer about our slip-and-fall injury case
in his private chambers.

The insurance lawyer said he had just increased his offer from
$10,000 to $15,000, which was five thousand more than the case
was worth, but that I had turned it down. Judge Driver turned
to me, his brow furrowed. Clearly his thinking was aligned with
that of the insurance lawyer. I felt like the odd man out. When I
first walked into the room they were chatting like they were old
fishing buddies. Both were in the same age group, 40-45, and I
was the new kid on the block.

"That's a generous offer," the judge said. "You better take it."

I told the judge that my client rejected the offer and preferred
to try the case. He glanced at the insurance company lawyer,
who was shaking his head, smiling. The judge returned his smile,
then said to me: "I had a case in here just a week or two ago
almost exactly like yours and the jury awarded the plaintiff ten

thousand dollars. Go talk to your client and tell her she's making a mistake. Talk some sense into her."

"There's only one problem with that, your honor."

"What's that?" he said.

"I agree with her."

Judge Driver's face tightened. "Okay, gentlemen. Let's pick a jury."

* * *

I cross-examined the medical doctor who had just testified that he performed an independent medical exam of my client and concluded that nothing was wrong with her, that she was a malingerer, which he defined for the jury to mean a person who exaggerates or feigns injury to either avoid work or obtain compensation. The doctor's testimony was damaging, mainly because of his exalted credentials. He was a board certified neurologist, did his residency at the Mayo Clinic and on and on.

Question: What medical records of hers did you review prior to your examination?[11]

Answer: Her chiropractor's report.

Question: Any others?

Answer: No.

Question: She went to Morton Plant Hospital after the accident. Did you view those records?

Defense: Objection. Asked and answered.

Judge: Sustained.

Question: Did you ask for the hospital records?

Answer: I didn't need them.

Question: My question was whether you asked for them.

Answer: No, because I didn't need them.

Question: Did you view the x-rays taken at Morton Plant Hospital?

Defense: Objection. Asked and answered.

Judge: Sustained. You made your point, counselor.

Plaintiff: Thank you, your honor.

Question:	How much were you paid for your examination of Ms. Bradford?
Answer:	I don't know.
Question:	You don't know your fees for independent examinations?
Defense:	Objection. Asked and answered. He said he didn't know.
Judge:	Sustained.
Plaintiff:	Your honor, in all due respect, that's a different question.
Judge:	Next question, counselor.
Plaintiff:	Thank you, your honor.
Question:	Who in your office bills the insurance company for your independent examinations?
Answer:	Well, I guess that would be my office manager.
Question:	Give me a name, please.
Defense:	Objection. Beyond the scope of direct examination, your honor.
Judge:	Sustained.
Plaintiff:	Your honor, I'm entitled to challenge the credibility of this witness. I'm trying to establish that his testimony is financially motivated, and if he doesn't know how much he billed the insurance company then I want to subpoena the person who does know.
Judge:	I'm not going to hold up this trial for you to do that. Next question.
Plaintiff:	Thank you, your honor.
Question:	How many independent examinations do you perform per year for insurance companies?
Answer:	(Snickers) I have no idea.
Question:	Give me your best estimate?
Defense:	Objection. Asked and answered. Calls for speculation.
Judge:	Sustained.

Question: How many independent medical examinations have you performed in the past week?

Answer: I don't know. A few. I'm not sure.

Question: Maybe five a day?

Defense: Objection. The witness said he didn't know.

Plaintiff: Your honor, please. The witness isn't trying.

Judge: Sustained. Next question.

Question: In a given day, how much of your practice is devoted to doing independent medical examinations for insurance companies?

Answer: I couldn't say for sure.

Question: Oh, come on. Give me your best estimate. Fifty percent?

Answer: It could be.

Question: Could it be more than fifty percent?

Defense: Objection. Asked and answered. Calls for speculation. This is ridiculous. Counsel has yet to ask a question directly related to the testimony of the witness on direct examination.

Judge: Sustained. Move on to something else, counselor.

Question: You're being paid for your testimony here today, aren't you?

Defense: Objection.

Question: I'm entitled to ask that, your honor.

Judge: Overruled. (To witness): Answer the question.

Answer: Yes.

Question: How much are you being paid for your testimony today?

Answer: I... I don't recall the terms.

Question: Give me your best recollection.

Defense: Objection.

Judge: Sustained. (To plaintiff counsel): How long is this going to go on?

Plaintiff: I'd be done if the witness was more forthright, your honor.

Judge: It would also help if you had more relevant questions to ask. I'm going to break for lunch. When we get back I expect you to bring your cross-examination to a quick conclusion.

* * *

Question: When we broke for lunch I had asked you how much you were being paid to testify today and you said you didn't recall. Has your memory improved since then?

Defense: Objection. Asked and answered.

Question: Different question, your honor.

Judge: Overruled. (To plaintiff counsel):   Remember my warning.

Plaintiff: Yes, your honor. I don't have much more.

Answer: I still don't recall the amount if that's what you mean.

Question: Can you give me a ballpark figure?

Defense: Objection.

Judge: Sustained.

Question: How many times have you testified on behalf of an insurance company this year?

Answer: (Looks at insurance lawyer with a smirk on his face). I couldn't say. I don't keep track.

Question: Give me your best estimate.

Defense: Objection. Asked and answered. Calls for speculation.

Judge: Sustained. I thought I told you to wrap it up.

Plaintiff: Your honor, I've come here to represent this lady and until you tell me to sit down I'm going to keep asking the questions I think need to be asked.

The judge leaned forward, glared and hissed at me between clenched teeth, "Proceed counselor," as if he wanted to come over the bench and tear off a piece of my young ass. It occurred to me that his words, taken alone, as the court reporter would

143

have transcribed them, were harmless. His tone and demeanor would be absent from the record. For all a reader of the court transcript would know the judge was speaking respectfully, maybe even in a sing-song, apologetic tone, as if to say: you're right, my error, you can proceed and I'll shut my trap and let you do your job. That's where experience came in. The judge knew how to body slam a lawyer without the record showing the smack-down.

Plaintiff: Thank you, your honor.

Question: How long did your examination of Ms. Bradford take?

Answer: I have no idea.

Question: None at all? Give me a ball park.

Defense: Objection. Asked and answered. Calls for speculation.

Judge: Sustained. Next question.

Question: You recall me being there, don't you?

Answer: Yes.

Question: I was in the waiting area when you came to get her and I was there when she was finished, isn't that correct?

Answer: Yes.

Question: I kept track on my watch. Would you argue with me if I said she was only gone twenty minutes?

Answer: That sounds about right.

Question: No further questions, your honor.

* * *

In closing arguments I told the jury that they were allowed to take into account the credibility of the witnesses and were free to entirely reject the testimony of the examining doctor, then said, "When you go back into that jury room, ask yourselves: did he come here to enlighten you as to Ms. Bradford's injuries and her required treatment, or did he come here as a hired gun on behalf of the insurance company?" I then hammered the doctor over his evasive testimony and compared his efforts to that of the treating chiropractor who had studied all her medical records, including those from the hospital, and had given her relief and hope for a future pain-free existence.

The jury returned a verdict in the amount of $36,000.

Bill Castagna, the city's most prominent plaintiff's trial lawyer, was standing by to try a case right after mine. He congratulated me, saying the verdict was a county record for soft tissue injuries, and invited me to join him for lunch next week. I left the courtroom with a bounce in my step. The theme song from the sitcom, *The Jeffersons*, played in my mind. *Well we're movin' on up, to the east side.*

* * *

A day or two later I dropped by Judge Driver's chambers. I told him I was there to make sure there were no hard feelings and to see whether I owed him an apology. He gave a surprised look and said, "No. No hard feelings at all." I told him I was just checking. He said I was only doing my job, then added, "You're welcome back in my courtroom anytime."

I was happy to hear the judge say that because I planned to be back.

Chapter 15

ON THE LAM

There's a silver lining to every cloud that sails about the heavens, if we could only see it.

— Katty Macane in
Marian; or, a Young Maid's Fortunes,
by Mrs. S. C. Hall

"We need you to leave the country. Pick any place in the world you want to go, all expenses paid." I could see in Tom Ritchie's face that he was serious.

I was dazed. "Why should I go anywhere?"

He said he was sorry to give me the news but all hell was about to break loose. There was a grand jury proceeding in Washington, D. C. at which top officials in the G.O. were targeted for criminal charges, and there could soon be grand juries in Florida; maybe they were already underway.

"What's that got to do with me? I wasn't involved in that stuff in D.C., and I didn't do anything illegal here. Neither did Fran, I'm sure."

"They might know you were working for the church and want to go after you as a witness and turn you against us."

I told him not to worry about me turning against anyone. It wouldn't happen. He said that wasn't the only concern. I would be the focal point of news stories and put under a spotlight and subjected to public ridicule and hatred, just like the church had been when it first arrived in Clearwater.

"I'm tougher and more capable of taking care of myself than you think. It will be embarrassing but the other side has more to hide than I do. I'm not afraid to talk about what I've done and why I did it." People in the State Attorney's Office and the St. Pete P.D. intel department buried evidence and covered up a counterintelligence program against the church. The FBI spearheaded the program. At the same time they were testifying before Congress and promising the American public they were no longer involved in those activities. "They broke the law. I didn't. You think they want to talk about what they did? I don't think so. Do you think Tampa INS wants to talk about helping a private party in litigation against the other party?"

I realized that Ritchie might not know about the INS intel op since it occurred before his time. "Did you know about that one?" He just looked at me. "Trust me. The Officer in Charge of Tampa INS doesn't want me talking publicly about it." After a pause I added, "By the way, has anyone at your end considered that an investigation here is not necessarily a bad thing?"

Ritchie swung his head from side to side in shocked disbelief. "Yes it is. You've seen the media dump on us before. They'll be in bed with government agencies. It will be everyone against the church, and you, too, if you stay."

"But back then you didn't have the evidence I uncovered in St. Pete P.D. intel files, and didn't know the source of the media attacks. Now you know. We could plan it out and strike first. Get the upper hand here in Florida and take some of the heat off the church in D.C."

He again shook his head, saying that the government had all of their documents but we didn't have theirs; that I only saw theirs; and that they have all the momentum and we wouldn't get our stories out. I conceded my lack of information. Still, running didn't feel like the best solution. "I guess what I'm asking is whether the people making this decision appreciate the evidence I uncovered and how it can be used legally? If not by them, then by me?"

"They know much more than you and I do," he said. "They have the big picture."

"Have they run it by lawyers who know these issues?" He said he was sure they had fully considered everything.

"Tom, they're putting me in a tough spot. I've got a six-year old who has friends and just started school. I've got a good job. My department is the top earning one in the firm now. We've been here a year and a half and like living here."

He said he was sorry and I could tell he meant it. As I mulled it over he shifted to a lighthearted approach. "Wouldn't you like an all-expense paid vacation to Paris? How about London?" He projected his voice like a game show host offering prizes. I laughed. I liked that about him. He was a nice guy, a fun guy, even in a tough situation. I told him I didn't want to go to either of those cities. "How about Switzerland? Or Australia?" I shook him off. He rattled off other locales with the same gleeful tone. I cracked up.

"Seriously, Ritzie," he said. "Look at this as a once-in-a-lifetime opportunity. All expenses paid. Kick back. See the sights."

"Seriously? Seriously, I'd prefer to face the music. Let it all hang out."

"You really think you can stand up to the media and grand juries and all that, even when you're isolated?"

"I won't be isolated, I assume the church will pay for an attorney for me if that happens, and he can work with the church's attorneys."

"Think about walking out of your office one day and there's a camera stuck in your face."

"I'm not afraid of cameras."

"What would you say to reporters who ask if you were an undercover agent for the church?"

"I'd refer them to my attorney." He let out a half-laugh gasp. "Seriously, I'm not going to let somebody ambush me."

He went silent, contemplating. My train of thought led to Alverzo. I would have to give up his name if I stayed and was subpoenaed to testify. "Ole Don sure pulled out in the nick of time, didn't he?"

Ritchie tightened up. "What do you mean?"

"Nothing, just that he left and never came back."

Ritchie returned to his meditation. Eventually, he took on a forlorn look and said, "I'm begging you, Ritzie. Think it over. Talk to Frannie and come up with a country you'd like to visit."

It was another sign that the order emanated from on high and not from someone Ritchie could reason with. I was forced to make a hard decision based on limited information. I needed time and space for that. Taking a break to speak with Fran was a good temporary solution. "Okay, since you put it that way."

He let loose his pent-up frustration and exclaimed, "You mean that's all I had to do?"

"No. I wanted to make you work for it. Test you out," I said. He broke up.

* * *

Fran was not happy with the idea. She wondered what she would tell her family and how it might adversely affect Angie. "We could tell them a business opportunity came up for me," I said. "Or whatever. We can work that out if we decide to leave." As for Angie, I agreed with her concern but said we could soften the blow by telling Angie it's a long vacation, not a move, and make it fun for her. "Tom said the move may only be for a month or two, just until the dust settles and they're on top of the situation."

She asked what I wanted to do. I told her I wanted to stay, I thought the decision-makers for the G.O. were overreacting, but it was impossible to know without more information. "The one thing I don't want to do is inadvertently harm the church or anyone else, like Don." I told her I suspected Alverzo might be tied in to the criminal charges in D.C. and might have done similar things in this area, but didn't explain my concern. She didn't know what Alverzo and I had done in St. Louis or about his ability to pick locks. Reminded of it, I wondered whether she had ever made internal files available to Molly or Don in either Gabe's campaign office or as a secretary to a lawyer in the firm Baynard, Lang, Ballard & McLeod, attorneys for the *St. Petersburg Times*. She said she hadn't, nor did she have access to files containing sensitive information in either place.

"Were you ever asked to provide a sketch of the offices and indicate on it where sensitive files may have been located?" She said she drew one of the law firm. I asked why a sketch was requested. She didn't know. In the end, I told her I thought we should leave. "It's possible we could be made witnesses against them, and I don't want to do that." Fran said she didn't either. My bigger concern was that she might possibly be dragged into a burglary but I didn't voice that one. I didn't want to alarm her.

* * *

"I'm at the hospital," Fran said from Toronto. "Angie broke her wrist." They had flown ahead while I wrapped things up in Florida, selling the Chevy Impala and lugging our belongings into storage. I was ready to hit the road in our 1976 Mazda to join them. Angie did not take the move well. She got sick and threw up on the airplane, and now this. Fran said it was a terrifying experience. Angie was running her right hand along an escalator handrail at a local shopping center when it got wedged between the moving rail and the non-moving base. Fran managed to pull her arm loose but not without considerable effort on her part, and a lot of pain for Angie.

Fran started to cry. The stress of the ordeal had caught up with her. I already regretted the decision to leave. I consoled Fran as best I could and promised her I would arrive in two days.

* * *

151

"This is a . . ." Angie hesitated when she came to the word "top." She looked at me for help. I was tutoring her in reading. Before we left Clearwater, her first grade teacher told us that Angie was having trouble reading and needed extra work. Our immediate plan was for me to help Angie learn to read while Fran looked for a job that did not require a work visa. As it turned out the "all-expenses" deal included a request that we do our best to offset expenses. We also wanted extra spending money. Fran found a job babysitting a couple of children. Angie and I drove her to and from the nearest subway station each week day.

"Sound it out," I said. She didn't know what I meant. I pointed to the "T." "What is that letter?" A "T," she told me. "Good. What sound does a "T" make?" She didn't know. I moved to the "P." She knew the letter but not the sound for it. I went over other consonants of the alphabet. She didn't know phonics at all. I found it hard to believe that her school would try to teach students to read without first teaching them phonics. I asked her about the middle letter, the "O." Same thing. She also didn't know that vowel sounds are pronounced with an open vocal tract in contrast to the sounds of consonants that are made by obstructing some point of the airway; the lips for a "B," the tongue for a "D," and so on.

She cast the book aside with a defeated look. "I don't like reading." She wanted to play instead. I told her I had a better idea. Shopping. Her face lit up.

Angie was a born shopper. I figured that out before she was two years old when I was looking for a form of discipline that didn't include spanking. I had swatted her on the butt once, and her first reaction was total shock. It couldn't have been from the pain because I barely tapped her, and she was wearing a padded diaper. She rolled over onto her seat, and wailed. I felt horrible. That wasn't the effect I wanted to create. I just wanted to instill a little discipline.

I began to read *Miracles for Breakfast*, a book written by Ruth Minshell, a young mother who based her work on principles of

Scientology. She stressed rewards and penalties. The missing ingredient in most justice systems was reward, she said. I implemented a system of good marks and bad marks. For a certain number of good marks per week Angie got $2. Plus, and this was the kicker that made the system really work for her: I would take her shopping and she could spend it on anything she wanted. Or she could save it for things she wanted but couldn't afford right away, but she still got to go shopping even if she was saving. She hated bad marks so much that I added a rule that she could wipe out a bad mark by doing two favors for either Fran or me. Man, the ink on the bad marks barely dried before her two favors were done. She hated the whole idea of a bad mark and would immediately snap out of whatever funk she was in that earned her one.

I drove her to the shopping center in Scarborough, a few miles east of the guesthouse we rented on the outskirts of Toronto. While Angie shopped and got ideas for things she wanted to buy I purchased a couple of books on phonics. I calculated the amount of money she would need to buy some of the items she put on her wish list and made her a deal so she could earn it: dollars for progress in phonics, a bonus for learning every sound associated with each letter of the alphabet.

That's how I taught her phonics and how to read. After she finished her readers from school I bought more readers and upped the reading level. And I kept my end of the deal: we also shopped and played.

One of the games she liked to play was house. She was the mommy and I was her little boy. During one of the early play periods she told me it was time for me to take a nap, and had me lie down on the couch. I lay down, but then said I wanted a plo. She giggled. "What did you say?"

"Plo. I wanna plo."

"You mean pillow?" she said.

"Yes. Plo."

She cracked up and ran off to get a pillow. She placed it under my head. "Little boy, this is a pillow." She broke it into syllables, speaking each one clearly. "Can you say pil-low?"

"Plo."

She laughed. "No. You said plo. It's pil-low. Say pil." She mouthed the "p" sound and "l" sound for me. I said it correctly, and she happily said, "Good. That was perfect. Say it again." She was using the tactics I had used on her and I could tell it was having a learning effect on her, switching roles like that. I decided to keep it up and have some fun in the process. She had me repeat it several times to ensure that I really got it down and could say pillow correctly, which I finally did.

Angie was elated. "Very good, little boy. I'm going to give you a good mark. Now we can go shopping."

She also loved to play hairdresser. Fran and I would compete to get our hair brushed. It was so relaxing I could fall asleep. Once, after her cast was removed and she had full use of both hands, Angie combed my hair. I started nodding off when she started using rubber bands and hairpins. Thinking of the time she cut her playmate Charity's hair, I admonished her, "No cutting." She knew what I was talking about. Grinning, she agreed.

I fell asleep. Sometime later I felt something on my lips. At first I thought I was dreaming, then I realized that Angie was applying lipstick. My alarm gave way when I heard her giggling. I let her have her fun, and kept my eyes shut. She worked over my entire face, eyelashes and all. She giggled along the way. I imagined how I must look.

Finally, she shook my shoulder. I pretended to slowly awaken. She had a mischievous look. I played dumb. She handed me a mirror. "Here, look." As I took the mirror, she could barely contain herself. One glance and I busted a gut. I had tufts of hair sticking out in all directions and all kinds of gaudy makeup. Angie was beside herself, literally rolling on the floor.

When she calmed down, she said, "I wish mom could see you."

"Should we pick her up from the subway with me looking like this?"

Her eyes lit up. "Yes!" she exclaimed. "Let's do that!"

At the station Angie was beside herself as she sat in the back of our little Mazda, leaning over the front seat, peering out the passenger side window. "There she is," Angie cried out when Fran stepped off the train car.

I turned away so Fran couldn't see my face until she got inside. Angie cupped her mouth, on the verge of breaking up. Fran opened the door and slid inside, and Angie let loose some of her suppressed laughter. Fran first looked at her, passing me over, but then did a double take. Her eyes landed squarely on me and popped out of their sockets. She shrieked. Angie totally lost it. I looked innocently from one to the other, as if I didn't know what was so funny.

"Ready to go to the restaurant?" I asked. It was Friday, the day we ate at a place that served the world's best homemade chicken noodle soup and oven-fresh bread. It was next to the public phone booth where Tom Ritchie called me every Friday evening.

"Yes!" Angie squealed at the same time Fran firmly said, "No!"

Fran got the last word. "No way will I let you go into the restaurant looking like that." Angie sighed. The joke had to end there, I told her.

Later that night I took Ritchie's call. He had no news. Same as last week. I was still not cleared to return to the U.S., not even to St. Louis. I pleaded with him. "Hang tight," he said. He would get me out of there as soon as possible. Everyone knew how badly we wanted out of Canada, he assured me.

By the middle of December I was pressing Ritchie hard. My parents expected me home for Christmas and I told him we did not want to return to Canada after that. He said everyone was working on it. The powers that be were the holdup and he would check in every day. I promised not to leave without his say-so.

Finally, Ritchie gave us the green light. We pulled out of Toronto on December 23 during a heavy snowfall, one year to the day after I entered my appearance in the Cazares case, and three months after I left Clearwater. We drove our little Mazda, packed to the brim, 750 miles straight through to my parents' house in Missouri. We stopped only for gas, food and restroom breaks.

The best result of my time in Canada was tutoring Angie in phonics. Her new teacher at Wentzville Elementary said she was far and away the best reader in her first grade class.

Chapter 16

ST. LOUIS LAWYER

There is no greater gift you can give or receive than to honor your calling. It's why you were born. And how you become most truly alive.

– Oprah Winfrey

"Fran and I have jobs in St. Louis, and we've decided not to return to Clearwater." I was speaking on the telephone to Norrie Gould. I had taken a two-month leave of absence and extended it. He asked how my mother was doing. Better, I told him. The cover story I gave him for leaving so abruptly was a medical emergency involving my mother. He said he understood and agreed to ship me the certificates still hanging on my office wall, which were left there not only to solidify my cover story, but also because I hoped to return. Tom Ritchie shipped us the items I placed in storage in Clearwater. So now the relocation was complete. We moved into a house in Wentzville across the street from my brother, Darrell, and his family.

"Stand pat and lie low," Ritchie told me. He promised to keep me updated on the legal cases surrounding the seized documents. Prior to leaving Clearwater, the search warrants used to seize papers from the D.C. and L.A. offices of the G.O. were ruled invalid. The documents were placed under seal with a district court in Los Angeles pending the government's appeal, which was successful, and the documents were returned to the government. Ritchie said they still did not know what was in them.

* * *

Tragedy struck in April, a real medical emergency. Darrell collapsed suddenly. Tests revealed he had suffered a brain aneurism and was sent to St. Louis University Hospital for brain surgery. On May 3, Fran and I waited in the lobby with his wife, Sue. We were all friends who had gone to the same high school in Sigourney, Iowa. Sue was in my class, Darrell was a year behind me, Fran two.

The surgery was a success but Darrell did not regain consciousness afterward. The next day Sue called me, distressed. The surgeon told her Darrell was in danger of slipping into a coma and if that happened he said, "We will lose him." If there was no improvement in the next 24 hours the surgeon wanted to operate again but warned that there was only a ten percent chance he would survive back-to-back brain surgeries.

"Can you do anything?" Sue asked, pleading. She meant with Scientology. The family knew of my personal success with the technology and how I had helped my youngest brother (of five brothers) who had issues related to congenital epilepsy. Even my parents had taken Scientology's basic Communication Course and said they had benefitted from it.

"Ask the doctor if I can be alone with Darrell," I said. She called me back a few minutes later and said yes.

Fran and I huddled with Sue outside the ICU. I told her not to say anything no matter what happened. She ushered me inside to Darrell's bed behind a curtain. The ICU was a creepy place. I had never been in one before. The ambience was dire, and cheerlessly quiet, except for the mechanized beeping of the monitors surrounding each patient. They were all barely clinging to life. Their fight for survival was palpable, and unsettling.

Darrell was lying there with his head completely bandaged. Tubes ran everywhere. I stood by his side, Sue to my left. Fran stood at the foot of the bed.

I spoke to Darrell gently, as though he could hear me. "I'm going to give you an assist." I took his left hand in mine. "I will give you a command. Do what I tell you to do and then squeeze my hand to let me know you have done it. Start of assist: You make that body lie on that bed," I said. I felt nothing.

I was trained what to do in that event: treat it as though he had complied; that he, as a spiritual being and not his body, had tried but just hadn't taken control of his body yet. So I said, "Thank you."

Actually, I had no idea whether the assist would work. We didn't have any unconscious persons lying around when I did my Scientology internship. We trained on a doll. But everything else I had trained on in Scientology worked, so I was confident I could help Darrell. If I couldn't bring him to full consciousness that day, then at least I could make an improvement sufficient to keep him from slipping into a coma. I was ready to repeat the process on successive days until he was fully conscious.

"You make that body lie on that bed," I repeated. No noticeable response. "Thank you." I repeated the commands for several minutes with no noticeable result. And then I felt the slightest tremor in response to one of my commands. So slight that I wasn't sure. "Thank you," I said and repeated the command. This time I was sure. A chill went up my spine. The response was still so feeble that I knew Fran and Sue couldn't see it and therefore didn't know what I knew: that the damn thing was working. "Thank you," I said again, bolstered with confidence.

Darrell's squeezes became more and more pronounced with each command. So much so that I knew without looking that Fran and Sue also saw them and knew the assist was working. I could feel their morale lift.

After about five minutes, Darrell squeezed so hard that it hurt. I felt like saying, "Not so damned hard, bro'," but all I said was "Thank you," and repeated the command.

Suddenly he popped up, tubes and all. He jabbered a bunch of incoherent nonsense, as his head and eyes flitted all about. Then he lay back down. His eyes were closed, but he now seemed to be sleeping peacefully – a vast improvement.

"End of assist," I said, and let go of his hand.

I returned the next day with Sue, prepared to repeat the process. We checked in at the nurse's station. The nurse said he was still unconscious but not deeply. His vital signs were much better. Sue told the nurse how happy she was to hear that.

Then we heard Darrell's voice from behind his curtain. "Is that you, mama?"

Sue and I glanced at each other, then at the nurse. We rushed to see him. He looked great. He asked what I was doing there and I told him I was there to see how he was doing. Obviously he didn't remember my assist from the day before. Nor was there any need to continue with it. Since I was there, I offered to do a process for an injured, conscious person called a "touch assist." I explained to him that it was meant to unblock the body's nerve channels and speed the recovery from shock or injury. He agreed, and I performed the procedure.[12]

The next day Sue called from the hospital. Darrell was being taken out of ICU and they were talking about a discharge date. Sue said the entire staff was amazed at his turnaround. It was the fastest recovery they had ever seen.

I was curious. "Did any doctors ask what I did for Darrell?" She said they hadn't. "Did *anyone* on the medical staff ask what I did?" Same answer. The lack of inquiry by the health care professionals astonished me considering the results of my visit.

Darrell was soon home and back to work.

* * *

I soon landed my ideal job at a law firm in Clayton, Missouri, a suburb of St. Louis. Compensation was based on production, not salaried. My income was a sliding scale of percentages of income I brought into the firm. I received the highest percentage on legal matters when I brought the client to the firm and also did the related legal work. Dolgin, Beilinson & Klein provided me an office, access to their library, and a shared secretary and receptionist. I loved the arrangement. A few clients followed me from the personal injury lawyer I initially worked for, so I started with some of my own cases, and there was plenty of work for me to do on the firm's cases. I thrived in that environment.

More news about the church came around the same time. Based on a review conducted by 20 federal agents over several weeks, the government filed an inventory of the seized documents with the federal court in Los Angeles. The *St. Louis Post-Dispatch* carried the story. Ritchie called me when the news broke. He assured me there was no mention of Fran or me (Merrell or Ritz) in either the national news reports or the actual inventory. He was not only keeping me updated, but I got the impression he was monitoring my team loyalty. He cautioned that the inventory was just a *summary* of the things seized. The G.O. staff still had not seen the actual documents.

The bad news for some individuals was that the seized documents were being submitted to a grand jury. These included orders from top G.O. officials to investigate certain government agencies, private businesses and individuals; secret CIA documents; "apparently original" Internal Revenue Service documents; and confidential letters between executive branch Cabinet members including one letter that appeared to have been drafted but never mailed. According to the inventory, the government also confiscated memos on how to obtain false identities and tap telephones; electronic eavesdropping equipment, and a lock-picking kit.

"Just continue to lie low and keep doing what you're doing," Ritchie said, and asked how I was doing.

"Great," I told him. And I was. My job was going well. I was kicking ass financially. I had paid off the 1977 Toyota Celica I purchased. We were completely debt-free and actually saving money on the side. We even entered talks with our landlord to purchase the house we were renting.

* * *

In August 1979, almost two years after I left Clearwater, eleven G.O. staff members were indicted on charges of electronically intercepting oral IRS communications, forging government passes, illegally entering government buildings, recruiting Scientologists to infiltrate the government, and stealing records belonging to the IRS and the U.S. Justice Department. Ritchie said the defendants were filing motions to suppress the seized documents. Prior rulings relating to the validity of the search warrants had been prompted by church filings regarding its property rights in the items taken. The defendants had separate due process rights and were entitled to challenge the search warrants and seizure of evidence being used against them.

I felt a sense of responsibility. I originally volunteered to help the church, not contribute to its downfall. I was an experienced lawyer; the Information Bureau obviously lacked proper legal oversight, and the church was suffering because of it. I wanted to help set things right. It coincided with another change: I became bored. The kind of legal work I was doing no longer satisfied me. I called Ritchie.

"Looks like you guys could use some help?"

We didn't know it at the time, but a grand jury had been convened in Tampa, too, and seized documents were sent from D.C. to the U.S. Attorney's Office there. Some of them referred to me by my code name, *Ritz*. They would become known as "The Ritz Documents."

Chapter 17

SECRET PROJECT

Some criticism will be honest, some won't. Some praise you will deserve, some you won't. You can't let praise or criticism get to you. It's a weakness to get caught up in either one.

> – John Wooden
> legendary college basketball coach

I arrived in Los Angeles in October 1979 with the expectation of joining the United States Guardian's Office. Not good timing, I was told. Nine of the eleven defendants had recently pleaded guilty based on a Stipulation of Facts. The other two were in England fighting extradition to the U.S. The nine waived a jury trial and awaited sentencing by U. S. District Court Judge Charles Richey. The plea deal allowed them to avoid a trial and cap their sentences while preserving their rights of appeal. A trial would provide lurid details to hungry media outlets and federal grand juries sitting in New York and Tampa.

The person briefing me was Duke Snider, one of the nine defendants. He wore fine clothes and had a sophisticated air about him. Joe Lisa was the other person in the room. He was the director of U.S.G.O.'s Information Bureau. Affable, stocky, pushing forty, he was proudly Italian with a thick New York accent – and not a defendant in the case. The room was in a large suite of offices behind a steel double door in a building that used to be the X-ray department of Cedars of Lebanon Hospital. There were no windows in any of the offices. A perfect hangout for intelligence officers.

Judge Richey unsealed the seized documents and made them available for public viewing. One of the persons poring over the 40 or so boxes of materials was Bette Orsini, the reporter for the *St. Petersburg Times* who helped orchestrate the campaign against Scientology in the Tampa Bay area. She had already written an article about some of the documents. I was told it did not mention Fran or me, although the Justice Department's documents related to G.O. activities in Clearwater might contain references to "Ritz." Since I could be dragged into the proceedings, the G.O. hierarchy preferred that I not join staff then.

Snider told me to keep a low profile and stay in touch with Joe. Now that I was in L.A., with time on my hands, I asked if there was anything I could do to help.

* * *

"We need these case files sorted out and put in order," said John Taussig, a member of the Los Angeles G.O. legal department. Joe had referred me to him.

My jaw dropped. There were a dozen or so legal boxes and papers strewn about a room that could have passed for either a small, windowless office or a large closet. I slowly turned to Taussig and he broke into laughter, saying, "It's a mess, I know." That was an understatement.

"Is this all one case?" I asked. Actually, there were three cases, he told me, but all of them involved one party. He asked if I had heard of Paulette Cooper. I said I had. She wrote the book *Scandal of Scientology* in the early 1970s. "All this is litigation against her?" He nodded and told me that the original libel suit over the book was settled in the church's favor, but subsequently Cooper began speaking out against Scientology in violation of the settlement agreement, so the church sued her again – twice – in California and in New York where she lived. Cooper countersued in both venues and also sued the church in a separate lawsuit in New York.

"How do you get any work done with files like this? It looks like people just throw stuff in here." He laughed and said, "Pretty much." The church had lawyers in New York and Los Angeles doing the legal work, he explained. His office just monitored the work. "I can't imagine how," I said, and he laughed again.

I took a deep breath. "Well, let me get started." He said to holler if I needed anything or had questions.

I worked every week day for two months organizing the files into an orderly system, one that anyone knowledgeable about litigation could easily work with. I broke each case down into boxes and file folders for each of various subjects: pleadings, discovery, attorney communications, and so on, and placed them all in chronological order with indexes. During the process I learned the details of each of the cases.

The church's original libel suit over Cooper's book was settled in 1976. She agreed not to republish or comment on the book, assigned her copyright to the church, and signed a statement admitting that 52 passages were "erroneous or at best misleading." In exchange, the church paid her legal fees.

Shortly after I first became involved in Scientology in Kansas City in 1972, someone told me I ought to check out Cooper's book. I read through the first fifty pages or so and thought it was garbage written by someone with an obvious agenda. Several passages I knew from personal experience to be false. To me it was like reading a book written by a member of the KKK about Martin Luther King, Jr.'s Southern Christian Leadership Conference, which is why I stopped reading it.

What troubled me was not so much what I saw in the legal files – her counter claims for harassment were largely unsupported by evidence and not credible given her penchant for making false and misleading statements about Scientology – but what I read in daily newspapers while working on the project. Reports based on the contents of documents seized from G.O. offices supported many of her harassment claims, and worse. As early as 1972, soon after her scandalous book had been published, a number of intelligence campaigns had been waged against Cooper.

Operation Daniel was a 1972 plan to attack her in as many ways as possible, including a wide-scale exposure of her sex life. This evidence supported her allegations that Scientologists were behind her name and phone number being posted on street walls, her receipt of obscene phone calls, and subscriptions in her name to pornographic mailing lists. She also claimed that she had received anonymous death threats and her neighbors were receiving anonymous letters claiming she had venereal disease.

Operation Dynamite involved a fake bomb threat typed on Cooper's stationery marked with her fingerprints and sent to the New York Church of Scientology in December of 1972. The operation led to her indictment in May 1973, but the charges were later dropped.

Operation Freakout was a 1976 covert plan to get her incarcerated in a mental institution or sent to jail, or in some way to hit her so hard that she would drop her attacks against the church. Cooper claimed in her harassment suits that Scientologists were behind the plot. She testified in discovery about her suspicions that certain people she allowed into her life during the time of the bomb threat letters were Scientologists, including a person named Jerry Levin and two of his female friends. Jerry Levin befriended Cooper and moved into her apartment building, and later into her apartment, in a platonic arrangement. She could not locate or connect these individuals to Scientology, however. Seized documents made the connection.

In interviews with news reporters Cooper spoke about one of the documents, a diary of her daily activities during the bomb threat period, and how close she was to suicide. "Wouldn't that be great for Scientology?" the person wrote in the seized report.

In interviews with news reporters she stated her belief that the writer could only have been Jerry Levin. She said he and his friends had been in and out of her old apartment during the time the threats were sent. They had access to stationery which contained her fingerprints.

The seized documents and Cooper's testimony were presented to the federal grand jury in Southern New York. All that evidence would surely find its way into the civil suits, creating significant legal problems for the church and for people like Jerry Levin, if that was his real name and authorities could locate him. This information certainly made clear to me why the criminal defendants had cut a deal with federal prosecutors. They knew what additional exposure they faced in New York.

All this had resulted from the publication of a crappy, insignificant book that was gathering dust on library shelves and written by a prejudiced author on a subject she knew nothing about.

I recalled Tom Ritchie telling me in Clearwater that the top decision-makers had the full picture. That may have been true. But they apparently had some warped ideas about how to frame and mount that picture. I thought the G.O. could use my help. That's why I moved to Los Angeles. Now, more than ever, I was glad I had come. What a legal mess this was. And I had only scratched the surface.

* * *

In January 1980, Duke Snider said I was cleared to apply to join the G.O. Their concern about me being overtly connected to the G.O. had disappeared. He wanted me to help him on an ultra secret project while my application was being processed. The individual criminal defendants, through one of their high-priced lawyers, had hired Richard Bast, one of the world's top private investigators. Bast was developing evidence from inside Judge Richey's security team to support a motion to recuse the judge. Bast and his employee, Fred Cain, a retired police officer, had developed a confidential relationship with a U.S. Marshall who was spilling intel on Judge Richey – on tape.

Snider asked me to transcribe the secret tapes and to occasionally courier others between Washington, D.C. and Los Angeles. The material was too sensitive to airmail. "Is this something that interests you?" I told him it did. He said I would report to him and I should not mention anything about the project to anyone, including Fran or the friends I had made since moving to L.A. I agreed.

The next day Snider took me to a small room above the U.S. Information Bureau offices and introduced me to Grace Marie Haddy. She was a hefty, top-heavy woman in her fifties with bad teeth and a friendly smile. She wore leather sandals and a loose fitting shirt and slacks that looked like Salvation Army clothing. I admonished myself to not judge a book by its cover. I returned her smile and shook her hand.

"Grace used to work for us, but she took a break," Snider said teasingly. She giggled and waggled her finger. "I just agreed to help on this one project, remember that." Snider continued the play, saying to me, "But she'll see what she's missed. It's all part of our plan to win her back." He explained that she used to be the executive secretary for the former U.S.G.O. Director of Information.

Two desks were set up with new IBM Selectric typewriters and tape decks with foot pedal controls and headsets. A stack of tapes filled a tray marked, "Tapes In." Two empty trays were marked "Transcripts" and "Tapes Done."

Snider announced that I was in charge of the transcription team. Grace Marie flashed a we-will-see-about-that look. A slight grin then formed on her lips. *Looks like she has some authority issues*, I thought. I made a mental note of it, but I really didn't care who was in charge.

I warmed up to her later. We chatted during our breaks. She had a huge record collection and was once well connected with the early Hollywood rock scene. She knew and partied with them all, she told me, and dropped a few names, including Jerry

Garcia and the rest of the Grateful Dead. "No shit? You hung out with Jerry Garcia?" She asked if I had ever been to one of their concerts. I hadn't but I liked their music.

She asked if I'd done drugs. "No," I said. "A puff or two on a couple of joints while in college was all." I told her I went from high school to the military and then to engineering school and then got married when I was only 21. A dull guy by her standards. She filled me in on some of her wild days and made me blush more than once. I would never have guessed it just by looking at her.

The second day on the job we were interrupted by a tap on the door. A short redheaded man peeked into the room and flashed a big grin at Grace Marie. She tore off her headset and excitedly exclaimed, "Jimmy!" They exchanged warm hugs. Then he stood back and struck a rather effeminate pose, with his right hand over his left wrist, a chain of keys dangling from his left that held a pack of Marlboro cigarettes. "Introduce me to your friend," he said to her.

Jimmy Mulligan, the Controller Aide for Information. The Controller was Mary Sue Hubbard, wife of L. Ron Hubbard and one of the nine defendants for her role in the infiltration of government offices. I was still deciphering the command structure. Jane Kember was the Guardian but somehow Mary Sue Hubbard oversaw the G.O. and was senior to Kember. Most of what I knew came from newspaper accounts about the seized documents. I felt uncomfortable asking questions of people who were extremely security conscious. I learned quickly that a very thin line separates an innocent question from an inappropriate probe. The former received a short answer; the latter, a heavy silence or withering stare. So I tended to keep my eyes and ears open, my mouth shut.

I remembered seeing Jimmy Mulligan's name in a number of damning seized documents. I didn't understand why he wasn't indicted when people above and below him in the chain of command had been. Luck of the Irish, perhaps. The idea that

Jimmy may have struck a secret deal with the government and was now a plant for the FBI did not occur to me at the time.

He extended his hand admiringly. "I've heard a lot about you." His handshake was wimpy, using just his fingers, a dainty touch. His reaction to me was clearly insincere and off-putting but I remained polite and respectful. "Good things, hopefully," I said.

"Oh, of course," he replied, fawning. "Your accomplishments are legendary."

"Really?" asked Grace Marie, glancing at me. "He's such a modest guy."

"What's your sign?" he asked. Sign? His question threw me. Grace Marie interjected, "When's your birthday?" I finally got it. What a weird question coming from a high-ranking Scientologist. "Oh that," I said. "The one with the fish." They both cracked up. Pisces, they told me. Jimmy decided that Grace Marie and I would get along just fine.

Finally, Jimmy pulled up a chair close to Grace Marie, gave her a love pat on the knee, and I went back to my work. As I donned my headset I heard, "So tell me, Grace Marie, what have you been up to?" I hit the start pedal.

Fred Cain was interviewing James Perry, one of two U.S. marshals who accompanied Judge Richey to Los Angeles the past summer to hear the defense motions to suppress the seized documents. Perry told Cain about some hookers Judge Richey procured while he was in L. A., and Cain wanted Perry to help track them down. I was thoroughly engrossed, typing away.

Jimmy became a frequent visitor. The two of them would gossip and cackle like happy chickens in a hen house. During those times I welcomed hearing the phone ring and Duke Snider's voice on the other end. "I need to see you," he said on one of the early days.

"Be right there," I told him.

* * *

Snider's office was deep inside the cavernous Information Bureau offices. I didn't have a key to the steel double entry door since I was not yet a member with the proper security clearance. I had to call in from a phone outside to gain entrance, and be escorted to and from his office.

"I need you to courier something to D.C. and pick up a couple of hot tapes," he said. "Will your wife mind you flying out on short notice like this?" It was almost 6 p.m. and he wanted me on the red eye that night. I said she wouldn't mind. He told me to deliver a sealed package to a man about my age. "He'll be wearing a cowboy hat and looking for you," he said. "Make the exchange, then hop back on a flight to L.A." That was it. Red eye there, early bird back. No luggage. Everything was arranged. A driver with my plane ticket would take me to LAX. "Be outside the horseshoe at ten-thirty." The "horseshoe" was a semi-circular driveway on the side of the building.

* * *

Soon after I began working on the Bast tape project, the *St. Petersburg Times* ran a fourteen part series of articles about the seized documents that pertained to Clearwater. There was no mention of me, Ritz or my activities, or of Fran and her activities. This bolstered my sense of security. Briefly. A legal shitstorm followed.

In late February my father called to say FBI agents showed up at my parents' house looking for me. My knees weakened. He didn't know the reason, only that they wanted to know where I was and how they could reach me.

"What did you tell them?"

"I gave them your phone number," he said. "I hope you're not in trouble," adding that he didn't know what I did in Clearwater but the agents asked if I was still part of Scientology, and he said I was. I told him I would give him the whole story someday and not to worry, that I hadn't done anything illegal.

When I returned to my apartment that evening I found the business card of an FBI agent wedged in my door. A handwritten note asked me to call the number on the card. Other Scientologists had just been subpoenaed to appear before the Tampa federal grand jury so I knew the agents wanted to serve me with a witness subpoena.

Snider arranged a meeting with the Safe Environment Fund (SEF), a nonprofit defense fund that was organized to solicit donations from Scientologists to pay lawyers and educate potential witnesses about grand jury procedures. I met most of the people I was reading about in newspaper accounts of the D.C. caper.

A lawyer who was expert in grand juries briefed us on our rights, legal issues, the best strategies, and so on. I was told that SEF would pay any legal fees and that I had a right to obtain independent counsel. In fact, church influence could amount to witness tampering or obstruction of justice. We were on our own but were told that the best strategy had been developed by anti-war and civil rights activists: hang together and do not cooperate, or risk being hung separately. That is, assert your Fifth Amendment right to remain silent if you were a target of the grand jury and were not granted immunity for your testimony; and, if granted immunity, which meant that you were not eligible for Fifth Amendment protection, take one for the team and refuse to testify, meaning that you would likely be held in contempt and sent to jail pending one of two events: either the grand jury's term expired or you changed your mind and decided to talk.

Fran and I met two lawyers selected for us by SEF but subject to our approval, Barry Litt and Peter Young. Fran was given a lawyer, too, because she could potentially become a witness, although FBI agents were not looking for her. Young had already spoken to the agent who left his card at my residence. I was a target of the grand jury, he informed me, and I told him I wanted to take the Fifth.

The next day Young called and told me that he had contacted the Assistant U.S. Attorney handling the Tampa grand jury, Terry Bostick. "He's inclined to temporarily release you from the subpoena since I told him you planned to take the Fifth." Young said we still needed to meet so we could prepare for a worst case scenario.

Before our meeting, seized documents regarding "Ritz" had somehow leaked from government files into the hands of Clearwater authorities and a few private parties, including my old nemesis Walt Logan, formerly of John T. Allen's office in St. Petersburg, the defense counsel for Mayor Cazares who counseled his client not to answer interrogatories in the case I was handling, and yet tried to force me to remain the attorney of record. Logan initiated a Bar complaint against me. A Pinellas County ethics committee notified me of the charges and gave me a Notice to Appear, which was sent to my residence in L.A., indicating that the FBI had likely provided him with my address.

I also received intel from the G.O. that Pinellas County State Attorney James Russell had convened a state level grand jury, and Walt Logan was preparing lawsuits against me on behalf of the Cazareses. If I attended the ethics complaint hearing, I would be hammered with subpoenas and further legal processes. I declined to appear "on advice of counsel."

In my absence, the committee recommended that the Florida Bar file formal charges. Gabriel and Maggie Cazares's suit was filed shortly thereafter, naming the church, L. Ron Hubbard, me and a few others. The media jumped into the fray. An article dated April 4, 1980, one of many on the subject, appeared on the front page of the Clearwater Sun. In large, bold type the headline blazed: "Lawyer's Days in Clearwater Spawn Mystery." The article was about me and used my real name.

* * *

I met Peter Young at his cluttered apartment on the west side of L.A.. His dimly lit living room was strewn with legal books

173

that seemed to have come from a wall of book shelves and had not found their way back. He sat at a small wooden desk with a typewriter, yellow legal pads, a stack of typing paper, and an ashtray overflowing with Winston cigarette butts and ashes. Burnt cigarette marks dotted the desktop. A haze of smoke lingered in the air mixed with a strong musty smell. It gave me an unsettled feeling about him. He lit a cigarette and asked my feelings about the bar charges against me.

"The charges are, uh, creative," I said. "Most of the six charges are false, or at least exaggerated beyond recognition."

"Did you represent the Mayor without telling him you were a Scientologist?" He was almost confrontational, which surprised me.

"Yes."

"That's enough, isn't it?"

"Hopefully not for the grand jury, which covers criminal conduct, not ethical violations."

"We'll see about that," he said. "I don't really know what evidence they have or what kind of legal theories they can come up with based on that evidence." He had me feeling uneasy. I welcomed his tough approach, though. He was professional in spite of his messy, stinky apartment. That's what I wanted in a lawyer.

I went over the whole case with him, starting with the scene in Clearwater when I first arrived there. I asked him if he had ever heard of the FBI's COINTELPRO. "Yes, of course." He said he worked on the famous Pentagon Papers case, which involved a secret Department of Defense history of the Vietnam War that was leaked to the *New York Times*. He said he had represented members of the Students for a Democratic Society and civil rights activists before grand juries and in criminal cases. "I represented Skyhorse and Mohawk, which is the longest criminal jury trial in American history." Paul Skyhorse and Richard Mohawk were American Indians who were tried for murder in Ventura County, California. They had been the subject of a far-reaching FBI counterintelligence program as part of a covert campaign waged against the American Indian Movement.

"What was the outcome of that trial?" I asked.

"I walked them," he said proudly. I loved hearing that.

When we finished a couple of hours later, Young said, "Listen, Merrell. I know what the government does to activists. There is one hard lesson I've learned and I wish people at the church would learn it, too, and that is: when you are a minority, you cannot afford to cut corners. You won't be given a fair shake. Government agents and people connected to the government can get away with murder. As a minority you have to cross every 'T' and dot every 'I.' There are better ways to handle the situations you witnessed. There always are. You have to be more creative and committed to only doing them the right way."

His comment struck home and confirmed conclusions I had already reached and thoughts I was still processing. I really liked this guy. I wish I had known him before I moved to Clearwater. Or even earlier, in St. Louis. Really early.

* * *

By the end of May the Bast project was winding down. Snider said they needed to bring it to a conclusion and file the motion to recuse Judge Richey, thereby blowing the cover of Bast and his undercover operation. Soon after, I transcribed a tape of Paulette Cooper dining with Bast. This wasn't my first recording of Paulette. Bast had her under contract, getting her to secretly tape other people. The cover story he used to entice her was his claim to be working for a wealthy Swiss national who had an axe to grind against Scientology and was willing to spend a lot of money to wield that axe, as long as it could be done without his fingerprints on it. But this recording of Paulette was different than the others in a way only I understood.

Jimmy Mulligan happened to visit right after I finished the transcription. I told him that the church should take Paulette

Cooper's deposition in her New York lawsuit before the Bast tapes are filed in the criminal cases.

He brushed off the idea with a wave of his hand. "No, that's not the purpose of the project. The motion to recuse Judge Richey is already in the works. We can't stop and worry about litigation with Paulette."

"You can do both," I insisted. "You can get one of her cases dismissed without slowing up the filing of the motion." I checked myself. "Well, maybe it'll delay the filing for a week. But it will be worth it. I guarantee it."

He asked me to explain. I told him I had become very familiar with the litigation between the church and Paulette. "In the tape I just transcribed she contradicted about fifty of her primary allegations in her New York case against the church. Take her deposition. Either obtain admissions from her that her allegations are false or force her to lie under oath. Either way, you win. Just file a Motion to Dismiss."

That seemed to flick Jimmy's switch. "Write that up," he said. "Explain it just the way you did to me and lay out the steps we need to take." As I settled into my desk, he asked how long it would take.

"Ten minutes."

"I'll be back in ten minutes," he said and rushed out the door. He soon returned and scanned my write up. "Excellent. Mary Sue (Hubbard) said you're heading up the mission to carry this out. Pack your bags. You're going to New York."

Before leaving I went through the transcript and prepared a list of precise questions Paulette should be asked and wrote an alert to the G.O.'s legal department in New York, asking that her deposition be immediately scheduled for the earliest possible date. Jimmy passed my written instructions through the proper channels. When I returned with an overnight bag, Jimmy had an airline ticket for me. He said the deposition was scheduled for next week. I was off.

* * *

"Are you a lawyer?" asked Jonathan Lubell, the church's New York libel lawyer. I told him I was but that I was not there in that capacity; I was attached to the G.O.'s Information Bureau. He nodded. After a little small talk he asked what I had for him. I handed him my list of questions. "We want you to ask Paulette these exact questions." He looked them over and said the questions were all relevant. "Yes, I can ask these. No problem."

I told him I was not at liberty to reveal everything, but that we had clear evidence of the true answer to each of these. "Paulette will either admit the truth, and in so doing will disprove the allegations in her complaint, or she will lie ..."

He interrupted me, clearly enthused, and said he got it. "How soon after her deposition will I get the evidence you mentioned?" he asked.

"The next day. The evidence will be revealed in a motion filed in an entirely separate case. The only thing you need to be careful of is to intersperse those questions with your own so you don't tip her off." He said that would be easy for him to do because he had many questions already prepared.

That was it. I had lunch with the G.O. staffer, retrieved my overnight bag, and headed back to Los Angeles.

The deposition went down as planned. Paulette perjured her ass off, testifying in exact opposition to her recorded statements. Her case was dead – and would later be dismissed in response to a motion filed by Lubell.

* * *

"I have a message for you from Mary Sue," Jimmy Mulligan proudly announced. Grace Marie and I were glued to him. He quoted her emphatically: "You are worth your weight in gold."

"Ah, nice," I said, smiling.

Jimmy threw his hands in the air. "That's all! Did you hear me? That was from Mary Sue!" He acted as though she were royalty bestowing knighthood on me or something. I didn't know how to react.

Grace Marie, who was laughing at Jimmy's reaction, jumped in. "Oh that's just the Midwestern in him."

Jimmy was aghast, his head cocked and his mouth agape. "Mary Sue. Mary Sue Hubbard said you were worth your weight in gold. She's never said that to anyone before." Well, that was more information, but I still didn't know how he expected me to respond. I almost felt embarrassed by the praise he was dishing out.

I finally said, "Tell Mary Sue that I really appreciate her saying that."

Chapter 18

DODGING A BULLET

Fortune brings in some boats that are not steered.

– William Shakespeare

Upon completion of the secret Bast tape project, I met with Joe Lisa and my former handler, Tom Ritchie, to go over my new duties. I was assigned a desk job in the U.S.G.O. Information Bureau. I reported to Richie who answered to Joe, the director.

All intelligence collected in the U. S. first went to my desk. I would then distribute it to the various area managers: Southeast U.S., Northeast U.S., Midwest U.S., and Western U.S. We were all stationed in one large room. He gave me a tour and introduced me to the others. I already knew the faces but didn't have names to go with them until now. My desk was identical to the others in the room, a gray metal tank with an IBM Selectric typewriter and two large bins on top marked "Intel In" and "Intel Out."

Ritchie said they wanted me to see every piece of intelligence to determine the legal significance of information that pertained to the church's court cases. One of my functions was to be the liaison with the Legal Bureau, to coordinate with that staff to determine how to aid their legal actions and make sure they got the intel they needed.

"But do it without compromising our sources and intel ops," Joe added.

"So clear it with me first before you turn intel over to Legal," Ritchie said.

Joe continued. "There is one other important thing I want you to do because of you being a lawyer. You have to approve every intel op done in the U.S., and make sure it's all legal." That was music to my ears, exactly what I wanted to see done. I remembered reading in a newspaper article that Mary Sue Hubbard publicly accepted full responsibility for the infiltration of government offices, electronic eavesdropping, etc. and stated that she would do everything within her power to see that nothing like that ever occurred again. It sounded like she meant it. My respect for her grew.

I gave a fist pump, exclaiming, "Yes!" They exchanged amused looks.

"Good for you," Joe said. "Keep my ass out of jail." He added that he had barely missed being indicted himself.

"I know," I said. "I read about your role in the newspapers."

He pointed at me and said, "That's it." He turned to Ritchie. "He just nailed it." Then to the both of us, he said, "Here's our new motto: 'If you don't want to read about it in the newspaper the next morning, don't do it.'"

Over the next few days I got an idea of the mountains of paper flow I would have to handle. I was pushing paper, as the saying goes, and it was a heavy load. I also got a chance to meet other members of the Information Bureau, most of whom knew of my exploits in Clearwater once they associated me with my code name "Ritz."

One of the guys I met was Jim Douglass. After our introduction, he said, "You walk around like you own the place." I was taken aback, but saw the smile on his face. He meant it as a compliment, somehow.

"Really? I would hate to leave people with that impression."

"No, no," he said, cackling. "That came out wrong. I meant it in a good way. You have a lot of confidence in yourself and don't feel less than other people."

"Oh? I haven't noticed people here feeling lower than others."

He laughed. "For a new guy, I meant."

"Ah. Well, I've been around some of these guys, like Tom Ritchie, for a while, so maybe that's it."

"Yeah, I know what you did in Clearwater," he said with a telling grin.

"Except I haven't seen Don Alverzo," I said. "I was hoping to run into him."

"You know that isn't his real name, don't you?"

His comment froze my brain. It had never occurred to me that Don Alverzo was not his real name. Since Douglass had a loose tongue, I thought I would take a shot at learning his real name. While studying the Paulette Cooper files, I got the distinct impression that the person who lived in her apartment building, and later in her apartment in a platonic relationship during the time of the fake bomb threat operation and went by the name Jerry Levin, was really Alverzo.

"Is it Jerry Levin?" I asked.

Douglass hesitated. His laugh evaporated into a thin smile. I could see his security gates dropping into place. "Well, if you don't know his real name I shouldn't comment on that."

"That's cool. Maybe you shouldn't." At least I came away from the conversation educated on one fact: My old buddy Don Alverzo wasn't who he said he was. I would no doubt learn more about him on the job.

* * *

As the days and weeks passed, Fran, Angie and I settled in to a comfortable Southern California lifestyle. Fran liked her job, and I liked mine. Angie adapted instantly to her new school and to our apartment complex, a two-story 12-unit building with an outdoor swimming pool in Burbank, a suburb of Los Angeles. Four other girls her age lived there, so she had friends and plenty to do.

The legal actions involving Fran and me had gone into an inactive period. The Florida Bar had yet to file formal administrative charges. Two civil suits that named me as a party (and one of which also named Fran) were tied up in procedural motions. Neither of us had been served. The Gabe Cazares case was transferred to Daytona Beach due to massive pretrial publicity in Clearwater. Only the Tampa federal grand jury seemed to be a current threat. The motion to dismiss it due to prejudicial publicity had been denied.

One Friday evening at the end of July, Fran and I were on our way to meet friends for a game of bridge when the phone rang. It was my grand jury attorney, Peter Young. "Merrell, I just received a tip that two members of the Pinellas County Sheriff's Office are in town and have obtained an arrest warrant for you and Fran. They plan to arrest both of you." I was stunned, and spit out something like, "You're kidding me." He was clearly dead serious, saying "You need to take a quick vacation."

"Arrest us for what?"

"As material witnesses before the Pinellas County state grand jury." I asked if he meant they planned to serve us with witness subpoenas. "No," he said. "They plan to arrest the two of you and fly you back to Clearwater under detention until after your testimony is given."

"Geez, can they do that?"

"They *are* doing that," Young said, his voice raised. "The only thing that's important right now is for you to leave quickly and tell your neighbors and landlord that you're taking a short vacation. We can talk later."

Fran overheard my end of the conversation. We decided to head up to Big Bear Lake for the weekend, a mountain resort about a hundred miles east of Los Angeles. It was 100 degrees in Burbank that day and would be cooler at 7,000 feet.

I briefed Fran as we packed our bags. We left Angie with our close friends who lived near Long Beach, just in case the deputies located us or were waiting for us when we returned. Fran rounded up Angie, who was playing with a neighbor girl.

I stopped by the apartment of Janet Lonon on the ground floor. She was on staff with the Los Angeles G.O.'s Information Bureau (as distinguished from U.S.G.O. in Los Angeles). She was on the phone and jotting down notes when I arrived. I told her husband, Ken, that we were taking off for the weekend. He asked where and I told him it was best if he didn't know. Janet got off the phone and said she had just been briefed by Rebecca Chambers from the U.S.G.O. Legal Department about what to do when the Sheriff Deputies showed up.

"Is she the one who got the tip?" I asked. As the question fell off my tongue, Young's words came back to me. "The only important thing is for you to leave quickly."

"What the hell is this about deputies showing up?" Ken said.

"Never mind," I said, waving my hands to both of them on my way toward the door. "I've got to hit the road. Later."

* * *

I called Young the next day on a pay phone from Big Bear Lake. "It's all under control," he said, adding that the deputies had arrived at 6 a.m. "They knocked on your door and your neighbor Janet told them you were on vacation and didn't know when you would return. They gave her a business card. I've already spoken with one of the deputies. I informed him I was accepting service on your behalf and that you intend to challenge the material witness certificate in a California court."

"Those assholes showed up at 6 a.m. to arrest Fran and me, with our nine year-old daughter there to witness it?"

Young sighed. "That was exactly their plan."

"What would have happened to Angie?"

He said he didn't know how that would have worked. "Merrell, it didn't happen. We out-maneuvered them. They're flying back to Clearwater right now without their quarry. Relish that, and forget what they tried to do." He told me to enjoy the weekend, that he and Barry Litt would file papers the first thing Monday morning.

"Before you hang up, Peter. Where did the tip come from?"

"L.A. County D.A.'s office," he said. The Pinellas County authorities were required to go through the local D.A.'s office in order to obtain the California certification necessary to arrest California citizens. They had a Florida material witness certificate, but needed to turn it into a California certificate.

"Does the church have a plant inside the D.A.'s office?" I asked, surprised that I would not have known about it. "No," he said. "The person who gave us the tip is not a Scientologist. I was just told that she's a friend of the church. As I understand it, her husband is a Scientologist."

"Do you have the husband's name?" He was evasive but I pressed him for it. "I might know him." Before revealing the name, he reminded me that she had done us a favor and asked me not to contact her or her husband or do anything that might get her in trouble.

I promised I wouldn't. And I haven't until now, many years after it could cause her trouble. "She's a young assistant district attorney named Marcia Clark." Her name meant nothing to me at the time. Years later she became famous as the lead prosecutor in the 1994 murder trial of O.J. Simpson and has been a familiar TV pundit ever since.

Chapter 19

TAMPA GRAND JURY

Never be bullied into silence. Never allow yourself to be made a victim. Accept no one's definition of your life; define yourself.

— Harvey Fierstein
American actor and playwright

The threat of being hauled before the Pinellas County grand jury faded into the fog of the California justice system. A procedural challenge to the material witness certification in the California Superior Court failed but was appealed. Out of sight, out of mind. Life went on.

The lull in legal action ended a year later, in June 1981. A new federal grand jury was convened in Tampa after the original one's term had expired. Fran and I were both summoned to appear before it. Fran appeared first, along with two other Scientologists. She flew to Florida while I stayed home with Angie. Fran was not a target, so she could be held in contempt if she refused to testify after prosecutors promised not to use her testimony against her.

She called from Tampa after her appearance. Her voice was shaking. She had refused to testify even after being granted immunity. She was awaiting a hearing before a district judge on a motion to have her held in contempt and sent to jail. Her lawyer for the proceeding, Jim Rief of New York, filed a

185

procedural challenge to the contempt charge, in which one issue was spousal privilege. Since I was a target of the grand jury her testimony could not be used against me. She was horrified at the prospect of going to jail and began to cry.

I reminded her that if she was held in contempt and sent to jail that she held the key to her own freedom. "I'm not going to testify against you or other Scientologists," she said resolutely, and assured me that she would be okay. Her tears gave way to sniffles. I wished her luck and told her how much I loved her.

An hour later, she called again, greatly relieved, saying, "I'm coming home." But, she added, she had to return the following week. The judge had taken the legal challenge under advisement. I asked her what questions she was asked before the grand jury. Only seven, she told me. The two she remembered involved whether she worked on the 1976 Congressional campaign of Gabriel Cazares and whether she had done so at the instruction of the Church of Scientology.

Seeing her off at the airport the following week was tough. I gave her a kiss and a big hug and told her I would be there to pick her up the next night. She said goodbye with quivering lips.

I sat next to the telephone during the time of her scheduled hearing. The motion was being held in the judge's chambers. Mitch Hermann was facing contempt charges at the same time. Mitch was one of the original nine persons found guilty and sentenced pending appeal for the infiltration of the federal government. Information contained in the seized documents revealed that Mitch had, from his management position at the U.S.G.O. Information Bureau, orchestrated a fake hit-and-run accident in Washington, D.C. involving Mayor Cazares during his Congressional campaign. A young woman picked up the Mayor in her car, struck a pedestrian and fled the scene. Both the woman driver and the faux victim pedestrian were Scientologists. The idea was to invent a scandal involving the married Cazares while he was in the company of another woman. The episode became the subject of the Tampa grand jury and Mitch had refused to testify after being granted immunity for his testimony. Prosecutors probably thought Fran knew something about the incident, but she later told me she didn't have a clue and had only read about it in the newspapers.

The phone finally rang. I answered before the first ring ended. "I'm coming home," Fran said for the second time in a week. She cried tears of relief. She gave me a rundown of the proceedings. Mitch's hearing came first. He was found in contempt, handcuffed and carted off to jail. For the first time Fran said it had really struck home that she, too, was going to jail. Her frantic first thought was: "What am I going to tell my mother?"

When Fran's motion was heard she was also held in contempt and she expected to be handcuffed and taken away like Mitch. However, the judge granted her bail pending an appeal based on the spousal privilege issue. An appeal would take many months, maybe even a year or more. A weight was lifted from me. At least Fran was off the hook.

* * *

I met with Peter Young to prepare for my grand jury appearance. He told me that he and the other two lawyers, after reviewing all of the seized documents, including the "Ritz Documents," could not pinpoint a crime I could be charged with.

I reiterated that the authorities and civil litigants assumed I knew more than I did and were leaning on me to spill beans that didn't exist. "They see me as Gabe's lawyer and assume that I took it on to sabotage his case. They don't understand intelligence and can't conceive that I was actually involved in an intelligence operation."

Young agreed that federal prosecutors were leaning on me since I had the most to lose – my law licenses – and that I might cut a deal and testify against others rather than risk an indictment or lose my right to practice law. They planned to jail Fran and then tighten the screws on me. I told him that I have never been concerned about being indicted. "So their power move isn't working, especially now that Fran hasn't been jailed."

Young sighed. "Remember the saying: a grand jury can indict a ham sandwich. And once you're indicted, even on false charges, the possibility of conviction always exists." He conceded that he felt positive about my chances of escaping an indictment, and added that he was happy I had not been involved in or knew anything about some of the crazy stuff that went on in Clearwater. I assured him that the G.O. had cleaned up its act and was no longer involved in criminal or destructive activity, and that the office now had a lawyer overseeing their intelligence operations – me.

He was pleased to hear that, and even more so when I revealed that he had been a positive influence on me. "What was missing was professional legal advice. The G.O. didn't trust outsiders. I came up through the Scientology ranks, first as a professional Scientology auditor, then as a G.O. volunteer, where I won their trust. And the fact that they got their hands slapped made them receptive to legal constraints."

"You know, Merrell, I warned them a year ahead of time that they were going to be raided." I asked him how he knew that, and he explained that he was hired to work for the church in July 1976, a year before the raid. A mailbag had been confiscated by U.S. Customs going from U.S.G.O. Information Bureau to G.O. World Headquarters in East Grinstead, Sussex, England. He was tasked with recovering the mail bag and its contents. He succeeded, winning an emergency court order two days later.

"The government was ordered to return the contents and destroy all copies. They returned the mail bag but of course they never obey court orders to destroy copies." He snuffed out a cigarette and added, "Based on my review of the contents of the mail bag I told the G.O. they were going to be raided."

"What was in the mail bag that caused you to reach that conclusion?"

"It showed a vast intelligence network with information coming from the highest levels of government, including the

White House and congressional offices, and from powerful law firms. Some were original letters and memos involving extremely sensitive matters between high-ranking Presidential staff and the CIA."

I was stupified. "Did anyone ask for your advice as to how they should prepare for a raid?" He said they hadn't. "Do you know what the Information Bureau did with all their incriminating documents? Some of them were only proposals for operations that were never approved or implemented. They put signs on their file cabinets that said 'Confessional Formularies—' as if the FBI would not look in them for fear of violating someone's First Amendment right to the free exercise of religion."

Young lowered and shook his head. "I know," he said. "Unbelievable."

We broke into a bit of gallows laughter. "It's sad," Young said. "If only they had asked for my advice on what measures to take they could have avoided most, if not all, criminal consequences. And you, my friend, and your wife Fran, would not be in this mess."

Young was originally retained by Paul Klopper, the head of the U.S.G.O. Legal Bureau, so I assumed Young had made his report to Klopper, but I didn't ask. I knew Klopper; he was a likeable, friendly soul. But he really dropped the ball on this, I thought. The idea that Klopper might be a plant working for the FBI did not enter my mind at the time.

* * *

Approximately twenty jurors sat scattered throughout a sloping, semicircular grand jury box. It looked similar to one of my classrooms in law school, except, instead of a professor's podium, the jurors looked down upon a witness box. I sat in the box. The prosecutor, Assistant U.S. Attorney Terry Bostick, stood to my right. He greeted me and asked the court reporter to swear me in.

He asked for my full name and address, which I gave, addressing my answers to the jurors. They seemed bored. I turned to Bostick, a tall and stocky man, about 30 years of age. I held a piece of note paper in my hand, awaiting his first question.

"Are you now or have you ever been a member of the Church of Scientology?"

I read from the note I was holding: "Based on the advice of my attorney, I respectfully assert my right under the Fifth Amendment of the United States Constitution and decline to answer the question."

"Have you ever held an office in the Church of Scientology?"

"Based on the advice of my attorney, I respectfully assert my right under the Fifth Amendment of the United States Constitution and decline to answer the question." The jurors appeared catatonic, as though they had checked out. I reminded myself that they had already seen this drill before with other Scientology witnesses, so I understood. I was bored myself with the needless exercise.

"In fall 1975, 1976, and 1977 did you ever reside in Pinellas County?"

"Based on the advice of my attorney, I respectfully assert my right under the Fifth Amendment of the United States Constitution and decline to answer the question."

"Have you ever attended or graduated from any law school in the United States?" As he asked the question, Bostick backed his hind end against the top of the wooden panel of the jury box and leaned against it on one arm. He dropped his left hand, the one that held his list of questions, giving off an air of irritation.

I hesitated and glanced at the jurors to see if they had been adversely affected by his drama. I didn't detect any animosity or change in the way they regarded me; they remained listless. I repeated my stock response. Bostick raised his cheat sheet and rattled off two more questions: "What state bars are you a member of? Aren't you a member of the Florida Bar?"

With each question Bostick lowered his sheet and I asserted the Fifth. He raised his sheet and asked another question. "In 1975, when you flew to Florida, did you come with your wife?" I took the Fifth. "Do you know Gabriel Cazares?" Fifth. "Did you ever have an attorney-client relationship with Gabe Cazares?" Fifth.

I wondered how long he would keep up the farce.

A hint of sarcasm laced his next question. His mannerism and tone became more obviously sarcastic with each subsequent question. Clearly he was playing to the grand jurors. I kept one eye on them. They did not seem to be affected, one way or another. "Were you ever employed in Pinellas or Hillsborough Counties as an attorney?" Fifth. "Did you ever obtain or seek a job with James Russell of the State Attorney's Office?" Fifth. "Do you know Mitch Hermann?" Fifth.

Bostick folded his arms, gave an exasperated look and scanned the jurors. Then he said, "What did you have for lunch today?" I cocked my head, wondering what he was up to now. He answered for me in a sing-song voice, "Based on the advice of my attorney ..." his voice trailed off.

That ticked me off. "Mr. Bostick, please don't mock me. You knew before I flew here from California that I intended to assert my Fifth Amendment right to not answer your questions."

Out of the corner of my eye I noticed jurors begin to stir.

Bostick said, "I'm just making the point that you don't –" He stopped. "Well, let me ask you this: do you have anything to say to these jurors before I let you go?"

I looked at the jurors. Their eyes were riveted on me. I considered rolling out Plan B, something I had spent many hours working on and mulling over, something Young had talked me out of based on his fear that I might waive my right to remain silent if I said anything at all.

I looked at Bostick who seemed surprised that I was even considering his question. Everything felt right. So I let it rip.

"Yes, as a matter of fact, I do."

Bostick gestured gallantly with his arms. "By all means. Say what you will."

"Ladies and gentlemen of the grand jury," I began, and with that they came alive. They straightened in their seats, stole glances at one another as if to say, finally, some action, and grabbed their pens and pads of papers.

I then made a statement that went something like this: "I respect the important jobs you have, and it is not my wish to remain silent. I would prefer to cooperate and assist your investigation. But, in my opinion, this is not an honest investigation."

Bostick stiffened. I continued. "In my opinion the U.S. Attorney's office, through Mr. Bostick, is on a witch hunt. I think they have an agenda to prosecute Scientologists to the exclusion of, and as a cover-up of corruption by, government officials."

Some jurors scratched notes. All were hanging on my every word, as Bostick fidgeted.

"Most people do not understand the role and history of the grand jury. Mr. Bostick may not have explained to you that the grand jury arose out of the Bill of Rights so that We the People have a means to investigate corruption within the government. The grand jury was not intended to be a tool of the government to go after its citizens. It was meant to be a tool for citizens to hold government officials in line.

"Ladies and gentlemen, Mr. Bostick probably did not tell you that it is you, not him, who controls the grand jury. In fact, you can ask him to leave the room if you wish."

Bostick clutched the jury box with one hand and looked rather pale, a shell of the former smart-aleck bully he had been. "You can tell him which witnesses to summon before you, and you can inquire of those witnesses as you wish. You can even ask for the assistance of a lawyer from outside the U.S. Attorney's Office."

I noticed from the expressions of the jurors that I had captivated them. Bostick must have known, too. He pushed off the jury box, and pulled out a pen. "Okay, Mr. Vannier, which witnesses do you think should be subpoenaed?"

I loved that question. It was a softball lobbed down the middle of the plate with the words "HIT ME" written on it. "Start with James T. Russell, State Attorney of Pinellas-Pasco Counties." Bostick jotted something on his sheet of paper. Jurors also were writing. "Ask him about a multi-agency investigation he participated in, the results of which were buried in the files of the St. Petersburg Police Department's Intelligence Division. Sergeant Meinhart of that division can testify to that and provide the files. Ask him whether those documents were requested under Florida's Sunshine Law and whether he turned them over or responded to indicate the existence of those documents, and if not, why not?

"Subpoena Gabriel Cazares, the former Mayor of Clearwater and ask him about his relationship to the FBI as an undercover operative beginning with a counterintelligence operation against the United Farm Workers and continuing against the Church of Scientology, and later against me, personally. "Subpoena Francis Mullen and Michael Lunsford of the FBI and ask them the same questions.

"Subpoena Bette Orsini of the *St. Petersburg Times*. Ask her about her receipt of information leaked to her either by the FBI or the multi-agency task force. Ask if she then reported that information to the public. Ask if she reported a false impression that she, the FBI and Mayor Cazares did not know beforehand that the Church of Scientology was behind the purchase of the Fort Harrison Hotel in Clearwater."

"Any others?" Bostick asked. I told him no. Actually, I had more names and things to say but I thought I had given the jurors enough to keep them busy for a while, and I had accomplished my purpose by speaking. "Okay. Thank you for that information. Is there anything else you would like to say to the grand jury?"

I thought about it for a moment. "Yes. One more thing." I addressed the jurors. "Ladies and gentlemen of the grand jury, if you do subpoena those people and ask them those questions and others you might think of ... if you do that, call me back. Mr. Bostick knows how to contact me through my attorney. You turn this into an honest investigation and I promise you I will return and I will testify fully. I also promise that you will not be disappointed, because I have a lot to say."

* * *

In the hallway, Peter Young and Tampa attorney Bennie Lazzara scurried up to me. (Attorneys from out of state need to work through an attorney licensed in the state in which they appear. Young was not licensed to practice in Florida, so Lazzara was retained as local counsel.) Young asked what took me so long and I told him I ended up giving my speech. He was crestfallen. "Oh no, Merrell, I hope that doesn't come back to haunt you."

"I'm sure it won't. I won them over. I might have even turned them." It was clear to me that I had not won *him* over. "Oh, brother," he said. "You know, I warned you against that. It rarely works and is not worth the risk." I put my hand on his shoulder. "I know, but you weren't in there. I thought it was the right thing to do."

Young shook his head. "I hope you're right."

* * *

Tom Ritchie picked me up at LAX. As soon as I hopped inside his car he said: "What happened? CAL is really pissed at you. She said you testified." CAL was Ann Mulligan, Mary Sue's aide for G.O. legal matters, and Jimmy Mulligan's wife. CAL stands for Controller Aide Legal and is pronounced like the man's name, Cal.

Until that moment I was flying higher than the plane back to L.A., even rethinking whether I'd really needed to move from Clearwater to Canada in the first place. Suddenly I was gobsmacked by Ritchie's comment. It provoked a number of thoughts and questions that collided in a ball of confusion and brought me back down to earth with a thud. I wondered how CAL could have known anything that hadn't come from me. Grand jury proceedings are secret. Only a witness is free to speak about his or her appearance and I had only spoken with my attorneys. *Did one of them debrief her?* Surely not without my authorization.

"Hey, Tom. First of all, no, I didn't testify. I gave a speech. There's a difference. Second of all, CAL is in a senior position to me in the church and is reproaching me through you, my supervisor, for my conduct before a federal grand jury. That is inappropriate. Someone needs to tell her that her actions could be interpreted as tampering with a witness or obstruction of justice. Both are felonies. If she or anyone else in the church has a problem with my appearance before the grand jury ... well, first they should get their facts straight, because they sure haven't heard them from me, but then they should take it up with my attorney through church counsel."

Ritchie backed off and I explained to him what really happened. I never heard another word about my appearance from CAL or anyone else in the church.

* * *

There are two postscripts to this story. One occurred six months later, in February 1982. The Fifth District Court of Appeal denied Fran's appeal of her contempt charge and the matter was returned to the U.S. Attorney for further action, that is, to take her into custody for her refusal to testify. But nothing happened. No one at our end knew why. Eventually, of course, the grand jury's term would have expired.

The second postscript explains the first one and occurred more than ten years later. I received a phone call from Dick Weigand. "Hey, man. You need to come over. I have a wild story for you." I dropped what I was doing and jumped into my car.

Weigand was the head of U.S.G.O.'s Information Bureau during the infiltration of government offices era, the same post Joe Lisa held when I arrived in the bureau. (Dick Weigand is not related to Doug Weigand, a name mentioned in Chapter 4.) Dick Weigand was indicted, pleaded guilty and spent thirteen months in federal prison. I first met him after subpoenas were served for the original Tampa grand jury. He was one of the persons at the Safe Environment Fund meeting mentioned earlier. He moved into a house in a neighboring community after he was released and we stayed in touch.

He had just returned from vacation in Key West, Florida. "Hey," he said at his house, clearly eager to relate his story. "When I was on vacation I met this guy. We were fishing on a pier. I went out there every day and so did he. We ended up introducing ourselves and talking it up. One day I told him I was a Scientologist." Weigand added that he was prepared for anything when he told someone that. I knew what he meant.

"The guy's immediate reaction was, 'I've heard about Scientology. I was on a grand jury in Tampa once on a Scientology case.'" Dick paused to get my reaction. I was blown away. "I thought you would like this. Wait, it gets better.

"The guy said a young lawyer came in one day to testify, a Scientologist." That would be me, I said, breaking in. "I know. Catch this: he said the lawyer was taking the Fifth like everyone else, and the prosecutor started making fun of him, and this young lawyer got on him, which woke everybody up, because this guy also thought the prosecutor was a bully, and he was glad to see this lawyer call him out for it."

Weigand began speaking as if he were the man on the pier. "The prosecutor then asked the lawyer if he had anything to say, and boy, *did* he. He came right out and called the whole thing a witch hunt, which also got our attention, because we talked about it later and everyone thought all along that something was fishy. Anyway, this young lawyer starts telling us about how grand juries work, how we can kick the prosecutor out of the room and run it ourselves, and he gave us a list of witnesses we should subpoena and things to ask them, and we were all taking notes on everything he said.

"After he finished, we told the prosecutor that we wanted to confer alone and got him out of there. Every one of us felt the same thing. We wanted to take over and do what the lawyer said we should do. We called the prosecutor back in and gave him a list of names to subpoena, all the names the lawyer gave us."

"Holy shit," I said. "It really *was* a runaway grand jury!" Weigand said he remembered me telling him my story. "So what happened to the grand jury?" I asked. "What happened to their subpoenas?"

"The guy said they never heard another word from the prosecutor after they turned over the list of names for him to subpoena. He said he guessed that the U. S. Attorney's Office didn't want them to go down that road."

Chapter 20

LAWYERS CONFERENCE

To know how to disguise is the knowledge of kings.

— Cardinal Richelieu

Tom Ritchie leaned in and spoke quietly. "I want you to attend a legal conference in downtown L.A. tomorrow." Sitting next to his desk, I felt the sands beneath my job description shifting. "A legal conference?"

He said the church had hired a new team of lawyers to handle the civil cases. "Legal is meeting with them tomorrow to go over the cases and strategy, that sort of thing. We want you there for an intel perspective."

I welcomed hearing about a new team of lawyers. The legal strategy and tactics I saw in a growing number of lawsuits were ass-backwards from what it took to win cases. In fairness to the legal staff and their current lawyers, there had been an explosion of lawsuits against the church in the aftermath of Judge Richey's release of the seized documents, which were like blood in the water to shark plaintiff lawyers. One in particular, Michael Flynn from Boston, was the great white shark of that group. He began drumming up sour former church members and filing lawsuits on their behalf, including a class action, and then he started farming out lawsuits to other lawyers. He established FAMCO, Flynn Associates Management Company, to fund the litigation.

The Information Bureau was busy gathering intel in order to put Flynn on the defensive and locate his funding sources.

"CAL (Mulligan) and the director of Legal (Klopper) will be there," he said. I had worked with Klopper before He was an easy-going, bearded, hippie-like guy who typically wore blue jeans and sandals.

"Have you met Ann Mulligan?" he asked. I hadn't. Didn't need to. Wasn't interested. Her reaction to my grand jury appearance confirmed my instinct to avoid her. I had seen her around with her husband Jimmy Mulligan, coming and going from the building. She was taller than him and rather hard looking. I thought they made an odd couple.

"No. What do I need to do? Are they expecting some kind of intel briefing?"

"No, no, no. You don't have to do anything. Just take it all in."

* * *

I arrived at the downtown law office and the receptionist pointed me to a conference room. Klopper and Mulligan were seated on one side of a large table and three men were taking seats on the opposite side. Already seated at the front of the room was Barry Litt, who represented Fran in her California material witness certification case. Until then I didn't know he also practiced civil litigation.

Litt and I greeted each other. I slapped Klopper on the back, said hi, and we shook hands. Mulligan motioned toward the far end of the table and said, "You should sit there." She did not introduce herself. Nor did Paul introduce her. Perhaps he thought we had previously met. She knew that we hadn't, though. I decided not to initiate an introduction and took the seat.

She introduced me as a representative of U.S.G.O.'s Information Bureau. Litt introduced the other lawyers: Tom Hunt, Jay Roth and Carson Taylor. Litt and I sat at opposite ends. Stacks of case files were laid out on the table. Everyone had a legal pad except me.

"Merrell practiced law in both Missouri and Florida," Litt said to the lawyers.

"What area of the law?" Tom Hunt asked.

"Civil litigation, mostly."

"And you're not in the legal department?" he responded.

"I fought for him, believe me." Klopper said.

"Information could use a lawyer, too," I said to Hunt, adding, "as recent events have shown." I was referring to the criminal actions. They laughed. I stole a glance at Ann. She was the only one not amused. There was no chill or animosity between us; just a sense a mutual disinterest, and I was okay with that. I continued: "It also helps with the civil cases. They can better support Legal with a lawyer on board."

Litt started his overview of the active civil suits – dozens of them. His opinion on the state of the defense's handling of them – shoddy. The consequences of not immediately changing the strategy – dire. I agreed with every word. I was relieved, even heartened that someone else in the room besides me knew how to litigate civil cases. I really liked Litt's straight talk, too. He didn't mince words.

I glanced at Mulligan and Klopper occasionally. Both were taking notes. Neither seemed personally offended, even though they were both responsible for the horrible condition of the cases. Another good sign. Leave pride and ego at the door; let's fix this mess.

When he was done, Litt turned the floor over to his fellow lawyers to discuss individual cases, give their proposals on how they would turn each one around, and an estimated budget for doing it. Each presentation was short and to the point, capturing the essence and status of each case and what needed to be done. I could tell these guys really knew their craft. Fabulous. Finally.

The entire briefing lasted a couple of hours, after which Litt and the other lawyers looked at Mulligan for her reaction and comments. "Gentlemen," she began. "Thank you for the briefing. Your obvious hard work and time are greatly appreciated. However, the strategies you propose don't align with the direction we want to take."

My eyes popped out of their sockets, starting with the word "however." She kept talking as I collected myself. She sounded very distant, as though she was at one end of a long tunnel and I was at the other. She said something about being more efficient in the handling of the cases and that an overhaul of the kind recommended was unnecessary. I caught her drift. What she was saying was idiotic and destructive to the church's legal interests, bottom line. It was really tough for me to sit through it with a straight face.

The attorneys, to my surprise, did not show any reaction. None of them threw down their pens and stormed out. No one shot incredulous glances at one another. No one screamed back at her what they must be thinking: *No wonder you're in this legal quagmire: the person in charge is a moron!* They just politely listened.

After she finished Litt said to me. "So what do you think, Merrell?" *Gee, thanks Barry. I owe you one.* Mulligan butted in, saving me. "His opinion doesn't matter. I'm in charge of Legal. He's only here on behalf of Information for liaison purposes."

"I know," Litt said. "I was just curious since he is an experienced trial lawyer himself." Turning to his associates, he added, "Merrell has tried a number of jury trials and was the head of the civil litigation department of a law firm in Clearwater."

"Oh?" said Jay Roth. "I'm curious, too." The other two lawyers chimed in as well.

Mulligan looked at me. "Go ahead. Tell us your opinion."

I took a few moments to calculate my response. Litt was smiling at me. The attention of each of the other lawyers was fixed on me. Even Klopper and Mulligan had their eyes locked on me. Words of diplomacy eluded me.

"I agree with them," I said, addressing Mulligan. "Every word. This is exactly what's needed to turn these cases around." I turned to the lawyers. "Guys, I was really impressed with your presentations. I know from experience that Barry is a top-notch lawyer and I am equally impressed with each of you based on what I've heard today." I did not look to see Mulligan's reaction. I didn't have to. I felt her eyes like cold steel daggers pressing into my head, which prompted me to conclude, "For what it's worth." Mulligan spoke emphatically. "Yes. As I've already told you, his opinion is worth nothing because I'm in charge of Legal." She started gathering her notes. The meeting was over. And I was probably toast.

* * *

Back on post later that day I was trying to concentrate on my intelligence traffic, going through all the paper that had piled up in my absence, when Ritchie showed up. He leaned over and whispered, "How did it go?"

I raised my head. "Don't ask."

He was taken aback. And I must have spoken too loudly. Tom spun his head around and I glanced over my shoulder to see other staffers ogling us.

"Let's go for a walk," he said.

After we turned the corner at Fountain Avenue, Ritchie repeated his question. I shook my head. "Tom, this is not a good time for me. I'll write a report in the morning."

He stopped me with a firm grip on my shoulder and looked me in the eye. "Wow. I've never seen you like this. What the fuck happened down there?"

"Trust me on this one. This is not a good time for me to say anything."

"Are the lawyers no good?"

"No, there's nothing wrong with the lawyers. They're great."

"Ann?"

I brushed his arm aside. "Tom, please don't press me on this. I mean it. I'm not in a sociable mood and will only get myself in deeper trouble if I speak now." I began to walk away. He jumped in front of me and put both his hands on my shoulders and said, "Why do you think we sent you down there?"

We? Did he have a mouse in his pocket? Ritchie didn't have the power to investigate Ann Mulligan. "Who's *we?*" I asked.

He backed off, a sly smile formed on his lips. "I can't answer that." And then it hit me. I recalled that Ritchie's wife Cora was a Scientology auditor for Jane Kember, the Guardian (who had been extradited to the U.S. from England and was now stationed in Los Angeles). Tom had mentioned in the past that he and Cora had gone out to dinner or gotten together with Kember. She also didn't have power over Ann Mulligan, either. But Mary Sue Hubbard did, and Mary Sue worked closely with Kember and Mary Sue had said I was "worth my weight in gold." So maybe Mary Sue suspected the civil cases were being mishandled by Mulligan and/or Klopper and sent me there to be her eyes and ears. Smart lady. Good for her. I felt better already.

"So tell me what happened," he said.

I laid it on him with both barrels, beginning with: "Ann Mulligan is incompetent. She's not qualified to carry my brief case much less run the legal department of an international organization. She's sabotaging the civil cases."

Chapter 21

COUP D'ÉTAT

There is an immeasurable distance between late and too late.

– Og Mandino
American author

Barely a week later, while absorbed in the routine intelligence traffic of my post, a disturbance erupted in the outer entrance. The sound of the bureau's heavy steel double door flying open and hard leather soles pounding against the tiled cement floors sent out a shock wave of panic. The patter of footsteps and agitated voices in the spacious hallway created an echo effect that amplified the excited commotion.

"We're being taken over! We're being taken over!"

I shot a glance at the others in the room. Only two of the six metal desks in the room were occupied, both by women. They sat erect, their faces masks of confusion. Then the sprinting footfalls of the harbinger of what was a palace revolution in progress skidded to a stop at the doorway to our office, his rapid deceleration assisted by arms grabbing the door jamb.

It was Jeff Shriver, a fellow staffer. A shock of light brown hair covered his brow. Panting, with one hand he threw back the hair, then blurted out between gasps for air, "Bill Franks is trying to take over the G.O.!"

Franks was the recently installed Executive Director International of the church. I didn't know him personally but had overheard from water cooler whispers things such as: "He's psychotic"; "Who appointed him?"; "He has ties to government intelligence"; and "He has *plant* characteristics (i.e., he is possibly a spy)."

The two women in the room rose and approached Jeff. One asked, "How can he do that?" Other bureau staffers advanced from behind Jeff with their own questions, castigation of Franks, and calls for action, creating a conspiratorial muddle. The gathering grew, and spilled into the hallway.

I remained at my desk. I refused to take sides; I didn't have enough information. As I considered my attitude, a more compelling basis for neutrality came to mind, one I wasn't inclined to share: Maybe the G.O. *should* be taken over. I was thinking of the legal conference I had recently attended and the lack of organizational legal acumen in general. I went back to work.

Before long, Joe Lisa's secretary rushed into the room calling my name. A petite young woman with a ready smile and friendly demeanor, she was now deadly serious and obviously harried. "Mary Sue wants you up in her office immediately."

I responded to the urgency in her voice. "Where's her office?"

"Follow me." She was halfway out the door when I rounded my desk. "Quickly."

I caught up to her in the hallway. "I'll brief you when we get on the elevator," she said into my ear. She pushed the button for the eighth floor, fell against the back wall of the car when inside and let out a huge sigh, "Phew!"

"Pretty hectic, huh?" I said. She nodded and allowed herself a small smile. I said, "I heard Bill Franks was trying to take over the G.O."

"Yes, and Mary Sue wants you to be a witness." I uttered my surprise, and she continued. "When you go in there, don't say anything, just listen and observe. Okay?"

I repeated her instruction, "Just listen and observe."

On the eighth floor she escorted me to a closed door on the other side of a wide hallway and motioned for me to go inside. She drifted away. I opened the door, unsure of what I was walking into.

Inside were five people, two of whom stood facing each other in the middle of the room. I recognized Jane Kember from pictures. She was the Guardian; statuesque with short dark hair, in her mid-forties, I guessed.

Standing opposite her was Bill Franks. He was tall and lean, with close-cropped blond hair, and dressed in a pressed white Sea Org uniform with shoulder epaulets that signified his officer's rank. Behind him stood two young women also dressed in Sea Org whites but without epaulets. The only person in the room I had met before was Mary Sue's executive secretary, Janet Lawrence, seated behind her desk in front of the wall opposite the entrance. There was a door behind her so I assumed we were in the anteroom to Mary Sue's office. Janet gave me a subtle smile and a nod, as if to thank me for showing up. The others in the room gave me the barest of glances.

Then the fireworks began.

"All I am saying, Bill, is that I want to see something from Ron." Kember spoke in a businesslike manner with her South African accent. She was referring to L. Ron Hubbard. "I was appointed ..."

Franks cut her off, shouting, "I am CMO, I speak for Ron." CMO stood for Commodore's Messenger Office. L. Ron Hubbard was the Commodore. I took from Franks' comment that, in addition to being the Executive Director International of the church and a member of the Sea Org, he was also a member of CMO. One of the uniformed women handed him a policy letter on cue. He read from it out loud, very loudly. His flustered state led me to believe that he had already tried but failed to make this point prior to my arrival.

The gist of the policy letter was that CMO messengers speak on behalf of L. Ron Hubbard and what they say, and the manner in which they say it, was to be taken as though LRH himself was saying it.

Jane kept a stiff upper lip and did not flinch at Franks' rude behavior. "Yes, Bill. I understand. However, I was appointed by LRH in the policy letter dated 1 March 66." She was referring to Hubbard's written directive that established the Guardian's Office and gave Kember a lifetime appointment as the "Guardian" and head of the office.

I first learned about the Sea Org soon after I joined the staff in St. Louis. There was only one Sea Org representative at that church, a very friendly and unassuming woman, out of about 200 staff members. To me the Sea Org seemed like a group of dedicated people who mostly worked with L. Ron Hubbard on the Flagship *Apollo*. My impression of Hubbard, formed from reading his books and listening to his lectures, was that he was wise, competent, sane, friendly and fair-minded. I expected, therefore, that his representatives would share the same traits. Until this moment, my experiences with Sea Org members, though limited, had confirmed my assumptions. Membership in the Sea Org was optional for G.O. staff: some were, some weren't. Sea Org members in the G.O. had no additional powers; they did not wear uniforms on post and did not exude any sort of superiority based on their Sea Org status.

Since my arrival in Los Angeles I learned that the Sea Org played a large role in the upper level of management of Scientology organizations. Its power and influence in Scientology was on a par with that of the G.O. This created a form of checks and balances. Although I had never seen it manifested before, I understood how tension could naturally develop between the two forces. I realized that I was witnessing the equivalent of a constitutional crisis in the American government; a contest of power between two branches of government.

The burning question in my mind was: had L. Ron Hubbard changed his mind and sanctioned a Sea Org takeover of the G.O., or was this an unauthorized power grab now that he was isolated and off church management lines. His isolation was brought about by the government raids of G.O. offices, the predicted wave of civil litigation that followed, and his desire to avoid being made a witness and deposed. The favored strategy of plaintiff lawyers in cases against the church was to name Hubbard as a party and press him into deposition.

Franks leaned into Jane, within a foot of her face. "I am Ron speaking, and I hereby cancel your goddamned appointment." The veins in his neck popped and his arm muscles rippled. "Do you fucking hear that, you fucking criminal?" I was startled, and concerned that he might physically attack her. I readied myself to intervene.

I also became very concerned about Franks taking over the G.O. As bad a condition the organization was in, at least the problems were being confronted and solved, and people were easy to work for. No shouting, cursing, or abusiveness. There was no way in the world I would put up with someone like Franks in my face like that, and wondered how he rose to such a high position. Surely someone would have flattened him by now.

Kember was as calm and diplomatic as Franks was mad dog. "Bill, I agree to abide by Ron's wishes. "All I seek is something in writing, given that my appointment was in writing."

Franks went off like a volcano. "He can't put anything in fucking writing, he can't fucking talk to you, because you goddamned criminal assholes have fucked everything up so bad that he can't even be in fucking contact with his own organization!" Franks threw his entire body into his words, his face was beet red, and it appeared that he was doing everything in his power to restrain himself from ripping her face off. I was aghast, and prepared to intervene.

Kember remained a model of decorum. She did not flinch or show any sign of being intimidated or offended, which amazed me. "I understand his predicament," she said, "but there surely must be a way for me to responsibly discharge the powers entrusted to me."

"Why didn't you fucking think of that before you started your crime spree," Franks fired back violently, spittle spraying from his lips. "Now it's too fucking late."

"Surely a secure communication can be arranged with his wife," Kember said. "I would be satisfied if Mary Sue confirmed Ron's intention for me to step down." A very reasonable point of compromise, I thought.

Not to Franks. "It isn't safe for him to fucking communicate with her, either," he said. "She's a fucking criminal herself. She's going to jail and I'll be goddamned if we're going to risk her taking LRH down with her. She's nothing but a squirrel." A squirrel is a derogatory term in Scientology that refers to someone who has altered the technology. "Her and her fucking Ouija boards and astrology bullshit. She's got homosexuals on her staff. She's so fucked up, LRH doesn't want to talk to her even if he could, and he can't because of you fucking criminals!"

Okay, that was a lot for me to digest. I had no idea what he was talking about with regard to the Ouija boards, homosexuals, or astrology, except that Jimmy Mulligan once asked me for my sign, so maybe Mary Sue was also interested in the subject. But I did know something about legally privileged communications, and Franks was wrong. A safe communication between Mary Sue and LRH could be arranged. I thought of several solutions off the top of my head. In addition to the husband-wife privilege, attorneys could be utilized by each party to further protect the communication and insulate the channel between them. I considered speaking up but remembered my instructions.

Besides, it was now clear that Franks was not looking for a compromise: this was a *coup d'état*.

Eventually the combatants agreed to contact Mary Sue. Janet Lawrence placed a phone call for Kember. After a brief discussion, Kember told Franks that Mary Sue was receptive to receiving an emissary from LRH and would drop her demand for something in writing from her husband if she could be satisfied that he had authorized a takeover. Franks agreed. The clash was over. Kember thanked me for showing up.

My head was reeling when I pushed the elevator call button. The idea of working under the command of a whack job like Franks gave me the jitters. I counted the time left on my contract. Thirteen months. Yikes. An eternity.

Chapter 22

MISSION ALL CLEAR

When any government, or any church for that matter, undertakes to say to its subjects, This you may not read, this you must not see, this you are forbidden to know, the end result is tyranny and oppression no matter how holy the motives.

– Robert A. Heinlein
American science fiction writer

Bill Franks and the Sea Org won out. The G.O. was taken over. Instead of sitting at a desk handing intelligence reports I was doing "deck work," hanging dry wall, taping it, sanding it and so forth. All G.O. staff members were assigned to the renovation of Lebanon Hall, the eight-story building that housed the Information Bureau.

A couple of days later we were herded together for a briefing by Bill Franks. It was more like a sermon preached with fire and brimstone. He was going to put a stop to all the criminality (which had already ended) and smash it out of existence. He damned the G.O. and its "criminal" staff. How dare they take on the FBI and the Justice Department when Scientology policy requires the organization to build friendly relations with the government.

I assumed he was referring to a number of hard-hitting articles published in the G.O.'s *Freedom Magazine* that the PR

Bureau published. The whole thing smacked of propaganda and I found it highly demeaning to be forced-fed the ravings of a madman in a mass collective. To a sane person, individuals have differing roles and degrees of responsibility for past bad acts and current conditions of an organization.

Eventually Franks wound down and we were permitted to return to renovation duty. Manual labor was a welcome relief from that gulag gathering.

In the evening we were gathered to begin the rehabilitation process. Three Sea Org members, led by Marion Meissler, instructed us each to write down all G.O. activities we had participated in, with particular emphasis and details of any criminal acts. A large course room had been arranged for us. Tables and chairs filled the room. Paper and pens were on each chair. We wrote. And wrote. Over a span of days. I finished mine and turned it in. Back to renovations until everyone else finished.

Not everyone survived the process. We were not told when someone failed or was let go, least of all the reasons why; they would just never return. Some did not even show up the first day. I heard a rumor that a group of G.O. staff members had resisted the takeover and were expelled from the staff. Some disappeared for reasons unknown. A sense of ambiguity about our fates hung in the air.

For the next step we went through the Scientology Ethics and Justice pack, one page at a time, reading it out loud to a "twin," a study partner in Scientology terminology. My twin was Tom Ritchie. We took turns reading. The one listening was required to stop the reader any time he faltered or stumbled over a word. This was a sign that the reader did not fully understand the word and had to "clear" the stumbled word by looking it up in a dictionary and using it in sentences until fully grasped.

We were well treated by the Sea Org missionaires, all of whom had sociable personalities, unlike Bill Franks, so the process was very doable. A little levity or a joke thrown out here and there was not stomped on.

One evening Marion Meissler called me aside. She had an admiring glow on her face. "You're done. You've been posted in the Mission All Clear Unit." I asked her what that was and she explained it was an autonomous unit established to oversee all legal cases in which L. Ron Hubbard was either named as a party or may be named, and that the purpose of the unit was to resolve all personal legal liabilities so he could return to church management lines. She made clear her high regard for the position, not only by her approving expression, but by saying, "The G.O.'s top legal personnel were specially selected to staff the unit."

I smiled and said okay. I could tell that she expected more. She seemed like a nice young woman but I'm sure she had no idea what it was like to be yanked off post, thrown onto manual labor and put through a so-called rehabilitation process as a group rather than be treated as an individual. So I didn't do cartwheels or whatever else she expected. I was in a wait-and-see mode.

She held her radiant attention on me, showering me with admiration. "Yes. You really made the grade. Thank you for all you've done." Given the secrecy and seemingly arbitrary nature of the handling of G.O. personnel, I had no idea what she was thanking me for. Listening to Franks, I got the impression I was viewed as a criminal as was everyone else. Now I was a hero. Go figure. I did not figure. I just wanted to run out my G.O. contract and contribute as much as I could during that period, doing something other than manual labor. I thanked her.

* * *

I met with my new boss, Kathy O'Gorman. Everyone called her K.O. She was in charge of the MAC Unit. She had been the head of the Flag G.O. during at least part of my spy days in Clearwater. I only knew that because Tom Ritchie often mentioned her name. I met her once. She showed up in the back seat of Ritchie's car one evening, and said she wanted to meet me, apparently just to put a face on Ritz. We exchanged pleasantries, nothing more.

K.O. was a chain-smoking, coffee-guzzling woman who had a great sense of humor and was very popular. I would soon find out why. She was an excellent executive, results oriented, and easy to work with.

She welcomed me to the job and put me in charge of all the Clearwater legal cases, lawsuit and grand jury matters. I would not act as a lawyer but as a manager of church lawyers and Flag (Clearwater) G.O. support staff. The grand juries were silent at the time so my main job was to see that the civil cases were whipped into shape and handled quickly to a desirable outcome. My Florida bar case was a personal matter, not part of the church project, but then, no formal complaint had yet been filed. Fingers crossed on that.

"K.O., I don't know whether you know about it or not, but when I was working undercover in Clearwater I stumbled onto an FBI counterintelligence campaign against the church. Nothing was done with the intel despite my recommendation." Given the sermon by Franks about being friendly with the FBI I wondered how she would react. An impish grin came to her lips. "I know. You're going to do something about it now. That's one of the reasons I wanted you for this unit." I felt energized.

"Look at this and tell me what you think." She opened a file on her desk and handed me two internal FBI documents. "The church obtained these through a FOIA (Freedom of Information Act) request."

The first document was dated March 10, 1976. I oriented myself. At that time I had just finished taking the Florida Bar exams and was probably on my way back to Kansas City after meeting with Don Alverzo and visiting Clearwater for a week. The document was a 302 Memo, an FBI internal record, of a call from Gabe Cazares to FBI agent Michael Lunsford about information Cazares wanted to share about the Church of Scientology but did not want to discuss on the telephone. I remembered Lunsford's name from the St. Petersburg PD Intel files. Lunsford referred Cazares to Special Agent James Kinne, a person he said was familiar with the church.

The second FBI memorandum was dated April 6, 1976. It suggested that Special Agent Lunsford was probably the person who had contacted Gabe, not the other way around. It stated that "Gabe has been contacted," and that Gabe's information was later reported in the media. I recognized this language to be FBI-speak for having planted information in the media, in this case through Gabe Cazares.

"COINTELPRO," I said. "They used Gabe to run media attacks on the church. This backs up what I saw in the St. Pete PD intel files."

K.O. agreed. "Cazares testified under oath in a deposition in our civil rights case against him, right after March 10, that he had not been in contact with anyone from the FBI."

Not only was this evidence of perjury but it was a potential basis to have his current case dismissed. Cazares was concurrently suing the Church of Scientology, L. Ron Hubbard, and others, for malicious prosecution for the church's 1976 civil rights case against him. In order to prevail he needed to show that the case was frivolous and that there was no merit for it having been filed in the first place. John T. Allen and Walter Logan represented Cazares in that case. They obtained a summary judgment (a court-ordered judgment before trial). Had the church been in possession of these two documents during the pendency of the prior lawsuit, the result of that case likely would have been different and the church would have been allowed to delve into FBI records and fully explore Gabe's relationship with the agency. And his current case would be seriously undermined.

"This is dynamite," I said.

"Isn't it?" She said, smiling broadly.

"Where did you find these?"

"U.S.G.O. Legal had them in their files but never shared them with anyone handling the civil cases."

"Nor with anyone in Information," I noted. As the liaison officer between the two bureaus, I should have received copies. I flashed back to the lawyer' conference and wondered what else Ann Mulligan and Paul Klopper had withheld.

K.O. said there would be coordination from now on. She planned to bring the church FOIA lawyers, Bill Walsh and Tony Basiglia, from D.C. to Los Angeles so we could meet. She also brought up the Lindberg case, another lawsuit the church had against the FBI involving raids of church facilities. Lindberg is the lead name in a list of FBI agents who participated in the raid and were being sued. "We can go after FBI documents from three directions at once," she said, referring to the FOIA actions, the Lindberg lawsuit, and the Cazares case. I was pretty jazzed. I felt like giving K.O. a big hug. We slapped palms. It appeared that the ranting of Bill Franks had limited application. Either that or K.O. was going out on a limb. If so, I was happy to climb out there with her.

* * *

In addition to my MAC Unit position I was required to attend a form of group counseling. Sea Org missionaires ran the encounter. All G.O. staffers were gathered and encouraged to discuss how and why the G.O. went off the rails. The idea was to isolate those departures, bring them into the open, and clear them from the culture of the group. Most of the people responsible for criminal actions were no longer on staff. Plenty remained who knew about or had some role, however. Don Alverzo's name came up as the person responsible for a particular B & E (Breaking & Entering).

Information Bureau Director Joe Lisa raised his hand to speak. "That's right. Don Alverzo did that one and many more. In fact, he started the criminal acts." He said he knew this with certainty from his former position as head of the Information Bureau for the New York church. He said Alverzo was from New York and joined Scientology, and later the G.O., there.

The earliest criminal act I knew about was *Operation Dynamite*, the scheme to frame Paulette Cooper for a fake bomb threat which occurred in New York in late 1972. Joe's comment dovetailed with the info I had run across that led me to conclude Don Alverzo was Jerry Levin, the person who befriended Paulette Cooper after she was charged with the crime and moved into her apartment building and soon became her roommate.

Joe said Alverzo was an expert in black bag jobs, which are clandestine entries into buildings or other private places, and included things like lock-picking and other illegal activities. Alverzo trained other G.O. members in black bag crafts and convinced Information Bureau staffers that these methods were standard covert intelligence techniques performed by the CIA overseas and the FBI domestically. The results obtained by these methods were so spectacular that they became popular and commonplace.

Others in the group with personal knowledge supported Joe's analysis. Unanimity soon developed and a firm group consensus emerged. Don Alverzo, which I knew wasn't his real name, was *the guy* most responsible for G.O. illegal activities.

This revelation was fascinating, its implications staggering. The Stipulation of Evidence entered into by the government and the G.O. members who were indicted for crimes against the federal government clearly revealed Alverzo's prominent role in the criminal enterprise. He taught and assisted G.O. operatives in the use of special electronic devices employed to bug IRS offices and lock-picking equipment used to breach offices where files on Scientology were kept. Yet *he* was not indicted.

G.O. offices were raided, senior executives prosecuted, the G.O. was weakened and made vulnerable to a takeover, and LRH had been forced into hiding, all of which traced back to one guy. Don Alverzo.

Don fit the classic pattern of an *agent provocateur*[13], an undercover agent who entices others to commit illegal acts on behalf of a police or intelligence agency for the purpose of discrediting or harming the group. *Which agency really ran Alverzo? And why was Bill Franks hammering Mary Sue and railing against the G.O. collectively for attacking the FBI?*

I met with K.O. the next day and asked her what she thought about the outcome of the group session. She shook her whole body as though the idea sent shivers through it. "You knew and worked with Don in Clearwater," I said. "Could he have been an agent provocateur in your mind?" She said she hadn't seen that in him. "Me neither," I responded. "But he was a smooth operator. Extremely skilled in covert operations, as though he had undergone specialized training. So I guess it could be true, huh?"

She agreed and said she was sure he would be "dealt with appropriately," which I took to mean by the Sea Org missionaires in charge of the G.O. takeover.

I wondered about the outcome and where he was. I could see legal uses of the information if he were indeed an agent provocateur. It fit with the strategy K.O. and I discussed. I also saw the risk in causing him to break away and turn against the church, as well as the risk of me knowing too much about him since I was still a potential witness in legal proceedings. I made mental notes and stored them.

* * *

My office was off the beaten path. I had to walk the corridors to meet with K.O. or attend "product conferences," which were meetings to go over tasks assigned to each person. Two Sea Org members oversaw the MAC Unit product conferences, Norm Starkey and Terri Gamboa. They were as different as night and day. Starkey was a big burly man who looked to be in his early forties. He was from South Africa and projected an intense demeanor, as though he was ready to jump down a person's throat at the slightest provocation. Gamboa was a young woman in her early to mid-twenties. She was upbeat, even bubbly, very respectful and always smiling. I never saw Starkey smile. At our weekly product conferences, each MAC Unit staff member had to present a report to Starkey and Gamboa on the status of his assigned tasks, give an update on progress, and cross off or add new items to the product list.

* * *

One day all G.O. staffers were summoned together inside a small room. Before us was Norman Starkey in his white Sea Org uniform. Once everyone was crammed in, Starkey launched into a tirade. "LRH was not involved in G.O. activities," he yelled. "He did not know about them. He did not plan them. He had no knowledge whatsoever of any G.O. activities." It turned out he was just warming up. Then he really let go: "The idea that he was involved is an enemy line! Anyone who thinks LRH was involved in or had anything to do with G.O. activities has hidden crimes!" Man, his voice packed a punch. An image of the print advertisement for Bose speakers, or whatever the brand was, came to mind. You know, the guy seated in front of a speaker, clinging to the arms of the chair to keep from being blown backward by the blare of the music coming from the speakers, his hair straight back and his clothes pressed against him. That's exactly how I felt, clinging on to my body to avoid being blown all the way back to St. Louis.

Starkey then revealed the situation that had made him come unglued, an explanation that might have helped us had we known about it at the outset. "Some G.O. members are saying that LRH knew about G.O. activities," he roared. I thought, *Good, go scream at them and let me get back to work, you imbecile.* I hated like hell being subjected to group punishment, and all this screaming.

While Starkey rammed his threats down our collective throats, dictating to us what we could think or not think, I considered his basic assertion that LRH had no knowledge of or involvement in G.O. activities. That was contrary to my understanding. I thought LRH was overseeing G.O. activities in

Clearwater when I first arrived there and *did* know about mine. I traced my opinion to things Alverzo said to me. I was willing to let go and chalk it up to a false impression he created in his role as an agent provocateur. But shouted threats at me did not persuade me to abandon the idea. Insisting that I had hidden crimes simply for having formed an opinion was even less effective with me, insulting even.

I saw a disturbing pattern with Franks and Starkey. These guys should be locked up, not holding high management positions. They ruled by domination and propaganda, the tools of a tyrant. Sane people rule with reason. *Who appointed these people? Who condoned this sort of conduct?*

I would soon learn that the new leadership had a special term for Starkey's rant; an SRA, a Severe Reality Adjustment. Somehow this insanity had become part of the culture of the new leadership and was considered acceptable behavior.

Starkey pounded away on all of us G.O. "criminals" to not drag LRH into our crimes. I lost track of his rambling tirade, and tuned him out. I decided not to permit him to invade my space. Instead I pondered a rational way to handle the situation he was addressing. A simple statement informing us that, contrary to some opinions, LRH had never been involved in, or even known about, the G.O. criminal acts would have been a good start.

Had it been my job I would have told staff members that church management is taking this position in legal and PR matters based on internal investigations into the issue. I would then ask those with any evidence contradicting that position to take a moment to write it down so that all contrary evidence could be investigated. I would have given the results of the final investigation to our lawyers and PR personnel and asked them to advise me on the best PR and legal positions to take in light of this evidence. There. End of story. Confront the facts and deal with them the best way possible, even if it means throwing big money at some legal cases to make them go away. Starkey's approach, besides being demeaning and abusive, could lead to the commission of more crimes, such as perjury and obstruction of justice, and recoil badly on the organization.

In this work atmosphere it was probably only a matter of time before Starkey or someone else blasted me to my face. I began contemplating how I should deal with it. Starkey finished his diatribe before I reached a full resolution; I had only decided that it would not happen a second time.

* * *

Back at work one of my investigative actions hit pay dirt. A Tampa private investigator gave me the name and phone number of Joe Burton, who had been an FBI informant for a major Tampa FBI COINTELPRO operation from 1972-74. Burton created the (Marxist-Leninist) Red Star Cadre as part of a government effort to infiltrate and disrupt a particular Communist ideological movement. In 1975 Burton went to the *New York Times* with his story, telling the world that the FBI did *not* discontinue COINTELPRO in 1971 as the Director of the FBI had reported to Congress and the media. He testified before Congressional committees and subcommittees as well.[14]

I dialed Burton up and introduced myself. He said he had followed the news stories about me as a lawyer for Mayor Cazares. "Speaking of that," I said, "I may as well get right to the point of my call. Was Gabe Cazares an FBI informant?"

"Mr. Vannier, you're going to like what I have to say. I once attended a leftist party on behalf of the FBI. My job was to report on who all attended and what they had to say. Gabe Cazares was there. This was in 1972 or '73. When I got to his name on my list, Special Agent Robert Heible, my FBI handler, said, 'Don't worry about him. We own him.'"

"What did you take that phrase, 'we own him,' to mean?"

"He's one of us. He's an informant like me. No question. That's how he would say something like that. He was telling me not to bother reporting on Cazares because he was working for the FBI, too."

"Will you state that in an affidavit?" I asked. Burton said he would, and I asked if he was willing to fly to Los Angeles if I covered his expenses. He was, so we scheduled a meeting.

At the next MAC Unit product conference, I reported this development to Starkey and Gamboa. I explained its significance by telling them that I had previously seen evidence of an FBI counterintelligence operation against the church in Clearwater and that K.O. and I wanted to develop the evidence to prove that Cazares was an FBI informant and part of the counterintelligence program. As I spoke my attention went back and forth between the two. Starkey had a weird reaction. He became shifty-eyed and could not hold eye contact with me. His distress made me uncomfortable, but I did my best not to reveal that I had noticed his reaction or was bothered by it.

When I finished my report he did not acknowledge me, creating an awkward silence. Gamboa jumped in. "Great." she said, beaming. "Very well done, Merrell. I can't wait to see his affidavit and what else you come up with. Thank you."

As the next staff member gave her report, I doodled on my product list, mulling over Starkey's reaction. Something about me and/or my report had freaked him out. In Scientology terminology, I had *missed a withhold*. A "withhold" is something a person has done but is not revealing, and "missed" means it was almost discovered or the person wondered whether it had been found out. It is better for a person's mental state to get caught than almost caught. These terms are mainly important in a Scientology auditing session. The auditor is trained to recognize these symptoms and to address them and not proceed with the counseling without drawing out the "withhold" and how it was "missed," otherwise the session will go badly and the subject will get upset without recognizing the true source of the upset.

I was trying to discern the withhold I missed in Starkey. Possibly he was intimidated by my legal expertise, meaning his withhold was that he was not very bright and could not follow me. I rejected that idea. There was much more to it than that. His withhold was a doozy; his manifestation was too glaring. I recalled vaguely seeing the exact same reaction before. The memory popped in and out of sight as I tried to pin it down. Then it came clearly into view. Gabe Cazares. At the fund-raiser when I first met him and again at the opera club meeting. The withhold I missed on Gabe was that he was secretly working for the FBI and knew all along that I was affiliated with the Church of Scientology. The two reactions, Gabe's and Starkey's, were nearly identical. Suddenly, the G.O. takeover, the propaganda and the domination all aligned.

Back in my office I grabbed a legal pad and jotted down my observations. "Franks and Starkey" I scribbled, "Domination, Propaganda; Gross generalities: *all* G.O. treated as criminals; mass punishments. Starkey manifests missed withholds. Same as Caz. Caz FBI. Starkey FBI? My talk of COINTELPRO prove-up freaked him out. Starkey COINTELPRO? Starkey not mastermind, too dumb. Franks? Probably not, too insane. Someone senior to both. Was takeover COINTELPRO? Don agent provocateur, black bag jobs/crimes, entices G.O. leaders to adopt his methods. Raid. Indictments – but not Don, not Jimmy Mulligan. G.O. weakened. LRH on run/isolated. Deals cut by people in between? By Starkey & someone else in between him and LRH. All fits."

I then questioned my findings and took a contrary view. I listed positive points arguing against my conclusions. "Legal cases handled better. Free rein to develop FBI COINTELPRO – so far! – by K.O., not necessarily top brass. Lots of dedicated Sea Org staff. Quick learners. Productive. Most are high-toned. Starkey and Franks, exceptions. Not contradictions necessarily. Need more data."

I tossed the legal pad aside. *What difference did it make? What could I do about it? Nothing, and I would get creamed trying. Plus if I spend my time thinking about it, I won't get my work done.* I tore the sheet of paper from the pad and began to wad it up to toss it in the trash can, but changed my mind. I shoved it in a desk drawer and decided to keep my eyes and ears open while also doing my job. Maybe something would develop. Maybe I would decide I was off base. I could revisit the list later and see if my thinking held up, add to it, or whatever.

* * *

A few days later I met with Rory Boulding, a lawyer from England who was a member of the G.O. and was working with the Information Bureau on the counterintelligence aspects of a 2255 motion, which is a last resort motion to overturn a sentence imposed in violation of the Constitution or U.S. laws. The motion was being prepared on behalf of Jane Kember and possibly Mary Sue Hubbard and others. He'd heard of my expertise in the area of FBI counterintelligence and cleared it through channels for me to assist him. K.O. agreed to loan me out, in other words.

"What do you think about our new leadership?" Boulding asked when we lunched that day. The question itself and his overall demeanor signaled his concern. Speaking behind the backs of senior managers in Scientology organizations –"natter," as it was known – was forbidden. I didn't agree with the policy. Employees who complain are part of life in a free society, and can be an effective check and balance against poor management. True, mutinous situations can arise when natter is permitted, but there are less repressive means to protect the security of an organization. Despite my personal views, however, I followed the church policy and was reluctant to violate it.

But Boulding had piqued my interest. "You first," I said.

Rory laughed. "We are lawyers, after all." He said this in his inimitable British accent and manner. "As lawyers we have certain professional obligations, don't you agree? We are trained and accustomed to thinking critically. We have a duty, you might say, to think professionally, to look at and recognize instantly the difference between evidence and opinion, for example, in time to lodge an objection."

I loved listening to him, whether or not he made sense. His voice and language went together with his dress: an ascot, dress shirt and jacket.

"So what do you think, Barrister Boulding?"

"Well, actually, I'm afraid I am only a Solicitor." In England a Barrister tries cases, a Solicitor does not. "But I have an opinion and will gladly share it with you, nevertheless, since you asked. I am concerned, to be perfectly frank, that these fellows who have taken over, at least the most visible and powerful ones, are poor examples of Scientologists – and of human beings, if I may also add. I do not believe LRH knowingly assigned them such power."

I was noncommittal. "Assuming for the sake of argument that I share your concern, what could you and I do to determine LRH's intention or uncover who masterminded the takeover?"

Aha," he said, leaning closer. "There is something *you* can do. You are in a position to do something, not me."

I wasn't following him. "I'm just a staff member handling legal cases."

"But not just any legal cases. You're handling LRH's personal legal cases." I looked at him, questioningly. "You should speak with Jane." I had not seen hide nor hair of her since the clash with Franks. I asked why I should do that.

"Because she wants to speak with you, if you are willing. She wants to discuss and help."

If Kember wanted to speak with me, Mary Sue wanted her to bring me in to help handle the situation. That also caused me to believe that Mary Sue had not relinquished power over the G.O. voluntarily and did not believe her husband knew or approved of the takeover. Those conclusions concerned me greatly.

"Where's Jane?" I asked.

Angie in Burbank apartment, 1979, age 8

Angie (center) & friends, Wentzville, Mo., 1978

Angie school picture, age 10

Angie with cast, Toronto apartment, fall 1977

Me on the road, 1985

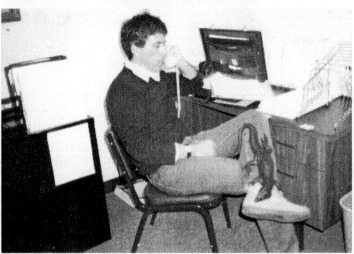

(Serious) Insurance Adjuster, 1984

Angie & John, June 1987

Fran & Angie, Southern Belles, circa 1985

Part 3

ARROWS IN THE DARK

Chapter 23

INTERNAL INTRIGUE

It is easy to dodge a spear in the daylight, but it is difficult to avoid an arrow in the dark.

— Unknown Author

Jane Kember greeted me from behind an executive-sized wooden desk in the middle of a large wall-less room on one of the unfinished floors of Lebanon Hall, the same building that housed the Information Bureau and where I was formerly hanging drywall. I walked across the dusty concrete floor, and she rose and extended her hand. I shook it.

I asked her if she had some position in the church. She didn't. She was given an office, such as it was, and permitted to work on her personal legal case.

She asked what I thought of the Bill Franks encounter. I told her it was unbelievable and praised her self-restraint and dignity in the face of his profane onslaught. She appreciated my compliment. "Do you think LRH would approve of his conduct?" she asked me. Because she had worked personally with Hubbard her question suggested the answer. I offered my view anyway. "I would certainly hope not."

"Of course he would not," she replied. "Let me tell you something about Bill Franks, Merrell. He was once the executive director of the Founding Church," the church in Washington,

235

D. C. "He was psychotic; he physically abused staff; and even assaulted one employee by striking him with the side of a pistol he kept in his office." She said he had significant connections in intelligence circles and had "plant" characteristics. "The G.O. forced his removal and disqualified him from ever again holding an executive position in Scientology. That explains some of the vitriol against the G.O. that you witnessed. He wants to get even with the G.O. We were on to him. You know what happens when you miss a withhold on someone, don't you?"

I nodded. They retaliate, often with vengeance. But I didn't say that. I just told her I was a fully trained Scientology auditor. "What do you want me to do?" I asked.

"Rory told me you're part of Mission All Clear. Is that right?" I nodded. "Because the cases you're handling concern LRH personally, and he wants to reconnect with the church, he will be in direct communication with the person who is ultimately in charge of your unit. Do you know who that person is?"

I shook my head. "I only know who shows up at our product conferences."

"Who is that?" She positioned her pencil and paper to take notes. I gave her the names of Starkey and Gamboa. She knew them both. "Terri Gamboa worked with LRH on the *Apollo*. She was a Watch Messenger working by his side at least eight hours a day, at his beck and call, delivering messages and making sure his orders were carried out. LRH was extremely selective over those he chose to be Watch Messengers. Terri is a trusted and capable Sea Org member. She is not the kind of person who would appoint Franks or run rough-shod over people," she said.

"Starkey carries out orders well. But he doesn't have the leadership skills or intelligence to lead a takeover of the G.O." I nodded, telling her that I agreed with her observation. I did not add my thoughts about his likely being an FBI plant.

"The question is, Merrell: Who is Starkey working for?"

"I don't know. All I know is that Terri and Norm and all the others running legal lines are part of ASI." She jotted it down like it was new to her so I spelled it out. "That's Authors

Service, Inc. It's a for-profit corporation that owns all of LRH's copyrights, both his fiction and Scientology writings and lectures. They have a building down Sunset." I gestured westward. "Near Highland, I believe." She wrote it all down. "Terri and Norm come and go from ASI to our product conferences. They don't have offices here at the complex, so it's impossible for me to know who they report to at ASI."

"We have to find out," Kember said. "I'm depending on you to be my eyes and ears, Merrell. Can I count on you? You may be our last hope."

I told her I would do what I could. The whole idea seemed half-baked to me. I mean, here she was working on her legal case in a dump of an office, dethroned from power, isolated and with one foot in the slammer. It was also clear to me that she was withholding information. But so was I. She had her reasons; I had mine. I only saw a single point where our interests converged: I was in a unique position to see those Sea Org members at the top level who might be in communication with LRH, and she knew so many Sea Org members, she could help me identify the right person.

I don't know what else she had in mind. She didn't say and I didn't ask. I was driven, not by a desire to reinstall Mary Sue or restore the autonomy of the G.O., but by a duty to determine whether the church was now controlled or influenced by outside forces, as my instincts suggested, and to remedy that if it was so – and if I could. I wasn't sure of Kember's motive, or of Mary Sue's. I certainly did not plan to be anyone's spy, their "eyes and ears," as Kember put it. I wanted to be on the steering committee, so to speak, not simply a gatherer of information that others used for their own ends. If I found the right person, Kember needed to let down her guard, open up to me, and allow me to develop a strategy on how to use the information, or at least let me co-create it. But I thought it was premature to bring that up. I might even change my mind about the venture with her.

* * *

Joe Burton came to my office and I asked him to read the FBI 302 Memo dated March 10, 1976. "Tell me what stands out to you."

"James Kinne is their wiretap man," Burton said after a few moments. He was referring to the notation by Special Agent Michael Lunsford, the author of the memo, that he had referred Cazares to Kinne as a person familiar with Scientology.

"Authorized or unauthorized wiretaps?"

"Both," he said. "He does all their wiretaps."

I made a note. "Good. Anything else stand out?"

"What's this classification?" he said, pointing to the number 92 in the file number. "Do you know their filing system?" I told him I did. "It means 'antiracketeering.'" Burton furrowed a brow. "That's odd. For a church?"

"Look at the office of origin," I said. The memo referred to "OO:MM."

"That's Miami," he said. I told him that Scientology's international management used to be based on ships sailing the Mediterranean Sea. "When they came ashore, part of the crew set up in Miami."

Next I showed him the 302 Memo dated April 10, 1976.

"This is COINTELPRO," Burton said while studying the memo. "Lunsford was planting a media story through Cazares." His comment confirmed my interpretation of the document.

"Who's running Cazares?" I asked. "Lunsford, Kinne, or someone from Tampa like Robert Heible or Francis Mullen?"

"Not Kinne," Burton said. "He was probably brought in to listen in on church telephone conversations in relation to the information planted in the media, probably trying to determine the internal chain of command or something like that. Heible ran him on the early stuff but I think he'd left by this time. So I would say either Mullen or Lunsford during this time period."

Burton read the report I wrote describing the documents I viewed at the St. Petersburg Police Department Intelligence

Division in June 1976. "Boy, they were all over you guys. This is definitely COINTELPRO."

We went into my report in depth. Burton figured that Mullen, the Tampa special agent in charge, had overall responsibility for the intel op against the church and that portions of it had been delegated to Lunsford, the senior resident agent in Clearwater. "Mullen is now head of the DEA,"[15] he said.

I pressed Burton for more details about Cazares' early days as an informant for Robert Heible, who was also Burton's FBI handler. He didn't have a lot of detail to contribute, saying he only had the single encounter with Cazares he already described to me over the phone. "Cazares was a left-wing activist. He was active with the United Farm Workers, as I recall."

"Would it surprise you, Joe, that Cazares initiated contact with Cesar Chavez, the head of the United Farm Workers? When Chavez announced that he was going to organize a march for farm workers in the area, Cazares contacted him and wormed his way into marching next to Chavez in the front line. I know because I had one of our attorneys interview Chavez."

"Typical informant work," Burton said.

* * *

In November Bill Franks was busted off post. Canned. I only picked up bits and pieces of the story. Franks met with Scientology mission holders in Clearwater. Missions are the front line of Scientology outreach, offering introductory services only. They feed the larger churches with people who seek higher level services.

There had been some sort of rebellion among mission holders and Franks tried to appease them. He took Joe Lisa along. The event went horribly wrong in the eyes of someone who obviously had more power than Franks. Lisa was sent packing, too. I heard that he had spoken to the mission holders and detailed some of the bad things the G.O. had done, supporting the Franks line that the G.O. was the source of their frustrations and that he had taken over the G.O. and would now resolve their issues.

I ran into Lisa on the street afterward. He looked cowed. I asked him for his version of the story. "I can't talk about that," he said. "I'm in enough trouble already."

Later I met with Jane Kember. She knew about the firings. "See, Merrell, Franks was not in charge in spite of his post title." (His post title was "Executive Director International," one that LRH personally held until 1966. Supposedly it was the most senior position in the Church of Scientology.) "We need to find out who's in charge."

I gave Kember more names of people from ASI I had run across. She jotted them down and said they were not the ones running Starkey. "What about the line to LRH?" she asked. "Have you made any progress with that?" I hadn't.

* * *

In February 1982, with eight months remaining on my G.O. contract, I returned from lunch one day and saw a terse note taped to my office door. "Report to Ethics." I took out my office key to enter and collect my personal items.

The key didn't fit. The lock had been changed.

Chapter 24

BUSTED

I have sworn upon the altar of God, eternal hostility against every form of tyranny over the mind of man.

— Thomas Jefferson

"What's this shit?" Brian Andrus was going through handwritten notes taken from my office. Other personal items of mine were on his desk, including my briefcase. Brian was a fellow Information Bureau staff member, now wearing a Sea Org uniform. I did not interface with him much while in the Bureau and mainly got to know him after the takeover. He was in charge of renovations.

Seated across from him, I was surprised as much by his furious reaction as I was confused by the changed lock and confiscation of my private papers. I was also trying to figure out what notes I had left behind that had him so riled up. He stopped at one of them and ran his finger down the page, reading: "Norm Starkey manifests missed withholds; FBI connection question mark."

Okay, now I knew what set him off. That was a hot one, the list of my thoughts and concerns about Starkey and whomever he reported to. He kept reading. "COINTELPRO question mark." He threw his hands up. "This is some crazy shit, Merrell."

241

"Those are private thoughts. I wrote them down to see how well they stood up to scrutiny. Is there anything wrong with having observations and thoughts?"

"Oh, come on. These guys are saving the church. Can't you see that?"

Brian may have only been seated four feet from me but we were a million miles apart in reality. Being a staff member, in my view, did not entail giving up one's rights – indeed, one's duty – to look and think. Brian evidently regarded his obligation to be blindly loyal and obedient, no matter his master. His role as an unindicted co-conspirator in the G.O. criminal case was laid out in the Stipulation of Facts. He was the person in charge of holding Michael Meissner captive in Los Angeles when he was hiding out from a federal arrest warrant for having infiltrated IRS offices in D.C. using a forged government ID card. Meissner eventually escaped Brian and his guards, called the FBI and became the sole witness against the church in support of the search warrants of G.O. premises.

Why did Brian do that? Because he had received an order to do it. The same reason given by Nazi officers at their war crimes trial in Nuremberg, Germany after World War II. They were only following orders. Brian did not stop and think that his actions in carrying out that order constituted a 15-year felony for harboring a fugitive and helped destroy the church requiring it to now be saved, according to him.

The moment I recalled Brian's role in the G.O. criminal case, I realized something else. Despite all the ranting by Franks and Starkey on G.O. crimes, here was Brian, who had committed the most serious felony of all – even though he had escaped prosecution – questioning my intentions. This made me wonder whether the standard used to retain G.O. staff was based not on one's role in criminal conduct, or loyalty to the old guard, but on one's willingness to transfer blind loyalty to the new regime. And if blind loyalty to them was what the new leaders wanted, I definitely did not qualify.

I did not take up his rhetorical question. "So where do we go from here?"

"You're off post and on the decks until further notice." That meant I was back on renovations doing manual labor. He added, "We need to get to the bottom of this," and then shook his head in disbelief while staring at me.

* * *

The next day I was escorted from renovation duty. I was told I had to undergo a security check, a kind of interrogation or forced "confessional." Scientology has a voluntary confessional that is designed to help absolve a person of past bad deeds. I had undergone confessionals before and derived tremendous benefit from them. The relief and soul-cleansing effect of the procedure could be phenomenal.

I had never had a Sec Check, as the forced variety is called. Hubbard canceled the practice in 1968 because it was so unpopular. I heard rumblings that some G.O. members were subjected to them after the takeover, so apparently the new leadership reinstituted the procedure. No problem. I had already decided to cooperate and tell all. I didn't care if I was terminated. My only concern was to remain in good standing so I could continue receiving services – training and auditing, which are personally very useful and productive in my life.

The basic arrangement for all Scientology auditing is simply a private room with an E-meter, a person reading the E-meter, and the person holding the cans. The word "audit," used in this sense, means to listen. That person operating the E-meter is the "auditor" and asks a certain series of questions, depending on the procedure being performed, watches the needle movement on the meter, and then takes the next step, which is often another question. There are many different auditing procedures, or processes, and not every auditor is trained to perform each one.

The technology involving use of an E-meter has been described, demonstrated, misinterpreted, and often lampooned in countless mainstream articles and television reports about the Church of Scientology. The fact is, it works.

My escort took me to a small room where I met my auditor, Tom Martiniano. He was roughly my age and size, dressed in a blue uniform. He invited me to sit across the table from him and pick up the cans. All I could see on the table was the back of the E-meter, not the needle. Before he began, Martiniano asked me a little bit about my background and we chatted for a while. When I mentioned my Navy service, he mentioned he had fought in Vietnam. He was friendly enough. I felt comfortable with him.

He started the session by saying, "I'm not auditing you," which reminded me that anything I said in the session would be written down and could be used against me in ethics and justice actions; it would not have the sanctity of an auditing (i.e., religious counseling) session, which is strictly confidential and cannot be used against a parishioner. I felt a chill. Even though I was willing to fully cooperate, the concept of my willing submission to authority, any authority, struck home in that instant. It was creepy and offensive. But I brushed those feelings aside. I wanted to get this over with.

Martiniano asked a number of questions: what was I up to, with whom had I spoken; what did I say, sparing no details. He covered every facet of my disaffection, my inner thoughts, and any actions I may have taken. I answered them all truthfully, giving up the names of Kember and Boulding in the process. Martiniano adjourned the session after a couple of hours and said we would continue it the next day. I went back to the "decks," taping and sanding drywall, cleaning up debris.

I saw Kember in the hallway the next day. We each had escorts. I was being led to an auditing room for another security check session, and she appeared to be coming from one. As we passed she glared hatefully at me. I was nonplused. If she was mad at me because I ratted her out, I didn't know what she expected. Even if I was inclined to lie or cover up, I would not have been able to do so effectively because I truly didn't know what prompted the investigation into my activities. For all I knew our conversations were taped.

The security check was completed within a week. Along the way, Martiniano maintained a friendly demeanor toward me. The security check, as opposed to what might result from it, turned out to be a walk in the park. In fact, my confidence rose significantly. The act of getting busted and accused of having crazy thoughts instilled a vague feeling that I somehow was missing some reality or deserved to be treated that way. Describing the details of what had actually occurred freed me of that specter. I felt good about myself and my actions and was ready and willing to part ways with anyone who thought differently.

Martiniano had other plans for me. After he wrapped up the security check he told me he was going to do a plant check, which is an action taken on the E-meter to determine whether a person has been sent into the church by an outside agency to either spy or cause internal damage. *Oh boy, that 's rich. I got busted for suspecting Starkey and one or more of his hidden superiors were FBI plants, and I'm the one getting a plant check.* I chuckled at the thought. Martiniano gave me a questioning eye.

"I'm not a plant," I said. "But feel free to inquire."

He started the plant check by asking if I had been sent into the church by someone. I passed that question and many other related ones. Then he asked if I had been implanted to join the church. The term "implanted" means a hidden command to spy or cause trouble is imbedded in a person's mind, usually by the use of drugs and hypnosis. The 1962 movie *The Manchurian Candidate*, depicts how it might be done. The character played by Frank Sinatra was implanted to become an unwitting assassin through brainwashing techniques involving hypnosis.

How this can occur is easily explained – and also remedied – by Dianetics, the precursor to Scientology. The most basic concept in Dianetics is that unwanted conditions stem from past moments of (some degree of) pain and unconsciousness, including hypnosis. During these moments, a person is highly susceptible to commands and words spoken, and will not remember them when they come to. Yet the spoken words and other perceptions in the incident have command value and can be triggered into action by subsequent stimuli in the person's environment which cause the subject to feel an urge to execute the command or experience pain, discomfort, illness, and emotional upset without recognizing the real source of the urge or symptoms.

The main use of the E-meter is to help a person locate those forgotten or unknown past incidents, view them fully, and thereby discharge the negative influence on the person presently. Sometimes the operator must steer the person in the proper direction with follow-up questions, aided by the E-meter readings. The needle reacts in the exact same way each time the person thinks the same thought that initially caused the meter to react.

Therefore, the person holding the cans and the person operating the E-meter must work as a team. A trusting relationship is vital for the process to work.

I trusted Martiniano. His eyes were on the E-meter when he asked me if I was implanted. Before I could respond he said, "What was that?" I said, "Nothing. I was just thinking, no, I hadn't been implanted."

He kept his eyes on the meter. "There. That. What are you looking at there?"

Because I was trained as an auditor, I assumed he was on to something I was not yet capable of seeing, and because I had experienced many previous, marvelous results when I followed an auditor's instructions, I fulfilled my role and looked deeper.

"Nope. Nothing there. You must be getting a false read." False reads can happen. An auditor can figure that out, too. A simple check (*Is this a false read?*) is all that is required. The needle will fall to the right if the prior read was false, and the initial read will not recur when the original question is repeated.

"Naw, come on," he said. "I'm getting something over here. Look again."

I did. As I did, he said, "There. What's that?" I told him I was just trying to find an answer and was thinking of possibilities. "Yeah, that, that," he said.

"I'm not looking at anything specific," I said. "All I did was search for times I may have been unconscious where an implant possibly could have happened."

"What's that? Yes, that. I keep getting the same read. Come on, what is that?"

"I was just thinking about a time when I was in a hospital."

"Yeah, yeah. What happened there in the hospital?"

I was starting to get upset. "Nothing happened. I just thought I'd take a look at when I was in the hospital and when I did I thought nothing like an implant had occurred. I was never unconscious."

Martiniano kept it up. "Right there. Tell me what happened there?"

"Nothing." I was ready to throw the cans at him. "I just wondered if it was possible something was done to me in my sleep and..."

"Yes. Right there. Tell me what happened in your sleep," he said.

I felt a sense of my reality slipping away. But I trusted Martiniano and, based on my prior positive experiences with auditing, I trusted the E-meter technology. So I proceeded into the unknown and the unreal. "I was just kind of, you know, imagining what could have occurred to get that needle reaction. I don't think it's real at all. But, okay, so maybe a doctor snuck into my room while I was asleep."

"Yes, that's it," he said. "I'm getting a lot of needle action. Something is there. Go on. Let's get to the bottom of this." I noticed him scribbling something on his work sheet. A shield between us obscured both the meter and his papers and pen. But I knew what he was doing. I also detected in him a sense of triumph, which I found odd.

The idea that I had really been implanted overwhelmed me and caused me to question my grip on reality. I was hoping my discomfort was only a temporary barrier I would pass through. He continued. Together we dug up a memory in which I had been implanted in 1968 to later join the church and destroy it. I was utterly devastated by the outcome. I distrusted myself and barely clung to my sanity. I walked out of the plant check a broken man, no longer questioning the new leadership; I had abandoned the thoughts I had been busted for having without even realizing it.

Back on renovation duty I became concerned about my fate now that I had basically confessed to being an enemy of the church, a spy – albeit an unwitting one. The possibility that I might be declared a suppressive person and denied further Scientology services entered my mind. Now more than ever, I felt I needed access to future auditing so that I could salvage myself spiritually. I was a mess, a basket case almost.

* * *

After a week of renovation work I was summoned to G.O. offices to see a church official who was involved in the transition of the formerly-autonomous G.O. into the command structure of the church. He said they had received legal advice that certain G.O. personnel should be removed from staff because of their high profile in past G.O. activities, and that my name was on the list. I smelled a rat.

"What about the sec check and plant check I just went through, and being busted from post?" I said. He shook his head. "That has nothing to do with it."

"What about my standing? Am I going to be allowed to receive services?"

He bobbed his head. "You have a clear record. You completed everything asked of you. This is an altogether different thing." He exuded certainty and smiled, friendly-like, as if working to create an air of camaraderie. "But I see your concern because of the timing."

I was leery. "Yeah, the timing," I said.

He insisted that all was good with me and the church. I still wasn't buying it. I was being shit-canned. The more I thought about it, however, the more I got over it. I agreed to resign from the G.O.

* * *

I was physically a free man, but mentally scarred and trapped. I steadily sank into a deep funk afterward. I could not find a decent job. No law firm would hire me as a non-licensed attorney (in California) and I could find nothing else. I settled for grunt jobs, making five dollars an hour here and there. I became introverted and deeply depressed. I wanted to walk away from my life and start over. I never once considered suicide but I was miserable day and night and wished my life would end.

My darkest hour came in December of 1982 when living had become absolutely unbearable. Lying in bed, with Fran asleep beside me, I took a hard view of my miserable condition. Something had to give. I recalled being happy and productive earlier in life and wondered when it had changed. My attention went straight to the plant check. I had completely forgotten about it. I recalled copping to having been implanted in 1968. "*Bullshit,*" I said to myself. "*It didn't fucking happen. I was never implanted.*" A ton of weight instantly lifted from me. My spirits rose. I looked closer still, examining each false memory I had agreed to regarding the imaginary incident. Each one I labeled "bullshit." More weight lifted; my mood further improved. My self-examination went into hyper speed. *Bullshit, bullshit, bullshit, bullshit. The whole damn thing was bullshit!* Indeed, the fictitiousness of the incident was so crystal clear to me that I wondered how I ever fell for it. My reality and sanity had returned full force. I peacefully fell asleep.

My life turned around immediately after that. My rise was as fast as my decline had been. I found a job working for an independent insurance adjusting company that was owned by a great guy. The pay scale was based on production, my kind of deal. In short order I became the company's top producer and was generating a healthy income.

* * *

Fast forward temporarily to June 2013, more than 20 years after the plant check. Tom Martiniano reached out to me by e-mail. I brought up the incident of the plant check he had given me. I told him how badly I had compromised my reality and how much I had been harmed by it, and only pulled myself out of it months later by realizing it was "all bullshit."

He replied, "Not only that but it was intentional bullshit." He added that he was ordered to do it by two people, one of whom was Norman Starkey.

Scientology has a term for what was done to me: "Black Dianetics." That simply means the reverse use of Scientology technology – to harm someone. Hubbard warns of the dangers of the practice, stating: "A person on whom Black Dianetics has been employed seldom retains the sanity or will to make a complaint, or does not know he has been victimized."[16]

Psychology also has a term for it: "gaslighting." Here is how Dr. George Simon, Ph.D., describes the term and those who engage in it:

"In recent years, the term 'gaslighting' has come to be applied to attempts by certain kinds of personalities, especially psychopaths — who are among the personalities most adept at sophisticated tactics of manipulation — to create so much doubt in the minds of their targets of exploitation that the victim no longer trusts their own judgment about things and buys into the assertions of the manipulator, thus coming under their power and control."[17]

Chapter 25

LIVES IN THE BALANCE

Trust your own instinct. Your mistakes might as well be your own, instead of someone else's.

– Billy Wilder
American filmmaker

"Merrell, I just spoke with John Fernandez." I was on the phone with Bennie Lazzara. It was March 1984, two years after I resigned from the G.O. staff. "He's on loan to the Florida Bar to prosecute charges against you. He's a very good trial lawyer. He used to work for James Russell, the state attorney in Clearwater. He was their death penalty lawyer."

His words hit me like a freight train. I had hoped that the Florida legal matters were behind me. I had not heard a single word about any action by either state or federal grand juries, and the Cazares civil suit was embroiled in legal challenges that did not require my involvement, and it was aimed at the church's deep pockets anyway.

The last time I checked I was told the Florida Bar's file on me was gathering dust. "I wonder if I stirred them into action by filing my application for admission to the California Bar," I said. I filed it in the fall of 1983, had just finished taking the bar examination, and was awaiting the result. Lazzara didn't know. He said Fernandez told him the Florida Board of Governors had mixed feelings about my case. "Half of them think it's too small to waste Bar resources on, but the other half can't understand why you haven't cooperated with authorities and in the civil cases."

In addition to refusing to answer questions before the Tampa federal grand jury pursuant to my Fifth Amendment rights in 1981, I also refused to answer key questions in depositions in the civil cases, including the Cazares lawsuit, and I effectively fought off the Pinellas County state grand jury with legal challenges in the California courts. I saw where Fernandez was going with his conversation with Lazzara.

"So they want to cut a deal?" I said. "I cooperate and the charges go away?"

"He didn't come out and say that, but reading between the lines, that's what he's saying. He said if they go forward they want your license and for you to never be able to practice again."

I let out a half-laugh. That was the death penalty for lawyers. A disbarred Florida lawyer was entitled to apply for reinstatement after 3 years. Lazzara was silent. "Do you think he can get my license?" I asked.

"That's not the point. He thinks he can, and he's a good prosecutor. I learned long ago to never tell a client the case against him cannot succeed." Lazzara was a former assistant state attorney who represented criminal defendants after leaving the prosecutor's office.

"Did you mention that he doesn't have the evidence to support the charges?"

"I did. He said in this environment he doesn't need evidence."

I was thunderstruck. Not just by its boldness but that it came from the mouth of a lawyer representing the Florida Bar in an ethics matter. "Do you believe that, Bennie?"

"I don't know. The sentiment against Scientology is very strong down here, as you know. Judge Hanlon is a good judge, a fair one, but he is an old, very devout Catholic, and I don't know how he will react to the junk Fernandez can throw at him." He was talking about state Circuit Court Judge Morton J. Hanlon, who was assigned as a Bar Referee to the inactive case. Bar charges are neither criminal nor civil; they are administrative proceedings with relaxed rules of evidence and no juries.

Lazzara asked how I wanted him to respond. I told him I was confident that I would pass the California Bar exam and wanted him to negotiate a fair resolution so I could put Florida behind me. He said he didn't know how to determine a fair resolution – he had never heard of a lawyer doing what I had done.

"Of course," I said, "I mean the type of charges. Conflict of interests." I suggested that we research every case over the past ten years. "Note the charges and punishment for each." He liked the idea and asked who would do that, me or him. "You," I replied, "so you're satisfied with the cases you find and can hold your own against Fernandez."

He sent me a copy of his research, a memorandum of 33 cases. Of the 11 that resulted in disbarment, all involved criminal conduct that caused their clients substantial monetary damage. The others ranged from public reprimands to suspensions, all but two of the suspensions had been for 90 days or less. Only one out of those 33 cases resulted in a permanent disbarment and that case involved a lawyer who had previously been disbarred and reinstated.

I told Lazzara to ask for a 90-day suspension. He said that was a non-starter given the stance Fernandez was taking. We discussed it and ultimately agreed that he would present his research findings to Fernandez, point out all the limited suspensions, and then use his judgment on how to proceed based on his reaction.

I heard back from Lazzara the next day. "He's playing hardball. No negotiations. Disbarment for life if he has to go forward." I told him I would talk to the church about cooperating with authorities and litigants. "I don't think I can hurt the church, do you?" He said he didn't know because he didn't know what all I had to say.

* * *

John Peterson was the church's in-house counsel. I knew him from when I was on staff. He had a private practice in Beverly Hills but spent a lot of time in an office on church premises. He was gentlemanly, a nice guy, easy to talk to.

"What do you want to do?" he asked.

"Cooperate. I think my testimony will help the church more than it will hurt. I'll have to give up two names, that's it." My former handlers, Don Alverzo and Tom Ritchie. I told him I was willing to coordinate with the church. He said he would get back to me.

A day or two later he called. "The church wants to moot court your testimony." Moot court is a play-acted case. He asked if I minded appearing in front of church lawyers, investigators, and legal staff. They wanted Lazzara to examine me as a witness in a morning session and for church lawyers to cross-examine me in the afternoon. Peterson would be the judge. "They want to hear what you have to say and test your demeanor under cross." I told him I was game.

* * *

The church showed up with two attorneys, a private investigator and two legal staffers, in addition to Peterson. I only knew one of the attorneys, Howard Steckel. The investigator was Gene Ingram, a former police officer with the LAPD. Lynn Farney and Warren McShane were present on behalf of church staff. They were holdovers from the G.O. I knew them both but not well.

Lazzara examined me, asking questions about my involvement with the G.O. in Clearwater: names, dates and details about my activities; why I did each thing, and so on and so forth. Everybody for the church took notes. Peterson ruled on objections made by church lawyers. There weren't many of those. When I finished we broke for lunch. That afternoon church lawyers tore into me. I thought I handled them well. We went late. I was exhausted and tired of talking when it ended.

I asked Lazzara how he thought it went. "You did fine." I asked him if he thought my testimony would hurt the church and he said he wanted to get feedback from church attorneys before answering.

* * *

"The church doesn't want you to testify in any proceeding, including your bar case," Peterson said. "In return for your cooperation, the church will fully fund the defense of your bar case."

I asked him for the basis of that decision. "Church lawyers think your testimony opens up a can of worms, making it difficult to predict the effect it will cause."

"Anything specific? Or is this just one of those decisions that falls in the category of 'no-one-ever-got-fired-for-buying-IBM.'" Peterson granted that it probably did fall into that category. "They thought it was powerful to hear a live witness testify as you did and were afraid of how a jury might react to it."

That appraisal surprised me. I started trying to reason with Peterson, telling him that things for the church could not be worse than they already were, what with the seized documents and unsupported allegations being hurled around in the media. None of what I said drew a comment or a reaction. His blank face said: "I'm only the messenger."

"You know, John, my taking the Fifth in Bar proceedings really puts me at a disadvantage." He said he knew. "The church is putting me in a tight spot." He knew that, too. "I mean, I have a legal career ahead of me. I probably passed my California bar exam and could save my Florida and Missouri licenses, too. That's a lot for the church to ask me to risk losing when it comes down to lawyers speculating and making safe, defensive decisions." He knew that, too.

"Merrell, if it makes a difference, on a personal level, and not as church counsel, I will understand if you choose to go against the wishes of the church. I would probably do that myself."

I paused to consider his statement and thought he better not let Norman Starkey or some others hear him say that. I appreciated his candor. "Thanks John. I'll be sure to call you as a witness at my Comm Ev." He laughed at my gallows humor. (A Committee of Evidence, or "Comm Ev," is the ecclesiastical procedure used to *declare*[18] someone a suppressive person and expel them from the church.) I would be roasted if I went against the wishes of current church leaders.

* * *

I went over the church offer with Lazzara. "As your lawyer, I feel I have an obligation to advise you that it is in your best legal interest to save your license. I understand what your relationship to the church means to you, and I will do what you instruct me to do, but I want to make clear what I think is in your best legal interest."

Lazzara had to say that. He was being paid by the church and was their lawyer on some church cases. Not that he would favor the interests of the hand that fed him. He wouldn't; he was a highly principled attorney.

"I hear you," I said. "I'll call you tomorrow."

* * *

I spoke with Fran that evening about the ramifications of testifying against the wishes of the church. We both had jobs working for companies that were owned by Scientologists. All our close friends in California – couples we played bridge with, went on vacations with, and spent most of our weekends socializing with – were all Scientologists. Angie went to Delphi Academy in Los Angeles, a school that was run by Scientologists and used Scientology study technology. Virtually all her friends were the sons and daughters of Scientologists. Almost all aspects of our lives were embedded in the Scientology community. If church management declared me a suppressive person, all that would go up in smoke – instantly.

The church's policy of forced disconnection required Scientologists to sever all ties to any declared person, and also to anyone who remained connected to the declared person, including family members – in my case, Fran and Angie. Those who did not disconnect from us were subject to being themselves declared suppressive by a twin policy. In practical terms, other Scientologists would have no choice but to cut ties with us. These policies were adopted in 1982 after the takeover of the G.O. When I first got involved with Scientology in 1972 disconnection did not exist. It had once existed in a voluntary form, but Hubbard cancelled it in 1968 along with security checks and the "Fair Game" policy as part of the Reform Code of Scientology.

Fran asked if I thought the church would *declare* me if I cooperated with Florida authorities and civil litigants against the church. "They might not *declare* me right away for legal reasons." By "they" I was thinking of those persons in control of the church who were calling the shots – those nameless, faceless souls in the chain of command between L. Ron Hubbard and Norman Starkey – which could have been a single person for all I knew. Based on what I had seen emanate from that control point, the temperament there was short-fused and ruthlessly domineering.

"They'll definitely be pissed off but will eventually get over it if everything turns out okay for the church. If it doesn't, if they feel my testimony harms them, I'm screwed. They'll *declare* me when it's safe to do so. The problem is I can't predict the outcome. I have my opinion. They have theirs. Who knows what will happen?"

She asked me what I thought my chances were for saving my license if I took the church's deal and refused to testify in any legal proceedings. "Fifty percent, max. Maybe less. If it's true he doesn't need evidence, then zero."

She said she trusted my judgment and fully supported whatever decision I made.

* * *

The next morning I called Lazzara. "Tell Fernandez to bring it on."

Chapter 26

HIDDEN FORCES

The most dangerous man, to any government, is the man who is able to think things out for himself, without regard to the prevailing superstitions and taboos. Almost invariably he comes to the conclusion that the government he lives under is dishonest, insane and intolerable, and so, if he is romantic, he tries to change it. And if he is not romantic personally, he is apt to spread discontent among those who are.

— H.L. Mencken
American journalist, essayist and editor

"You've got an urgent call from the church." I was on the road doing insurance adjusting field work and called the office from a pay phone to check my messages. I immediately returned the call to Judy Taussig. She was part of the newly organized MAC Unit that was now part of Office of Special Affairs, the organization that replaced the G.O. I knew her well since she was part of the original MAC Unit and her husband, John Taussig, was a lawyer and friend who currently worked in the IRS Unit of the church's legal department. He was the guy who showed me the Paulette Cooper legal files I organized when I first arrived in Los Angeles. He was still studying law and not yet licensed to practice then.

Judy said she wanted to talk about my bar case. "What about it?" I asked, baffled at what could be so urgent. She thought I should consider resigning from the Florida Bar and accepting disbarment. I told her I had already done that. "I worked out what to do with the church through Peterson and a bunch of other people."

She said the church now wants me to not fight the Bar case. My head was spinning. "Church? Who in the church?" Church management, is all she would say. Based on advice they received from Florida attorneys. "Which attorneys?" I asked. She mentioned Paul Johnson, the church's lead attorney for Florida litigation, but added that others were saying the same thing.

I told her I couldn't believe that advice came from attorneys. "If I accept a disbarment pending charges, those charges can be used as admissions against the church in the Florida civil cases. I may as well testify. My testimony will be much more favorable for the church than the charges against me."

She repeated that I should accept disbarment. The tone in her voice was a little forceful and condescending this time. Just as I started to get annoyed with her I saw what was going on. "Do you have an order to get me to do this?" I asked. She admitted she did. I asked for the source of the order but she dodged the question.

I told her I was on the road and had an appointment to make. "I'll call Bennie Lazzara when I get back and sort it out with him." She asked me to call her back after I had done that. I told her I would.

I immediately phoned Lazzara and asked if he knew which attorneys in Florida might be telling church staffers that I should resign and accept disbarment. He said he hadn't heard anything like that, but would look into it.

I received a call from Judy upon my return to the office, before I had even settled in. "Did you make a decision?" she asked. I couldn't believe the pressure she must be under. I told her I hadn't finished with Lazzara yet. "Give me a day or two." She said she needed something now, and was adamant.

"Okay. If you need an answer now, the answer is no."

"Merrell, this is your church. If you don't go along, things could go bad for you." I was taken aback. This was not the Judy Taussig I knew. I asked her what she meant by that. "Is the church going to *declare* me if I don't go along?" She told me to knock it off, and I told her our conversation was over.

I took a few minutes to regain my bearings then mentally replayed my calls with her and Lazzara. An idea struck me. I placed a call to Paul Johnson in Florida. "Hey, Paul. I got an order from church staff to resign and accept a permanent disbarment."

"What? This is the first I've heard about a permanent disbarment. Is that what the Bar wants?"

"Yep."

"That's absolutely ridiculous," he said. "You shouldn't accept that."

"Did you advise the church that I should resign or anything like that?" He said he hadn't. The only thing he said to anyone was that he was worried about what might go on the record of the bar case and later become public. "If you resign, the charges against you can be deemed admissions in the civil suits here. That will harm the church. I wouldn't want that to happen."

"That's exactly what I told them."

He said they must have confused something he said to them, so he would call and straighten it out. I gave him Judy's number and thanked him. Maybe Johnson thought he was misunderstood by church staff but I drew a different conclusion.

I phoned Peterson. "John, do we have a deal or not?" I filled him in on the day's events. He said we had a deal and that he would talk to church staff. He started to sign off. "Not so quick, please. I'm really troubled by Judy's call and what it might signify. Maybe it's not too late to get the Florida Bar to put their deal back on the table and ..."

He interrupted me. "No, there's no need to do that. I'll sort everything out." He was again ready to hang up. I asked him to hear me out. "How high in the church did you go to get your authority for our agreement?"

"All the way."

"To whom? Can you give me a name and a post title?" He said he could not since my question asked for confidential information that he was duty-bound not to reveal. *Man alive, the mystery surrounding who's in charge was amazing, truly amazing.*

"I just want to make sure my deal is ironclad and signed onto by the top decision makers because it sure doesn't look that way. It looks to me like somebody high up in the church, someone hidden from my view, deliberately misled me into turning down a chance to save my license by cooperating with Florida authorities when I had the chance, then once I let that opportunity pass, they pulled the rug out from under me. The net effect of that is an order under threat of a Declare[19] to neither cooperate with authorities *nor defend my license.*"

Peterson saw how I could view it that way, but promised it was not the case. He would never involve himself in a scheme like that. He apologized profusely and promised that he would sort everything out. I backed off, but insisted, "I don't want staff members giving me orders, John. I'm a party to litigation. I'm not some flunky staff member. I'm also a potential witness before state and federal grand juries. I mean, treating me like she did creates legal land mines for the church, too."

He agreed and said he would get on it. "You know how it is. You used to work here." Actually I didn't know how it was. Things had changed. But it was clear to me that Peterson felt a deal was in place and he was trying to maintain it. "Just call me if you have any more problems," he said, "and I will sort things out at my end."

I thanked him and let him go. I didn't hear any more from Judy Taussig or other staff members about accepting disbarment, so it looked like Peterson had come through. Shortly thereafter, Lazzara called me to say that John Fernandez told him the Florida Bar does not want to litigate my case and was now offering a resignation with me agreeing not to reapply for a certain agreed upon number of years. His offer was eerily similar to Judy Taussig's order. Since Lazzara also worked on other church cases, I suspected that someone from the church was lobbying him for my resignation. I asked him who initiated the settlement talk.

"Fernandez," he said. "He's working with Louis Adcock, a member of the board of governors. He reports to the forty-member Board. They don't understand why you're fighting this."

I laughed. "Then they're not very smart. Or they're misinformed. Offer a suspension and watch how fast this case goes away. Did you tell him that?" Lazzara said he had. "The problem with suspension is that one of the Board members wants to slam dunk you. He's pushing hard for disbarment."

"Who? Did you get a name?" Lazzara said he didn't. "Next time you talk with Fernandez will you try to squeeze that out of him? Maybe we can do an end around that guy." He said he would.

"Fernandez told me the board in general is dark about a lot of things. He told them he had no evidence that you actually harmed the Cazareses. Their biggest problem with your conduct is that you used the skills of espionage to gather information for the enemy of the client you represented – and that it occurred *before* the representation."

"Okay, yeah, I did that. But it was isolated conduct and happened eight fucking years ago. I was only a year out of law school, for Pete's sake. We're hung up on penalty, not wrongdoing. And context. There were other lawyers at the SAO (state attorney's office) who were also engaged in wrongdoing, except they're covering it up and putting the spotlight on me. The SAO and Gabe Cazares, the main people pressing the bar charges against me, were both involved in espionage against the church and everyone is helping cover it up. If they can engage in espionage against the church, why can't the church engage in espionage against them?"

"Who says they can't? You're a lawyer. You can't engage in espionage against someone you later represent, is what they're saying."

He made an excellent point. "Okay. Let me rephrase that."

"But isn't that the issue? This is a hearing against a member of the Florida Bar, not a hearing against the church."

"Of course it is. Let me put it this way: The SAO needs to either back off its allegations against me, which are bullshit anyway, or talk about the COINTELPRO it was involved in and helped cover up. And the FBI needs to get their agent informant Gabe Cazares to drop his charges against me or else turn over all their documents regarding their relationship with him. Then I'll sit down and discuss whether my moral character is so flawed that I'm beyond redemption, because that's the only time disbarment is supposed to be imposed as a penalty according to the Florida Supreme Court."

"They won't admit that and the Bar wants to avoid litigation," he said.

"The Florida Bar is being used by private litigants and law enforcement who want to either turn me against the church or punish me for not turning against it. The SAO and FBI covered it up back then, and they're covering it up now. They're using the Bar to either turn me or silence me. Either I become one of them and help cover up what they did, or they label me with the scarlet letter "D" to discredit me if I ever speak out against what they did. I'm fighting them, not the Florida Bar.

"Fernandez used to work for the SAO. He's one of them. The governor guy who wants to slam dunk me is probably in cahoots with them and engineered the appointment of Fernandez. I refuse to cave in to their strong-arm tactics. I would rather lose my license fighting them every step of the way."

I was worked up. I could tell that Lazzara really wanted me to settle the case and that I was now fighting against him, too. I appreciated his help and skills and did not want to blow him off. I took a deep breath and let it out. He didn't press the issue.

"By the way, Bennie. Someone in the church and someone in the Florida Bar both suddenly want me to settle for disbarment. Is that just a coincidence or am I being paranoid?" The thought had just occurred to me and it came out unfiltered. I felt a confused, uneasy silence on the other end.

"Forget I said that. I'm just venting."

Chapter 27

FEET TO THE FIRE

Stripped of ethical rationalizations and philosophical pretensions, a crime is anything that a group in power chooses to prohibit.

– Freda Adler
criminologist/educator

Lazzara deposed Denis Quilligan, an investigator for the SAO. "The Florida Bar charged Mr. Vannier in count six with obtaining employment at the State Attorney's Office as an agent of the church for the purpose of gaining access to an ongoing criminal investigation of the church, and you are listed as the only witness in support of the charge. So, Mr. Quilligan, what documents have you brought with you today in response to the subpoena for deposition?"

Our strategy was simple: make the SAO talk about the counterintelligence files I saw at the St. Petersburg PD intel division, and produce the records, or go home.

Quilligan: None. I no longer work at the State Attorney's Office and do not have access to them.[20]

Lazzara: Did you ever see a job application from Mr. Vannier?

Quilligan: There was none. He did not submit one.

Lazzara: Did Mr. Vannier lie to the State Attorney's Office about his affiliation with the Church of Scientology?

Quilligan:	No. The State Attorney's Office does not ask employees about their religious affiliation.
Lazzara:	In fact, it would have been improper to deny him a job based on his religious affiliation, right?
Quilligan:	Yes.
Lazzara:	Was there an ongoing investigation into Scientology at the time Mr. Vannier worked at the State Attorney's Office?
Quilligan:	Yes, but Mr. Vannier did not have access to it because it was housed in a different building and the investigation was kept on a strict need-to-know basis.
Lazzara:	Do you have any evidence that either Mr. Vannier or the Church of Scientology knew about the investigation before he went to work for the State Attorney's Office?
Quilligan:	No. It was not public information.
Lazzara:	Did Mr. Vannier have access to any records relating to the Church of Scientology when he worked in the State Attorney's St. Petersburg office?
Quilligan:	I don't know what he had access to. Maybe just the library.

Lazzara presented a copy of a 1980 affidavit signed by Denis Quilligan that was attached to the Florida Bar's charges of wrongdoing and was also the supporting affidavit for the material witness certificate used in the SAO's failed attempt to arrest Fran and me to compel us to testify as material witnesses to the Pinellas County grand jury in July 1980.

Lazzara:	Was any information you relied on while preparing the affidavit contained in any files at the State Attorney's Office?
Quilligan:	Yes.
Lazzara:	Where are those files today?
Quilligan:	At the State Attorney's Office.
Lazzara:	Do you have access to those files?

Quilligan: No.

Immediately after the deposition, we subpoenaed the SAO for the files Quilligan relied on while working on his affidavit. The SAO filed a motion for a protective order, asking Judge Hanlon, the bar referee, to excuse it from turning over the files on the grounds of prosecutorial privileges set forth in Florida Law. We opposed the motion, claiming a Constitutional right to inquire into the charges against me.

Hanlon ruled that the State Attorney's Office may withhold the documents but the Florida Bar cannot use Denis Quilligan or his affidavit at a hearing on the bar charges if it chooses to withhold documents. The SAO refused to turn them over.

We celebrated. Count VI, the SAO charge, was dead. One down, five to go.

* * *

"Good news," Lazzara said, after the pre-trial conference. "Fernandez conceded that he has no evidence you did anything to harm Cazares. He said he will not argue at trial that you did."

"Three down, three to go," I said. Counts IV and V alleged, respectively, that I had tried to get Cazares to dismiss his case and enter into a retraction/apology statement with the church.

"Fernandez thinks you were duped by the church and suggested that we amend our response to the bar charges and allege lack of *mens rea*." In criminal law *mens rea* (Latin for "guilty mind") is necessary to prove some crimes. A bar case is not a criminal case and I had never seen anything in all of my legal research that the Bar was required to prove guilty intent. "He thinks this is the weakest part of his case," Lazzara added.

"Oh, so he's helping me now?"

"No. We were just talking lawyer-to-lawyer about the case." He asked me what I thought about the idea.

"I wasn't duped," I said. "That's his religious prejudice against Scientology coming out." The mere idea he thought I had been duped touched a nerve. Inherent in that opinion are the presumptions that Scientology lacks legitimacy and a right to survive, that my motives were baseless, and that I was a victim. What the hell did Fernandez know about Scientology? Nothing, that's what. Were things done wrong by Scientologists? Yes. Different subject. Address those things. I vented on Lazzara. Not angrily but intently. I wanted to make sure I got my point of view across.

"The reason I became a Scientologist and still am one today is because the technology works for me. It makes my life better. It makes me a better person. The reason I used the tools of espionage against Gabe Cazares before I represented him, which is what Fernandez said bothered the board of governors most, is because I saw that the free exercise of my religion, including the use of that technology, and the establishment of the church's hierarchy in Clearwater, were under attack by elements in the intelligence community. I also discovered that Cazares was part of those covert operations and I wanted to do something about it. I saw the St. Pete PD intel files. I know what I saw in those files. I am now an expert on FBI COINTELPRO, and am more convinced than ever of what I saw.

"The reason I decided to represent Cazares was because the INS order to deport seventy-five percent of Flag staff members would, in effect, seriously harm, if not completely destroy, the free practice of my religion. The INS order itself was based on bias and false evidence. Once we uncovered the source of the false evidence and brought it to the attention of a responsible INS official, the problem was resolved. The only reason I was given access to the INS files that revealed the source of that false evidence is because the officer in charge of Tampa INS was also biased against Scientology and was willing to violate his oath of office to faithfully execute the laws of the United States and respect the rights of all citizens to equal protection under the law. He willingly cooperated with me, the person he thought was the attorney for a party adverse to the church he was working to destroy by deporting the bulk of its leadership.

"I wasn't duped. What the Florida Bar sees in my misconduct is a young, green attorney who didn't have the professional standards I do now, which are: every problem an organization faces can and should be solved within the bounds of the law and, for an attorney, within the Code of Professional Responsibility. I was responsible for each and every decision I made and for each and every act I engaged in or failed to engage in.

"I refuse to take the legal position of a victim."

Chapter 28

BLUE WALL OF SILENCE

I find a pattern of lying by [FBI] informers and agents, the falsifying of documents, and denial of responsibility for 'dirty tricks.' For many years the FBI also concealed their records systems and resisted disclosure under the [Freedom of Information Act] as part of the maintenance of a Blue Wall of Silence.[21]

– Ivan Greenburg
American author/civil libertarian

"In their minds, they aren't lying," said Wes Swearingen, former Special Agent in Charge of the FBI's Los Angeles Field Office. He was at this point a private investigator in San Diego. I contacted him in preparation for the FBI depositions we scheduled in the Bar case. "The FBI thought is, 'If someone on the outside doesn't deserve an honest answer, then they're not lying. They don't always lie totally. They give half-truths. Just be sure to follow-up your questions. Assume they're lying, and ask as many questions as you can."

I told him we were looking for a consultant and could pay him. He said he doesn't consult anymore on FBI matters. He referred me to two books on the subject of COINTELPRO. I told him I had studied both books in depth. "Well then you have a good idea of how they're dealing with you," he said. "All FBI offices conduct COINTELPRO essentially the same way."

I asked if he could refer me to a consultant. He said he didn't know anyone, adding, "Not anyone who really knows something." He asked me what we were trying to prove.

"What we really want to prove is that Gabe Cazares, who was then the mayor of Clearwater, Florida, was sent in on me, to hire me as his lawyer while knowing about my affiliation with the Church of Scientology. Kind of a spy vs. spy thing. Are we off base? Is that something they might have done, sent in an informant on a lawyer they know is a spy for a group they've targeted?"

Swearingen said, "Whatever you can imagine, the FBI probably did it." I was keeping notes of the call and wrote down this statement verbatim.

I told him that we more than imagined it. I gave him a summary about the files in the St. Petersburg Police Department Intelligence Division, the two FBI memos dated March 10 and April 6, 1976, and Joe Burton's testimony that he was told by his FBI handler, Robert Heible, when speaking of Cazares, that "we own him."

"Looks like you're on to something," he said. I asked if he could give us any tips for taking the depositions of FBI agents. "Loss of memory is a key thing," he said. "It's part of their training at school. Agents are given inspections and examinations annually on the rules, regulations, and the FBI handbook. They're instructed that 'don't remember' is perjury only if it becomes a pattern. So keep that in mind. Tell your lawyers not to accept 'this is all we have,' or other non-answers. Keep asking. And remember, the key thing is to dig for documents. After you're done with your depositions, get back to me."

I jotted a note: *Consultation!!*

* * *

Carl Kohlweck was my California attorney taking the FBI depositions in Florida along with Bennie Lazzara. Kohlweck had been my attorney ever since I was first served with the lawsuits. I wanted someone nearby I could work with who did not separately represent the church. Kohlweck once did represent the church but had been fired during the two-year lull in activity on my cases. I was given two different reasons for his firing by two different staff members: he screwed up on a case, and he had become disaffected. When my Bar case heated up I was told I couldn't use him. I tried to get to the bottom of his firing and sort it out, but ran into red tape. I finally called him on my own.

He told me he was fired because he recommended that the church settle the Wollersheim case. Larry Wollersheim was a former Scientologist who sued the church for millions of dollars after he had been declared a suppressive person. In his lawsuit, Wollersheim alleged that the church had waged a campaign to destroy him and his retail art business, as part of the church's "Fair Game" policy after he was *declared.*

Although it was officially cancelled by L. Ron Hubbard in 1968 because of the negative publicity it caused, the "Fair Game" policy authorized the punishment and harassment using any and all means possible of any person who was judged to be a threat to Scientology. Wollersheim claimed that, in addition to all of his Scientology employees, friends and acquaintances being forced to disconnect from him, the church contacted Scientologists who owed him money and told them not to repay him.

I didn't know Wollersheim and had no knowledge of the facts in his case. I did know, however, that he was represented by legendary trial lawyer Charles O'Reilly. Most attorneys who sued the church were either not very good or not funded well enough to take on the church. Not so with O'Reilly and his law firm.

I asked Kohlweck how much he tried to settle the case for. His answer: $250,000. Then he explained how it came about. He was taking Wollersheim's deposition and being extremely exhaustive about it. On day five of the deposition, O'Reilly asked him if they could take a break and talk. "We went into the hallway and he said that I was killing his case so bad he wanted out and asked why the church would not settle. I told him, 'Well, maybe it's because your last offer to settle was for a million dollars and they don't want to pay that much.' He pleaded with me to give him a number, and I thought about it and told him, 'I'll tell you what. If you will accept a quarter million, I will take it to them and twist arms if I have to,' and O'Reilly jumped on the offer."

Kohlweck said he sent his recommendation to the church, and in response he was fired. "Really?" I said. "A quarter of a million is a steal for that case." Kohlweck said that he thought the same thing, adding, "They're spending almost that much each month to prepare it for trial."[22]

His story rang true. Armed with that information and no other California lawyer to turn to, I made a power move. I called John Peterson. He knew the story. I had already sought his assistance on this matter twice before, and he had put in a request that I be allowed to use Kohlweck more than a month earlier.

"Did you get it worked out to use Kohlweck?" he asked.

I told him I hadn't. "I can't put this off any longer, John. I decided to relocate to Florida, enter my appearance as co-counsel and take the depositions myself. I'm buying my plane tickets tomorrow."

"No. Don't do that," he said in panic mode. "I'll get Carl's clearance."

He did, too. That very day.

Kohlweck called me from Florida during a break in the FBI depositions. "The documents the FBI turned over to the church pursuant to the FOIA were doctored," he said, referring to the FBI internal memos K.O. showed me on my first day on the job in the MAC Unit. "The April 6, 1976 memo the FBI just turned over to us in response to the subpoena has additional markings on it in the lower right hand corner, a number: "66-672-672 Sub 1-18cc."

"That's a subfile," I said, excitedly. "Holy shit. That's huge. That could be Gabe's informant file." A sub file is one that is somehow associated with this particular memo. The "18" means that the memo is the 18th document in the sub file. The "66" is a classification for "administrative matters," which covers supplies, automobiles, salary matters and vouchers – and is frequently used for an informant file. The middle numbers, "672-672" are the file number.

In the deposition Kohlweck questioned the author of the document, an FBI agent who was also the agent who met with Cazares, Michael Lunsford.

Kohlweck: The document refers to the existence of a sub file. What do you know about this sub file?
Lunsford: I don't know anything about it.
Kohlweck: Could it be an informant file for Cazares?
Lunsford: I don't know what it is.

Kohlweck produced our copy of the same memo, placed it side-by-side with the one the FBI had turned over in response to the subpoena for deposition, and asked Lunsford to view both of them.

Kohlweck: The copy I'm showing you was produced by the FBI in response to a Freedom of Information Act request. Do you agree that they are the same document except for one difference?
Lunsford: It appears so.
Kohlweck: Why does one copy contain a sub file marking and the other one does not?
Lunsford: I don't know.
Kohlweck: On April 6, 1976, the date of this memo, was Gabe Cazares an FBI informant?
Lunsford: I would not characterize him that way.
Kohlweck: How would you characterize him?
Lunsford: The Mayor of a city who was concerned about the new occupants of the Fort Harrison Hotel (the landmark building in Clearwater that became Scientology's Flag Land Base).

Kohlweck: It appears from the second FBI memo that you were the one who contacted him. Is that correct?

Lunsford: I don't really recall, so I will have to rely on the language in the memo.

Kohlweck: You met with him and then an article appeared in the newspaper. Did you ask Cazares to go to the media?

Lunsford: That is not something I would normally do.

Kohlweck: Did you do it this time?

Lunsford: Looking at this memo eight years later I would have to say no.

Kohlweck then went over each of the meetings memorialized in the two FBI documents in depth, and then referred to a comment in the April 6 memo.

Kohlweck: It says you had contact with Cazares "on several occasions." How many times exactly did you have contact with him?

Lunsford: Well, the memo says several, so that's my answer.

Kohlweck: When did those other contacts occur?

Lunsford: I don't recall any specific other contacts.

Kohlweck: Isn't it true that FBI rules and regulations require you to write an FD 302 memo for each contact?

Lunsford: Yes.

Kohlweck: Did you write memos for each contact you had with Cazares?

Lunsford: I don't recall specifically, but I probably did.

Kohlweck: Where are the memos for the other contacts?

Lunsford: I don't know.

Kohlweck: Could they be contained in the sub file referenced in this document?

Lunsford: I don't know.

Kohlweck: Did you meet with Cazares prior to the date of the March 1, 1976 memo?

Lunsford: Probably.

Kohlweck: When would that prior meeting have occurred?

Lunsford: I don't know.

Kohlweck: Give me your best estimate.

Lunsford: Maybe a month or two earlier.

Kohlweck was trying to pin down a date because Cazares had initially been friendly to church officials when they arrived in Clearwater, but then suddenly went to the media asking who these people were, perhaps as directed by Lunsford.

Kohlweck: So, you met with Cazares as early as the first of January 1976?

Lunsford: Possibly.

Next up for deposition was former Special Agent in Charge of the Tampa FBI Office, Phil McNiff. Kohlweck first inquired about the document request we attached to his deposition subpoena.

Kohlweck: The documents you produced appear to be the same ones the custodian of FBI records gave us. Is that correct?

McNiff: I didn't find any additional documents.

Kohlweck: What indexes did you check?

McNiff: I asked my staff for documents that fit your request. Indexing responsibility is delegated.

Kohlweck: So you did not personally check any of the FBI indexes?

McNiff: No. As I said, indexing responsibility is delegated.

Kohlweck: You didn't check the main index?

McNiff: No.

Kohlweck repeated the same question for all the various indexes, including the ELSUR (electronic surveillance) and FISUR (physical surveillance) indexes, and McNiff gave the same answer. Kohlweck then presented the April 6, 1976 FBI memo and referred McNiff to the sub file number.

Kohlweck: What do you know about this sub file?

McNiff: I have no knowledge about it.

279

Kohlweck: Do you maintain any confidential files in your special agent in charge safe that relate to Cazares?

McNiff: No.

Kohlweck: Do you have any "DO NOT FILE" documents related to Cazares?

McNiff: No.

Kohlweck presented a copy of an FBI memo dated August 17, 1977, which was obtained in another church legal case and given to us by legal staff. He asked McNiff to review it.

Kohlweck: Does this document appear to be genuine to you?

McNiff: Yes.

Kohlweck: It states that you and Special Agent Carl Hall met with Gabe Cazares on the preceding day, which would have been August 16, 1977, and discussed Merrell Vannier and his affiliation with the Church of Scientology, true?

(To place the document in context, Cazares dismissed the case I had been handling in May 1977. The FBI raid of church facilities in L.A. and D.C. occurred in July 1977, on the same day I was asked to shut down all intelligence activities, and I left for Canada in October, two months after this meeting between the FBI and Cazares.)

McNiff: That's what it says.

Kohlweck: Is that what occurred?

McNiff: Yes.

Kohlweck: Did you meet with Cazares previously when the subject of the meeting involved Merrell Vannier and his affiliation with the Church of Scientology.

McNiff: Yes.

Kohlweck: When did that previous meeting occur?

McNiff: I don't recall.

Kohlweck: Give me your best estimate.

McNiff: Four or five months earlier, perhaps.

Gabe and Maggie had contacted me on December 21, 1976, during the panicked phone call described in Chapter 9, and asked me to represent them in their libel case against the church. I entered my appearance on the twenty-third and Gabe called me on the twenty-eighth and instructed me not to undertake any actions on the case.

Kohlweck: Please clarify that the prior meeting with Cazares, in which you discussed Merrell Vannier and his affiliation with the Church of Scientology, may have occurred as early as February 1977.

McNiff: To the best of my recollection, yes.

Kohlweck: Could the prior meeting with Cazares, in which you discussed Merrell Vannier and his affiliation with the Church of Scientology, have occurred as early as January 1977.

McNiff: Possibly.

Kohlweck: Could the prior meeting have occurred as early as December 1976?

McNiff: I doubt it was that early, but possibly.

Kohlweck: Is it possible that you met with Cazares prior to December 21, 1976 and discussed Merrell Vannier's affiliation with the Church of Scientology?

McNiff: Possibly.

Kohlweck: Did you prepare an FBI memo regarding the prior meeting with Cazares, in which you discussed Merrell Vannier and his affiliation with the Church of Scientology, no matter when the meeting occurred?

McNiff: I do not specifically recall writing a memo.

Kohlweck: FBI rules and regulations require that you write a memo, don't they?

McNiff: Yes.

Kohlweck: So where is that memo, Mr. McNiff?

McNiff: I don't specifically recall writing one, so I wouldn't know.

Kohlweck turned to McNiff's attorney, Assistant U.S. Attorney Thomas Doughty. "Mr. Doughty, will you please have your client locate the document and then turn it over to me?" Doughty said he would.

* * *

"McNiff is playing with words when he says indexing responsibility is delegated," Wes Swearingen said in a conference call with Kohlweck and me. "That's not true. If a special agent in charge wanted to find documents he could go in and get them."

Kohlweck said Michael Lunsford claimed he didn't know if Cazares was an informant and we went over the questions and his answers in that regard. Swearingen told Kohlweck that he had let Lunsford slip through his fingers. "You should have kept asking questions. A senior resident agent (Lunsford's title) is responsible for everything that happens in his area. So he knew what other agents were doing in this territory even if he was not the personal handler for Cazares.

"But don't worry about it," he added. "Documents are key. Get the document showing the prior meeting of McNiff and Cazares and you'll have the evidence you're looking for."

He asked how much time we had before trial. It was January 18, 1985. The bar hearing was set for January 30. "The hearing starts then," Kohlweck said, "but the bar referee is a sitting Circuit Court judge with a full calendar and cannot finish Merrell's hearing in one sitting. We will only go three days beginning January thirtieth and then take a long break. The trial will conclude sometime in April or May. So we have time to get the document."

A few days after the FBI depositions, Assistant U. S. Attorney Thomas Doughty told Kohlweck that the document we were looking for was at FBI Headquarters in Washington. Kohlweck asked what it was doing there. Doughty said some documents from Tampa had been transferred there. Headquarters will turn it over but only in response to a formal request. Kohlweck said he would get him one.

Finally, we were "this close" to exposing the FBI's COINTELPRO operations against the Church of Scientology in Clearwater and Gabe Cazares' role as an FBI informant, thereby achieving all of our litigation objectives.

Chapter 29

BLIND-SIDED

When there is no enemy within, the enemies outside cannot hurt you.

– Winston Churchill

"Mr. Vannier solicited my case several times both by phone and in person," Gabe Cazares testified at trial. "I never once initiated his services." Fernandez, the Florida Bar prosecutor, was examining him. Cazares also testified: I told Mr. Vannier every little thing about myself, my finances, everything. I trusted him. The thought that he may have been a Scientologist never entered my mind. He then told me I had to drop the case with prejudice. That was the only way he could drop the case, he said."

One of the charges Fernandez was trying to prove was that I had solicited Cazares as a client. That was Count I of the six charges against me. Ethics rules forbid a lawyer from directly soliciting clients for legal work.

There were no other witnesses or evidence to support this charge. It was his word against mine. And I didn't plan to testify. All we could do, therefore, was cross-examine Cazares and hope to destroy his credibility.

Lazzara got Cazares to admit that he began seeking new counsel as soon as Pat Doherty, his previous counsel, talked about withdrawing from his case. Lazzara asked Cazares if he found anyone willing to take his case other than Mr. Vannier and he said he had not. Lazzara then brought to his attention a letter from Mr. Doherty dated December 16, 1976.

Lazzara: Do you recognize that letter?
Cazares: Yes.
Lazzara: Mr. Doherty threatened to begin charging you his regular hourly rate for his time if you did not provide him with new counsel by December twenty-third, a week after the date of the letter, didn't he?
Cazares: Yes.
Lazzara: But you didn't have another lawyer who would take the case. Your back was against the wall. You were desperate. So you contacted Mr. Vannier, isn't that what happened?
Cazares: He contacted me to the best of my recollection.

Lazzara asked Cazares about his relationship with the FBI. We didn't expect Cazares to confess but we wanted to poke holes in his credibility and also lock him into testimony that we planned to demolish in the second phase of the trial, after we obtained the missing document from the FBI about his early meeting with FBI agent Phil McNiff in which they discussed me and my affiliation with the church.

Cazares testified that he had no relationship with the FBI and he denied being an FBI informant when specifically asked. Lazzara produced copies of the two FBI memos that showed contact between Cazares and FBI Agent Lunsford. Cazares admitted the meetings occurred but said he didn't recall what they were about.

Lazzara: Do you remember testifying in depositions in a lawsuit filed by the Church of Scientology, one in March of that year and the other in April, that you had no contact at all with the FBI?
Cazares: I forgot about those contacts.

Lazzara: You had two meetings within a couple of weeks of your depositions and you didn't remember them?

Cazares: I forgot about them.

Lazzara: You testified that the thought never entered your mind that Mr. Vannier was affiliated with the Church of Scientology, correct?

Cazares: Yes.

Lazzara: And you testified in a prior deposition that you did not learn about Mr. Vannier's affiliation with Scientology until November 1979 when church documents were released in the media, correct?

Cazares: Yes.

Lazzara: In fact, though, you had a meeting with FBI Special Agents Phil McNiff and Carl Hall on August 16, 1977 in which they discussed with you Mr. Vannier and his affiliation with the church, correct?

Cazares: If I did, I forgot about it.

Lazzara showed him a copy of the FBI memorandum to read and asked him if the document refreshed his memory.

Cazares: I seem to recall it now.

Lazzara: You also met with agent McNiff prior to that meeting in which Mr. Vannier and his affiliation with the church was discussed.

Cazares: I don't recall a prior meeting.

Lazzara: If agent McNiff said an earlier one occurred would you disagree?

Cazares: It may have happened if he said it did, but I don't recall it.

Lazzara: In fact you and agent McNiff discussed Mr. Vannier and his affiliation with the Church of Scientology prior to you asking him to represent you in your case against the church.

Cazares: No, he asked me to take the case and I did not know his affiliation.

* * *

Fernandez announced his next witness, James T. Russell, Pinellas County state attorney. Lazzara leapt to his feet. "Objection, your honor. Mr. Russell is not listed as a potential witness. The State Attorney's Office refused to turn over evidence in discovery and Your Honor admonished the Florida Bar and said that no one from the State Attorney's Office could be a witness against Mr. Vannier unless they submitted to discovery and turned over evidence. This is an outrage to the basic due process rights of a member attorney. You can't let this man testify."

Judge Hanlon said he wanted to hear what Russell had to say now that he was there, and Hanlon told Lazzara that he could request documents from the State Attorney's Office and take Russell's deposition during the hiatus of the trial and call him as a witness when the hearing resumes.

Russell testified that state law enforcement agencies, including his office, had received requests for information from the Church of Scientology to turn over their files regarding the church, and that those other agencies had turned to the State Attorney's Office for legal advice on how to respond. Russell testified that he heard something by someone about Mr. Vannier handling one of those calls to the State Attorney's Office, and that the officer who called was skeptical about the advice he received.

Russell: When I heard that, bells and gongs went off in my head. I told Myron Mensh (head of the St. Petersburg SAO) that we don't need that man anymore.

Fernandez: (to Lazzara): "Your witness."

Lazzara: Mr. Russell, can you identify for me the name of the person who told you about the call Mr. Vannier took from one of the law enforcement agencies?

Russell: No I can't. I don't recall who it was.

Lazzara: Can you identify that person's position?

Russell: No, I don't recall.

Lazzara: Did you receive that information by telephone or in person?

Russell: I don't remember that, either.

Lazzara: Can you provide the court with any details about the call Mr. Vannier received concerning that request for public information?

Russell: No, I don't recall any of the details.

Lazzara: So you have no personal information about the call?

Russell: No.

Lazzara: Your information is at least second hand, is that correct?

Russell: Yes.

Lazzara: Could it be that the person you heard the information from also received his information second hand?

Russell: Yes, that's possible.

Lazzara: Maybe even third hand?

Russell: I suppose that is also possible.

Lazzara: You testified that your investigation into the Church of Scientology was public knowledge. The Florida Bar has charged Mr. Vannier with applying for a position at the State Attorney's Office knowing there was an ongoing investigation of the church. Do you have any evidence that Mr. Vannier knew about the investigation prior to him going to work at the St. Petersburg office?

Russell: It was reported in the St. Petersburg Times.

Lazzara: Do you have any evidence that Mr. Vannier read that article in the St. Petersburg Times?

Russell: No, but if it was written in the Times then the Church of Scientology would have known about it.

Lazzara: I'm asking about Mr. Vannier's knowledge. He's the person charged with violating an ethics rule.

Russell: I have no direct evidence of Mr. Vannier's knowledge.

Lazzara: Mr. Russell do you know if one of the agencies that called the State Attorney's Office for advice may have been the St. Petersburg Police Department Intelligence Division?

Russell: That may have been the agency that Mr. Vannier took the call from.

Lazzara: Can you identify what files that agency may have had concerning the Church of Scientology?

Russell: They had no such files. I know that personally.

Lazzara: So why would that agency have a need for advice?

Russell: I've tried to alert you to the fact that I'm not even sure it was a member of the St. Petersburg Police Department who called him?

Lazzara: (to Judge Hanlon): Your Honor I move to strike the entirety of Mr. Russell's testimony and move to dismiss Count Six. It is clear that Mr. Russell has no personal knowledge that Mr. Vannier joined his office knowing about an ongoing investigation, and the investigation did not even exist in the office where he worked. Mr. Vannier cannot be charged with wrongdoing merely because he did not reveal his religious preferences or affiliations to a prospective employer. And Mr. Russell has no personal knowledge that Mr. Vannier engaged in improper conduct while working at his office. His testimony is entirely hearsay, and possibly hearsay upon hearsay upon hearsay, and therefore, is entirely worthless and a waste of everyone's time. I request that you strike it entirely.

Hanlon: Motion denied. But I will give it the weight it deserves.

Lazzara: It deserves no weight whatsoever.

Hanlon: Well, in that case, Mr. Lazzara, you have nothing to worry about.

Lazzara: Your Honor, if you're not going to strike his testimony then I demand an order that I be allowed to request documents from the State Attorney's Office and take the deposition of Mr. Russell.

Over Fernandez's objection, Judge Hanlon granted the request for discovery.

So ended the first phase of the trial. It was scheduled to resume on April 30, almost a full three months later.

* * *

"Let's nail the bastard for perjury," I said to Kohlweck and Lazzara in a telephone conference call. We were planning and budgeting our next moves. "Russell says there were no intel files, yet bells and gongs went off in his mind after I took a call from the Intel division. He can't have it both ways." Lazzara said he would subpoena for deposition both Russell's testimony and the SAO documents.

We also agreed that I would talk to a private investigator who had intelligence connections in the area, and get him to track down Sergeant Meinhart, the person from the Intel unit who had called me.

"Where are we at on the FBI commissions?" I asked Carl. A commission is the paperwork required to obtain out-of-state subpoenas for documents. Our main target was the FBI internal memo showing the earliest meeting between Agent McNiff and Gabe Cazares. Kohlweck said they were ready to move forward; he just had to get with Assistant U.S. Attorney Thomas Doughty and agree on dates for the turnover of documents. We were looking at March.

Kohlweck called me on March 1. He had dates from Doughty. Lazzara reported in, too. Depositions for the SAO documents and Russell's testimony were set.

* * *

"I just got off the phone with Doughty," Kohlweck said on the eve of the FBI's production of documents. "The FBI custodians of records have all been ordered not to appear at their depositions."

"What? Doughty agreed to it. What changed?"

"He just said that headquarters shut them down; that they feel they have given us enough." I asked him what he thought we should do. "We need a federal court order. Simple as that. A state bar referee cannot order the federal government to do anything."

We got Lazzara on the line. After updating him, I asked, "What will it take for you to go into federal court and get an order?" He said he would get me the numbers and, when he later did, I submitted a supplemental budget request to the church for approximately $25,000, and it was approved.

A few days later, Lazzara called. "The State Attorney's Office filed a motion for a protective order." That meant their depositions were on hold until the bar referee ruled on the motion. "Great," I said. "All of law enforcement is shutting down." Lazzara said he would oppose the motion and get a hearing as soon as possible.

* * *

"Sergeant Meinhart still works for the St. Petersburg Police Department's Intelligence Division," said Clayton Briggs, the private investigator. "He said he never heard your name, and that the only files they ever had relating to the Church of Scientology contained only newspaper clippings. They only monitored the news on Scientology."

"Of course they did," I said. "That's why they buried the files and labeled them the 'District 6 Investigation,' and the captain told them not to turn them over. God forbid that Scientologists find out the police were clipping newspaper articles about them."

Briggs said the commanding officer back then was not a captain, but Lieutenant Larry Reese. "He retired four years ago. "He also claims he never heard your name and doesn't know about any investigations related to Scientology, nor any files maintained by his office."

We had reached a dead end. The only remaining question was whether it was worth the time and money to subpoena them for depositions and force them to lie under oath. Neither the state attorney's office nor the U. S. Attorney would pursue criminal charges for perjury, so the question answered itself: it was a waste of resources.

* * *

"Judge Hanlon ruled that the state attorney has to turn over everything except documents that might be related to an ongoing investigation," Lazzara said.

"That could cover anything," I complained.

"That's what I said to the judge, but he said he refused to pre-judge what they should turn over. He made it clear, though, that they had to turn over any and all documents related to you by name or under the code name Ritz." I was skeptical. "It's probably okay," he said encouragingly. "I'll let you know how it goes."

Lazzara reported back to me at the end of the day. Russell was the only witness who appeared, testifying both as the custodian of records and in response to his witness subpoena. As custodian, he said he had no records at all to produce. "He said he couldn't find any regarding you. He refused to answer any questions about his filing system and what places he searched for documents. It doesn't appear his office made a diligent search."

I could see where the briefing was going. As with the FBI, the SAO had locked down. It appeared to be a joint strategy. We would have to fight to get anything else.

Lazzara went on, "Russell said he's been thinking a lot about this and is starting to remember things better. He now remembers a gap between the St. Petersburg Police Department call he received and the bells and gongs that went off in his head."

"Fucking liar. What a piece of work. And I'm the one under Bar charges. This guy should be in prison."

* * *

The following day I received a phone call that changed everything.

"Is this a good time?" The caller was K.O., former head of the MAC Unit when I was on church staff. Right away I knew something was wrong. For one thing, she was not the person I normally dealt with. For another, she seemed uncomfortable.

"Yeah, go ahead."

"I have bad news. Your supplemental budget has been cut."

I was stunned and took a moment to collect myself. "No. You can't let that happen, K.O." She said it wasn't her decision, that she couldn't do anything about it.

"Whose decision was it?"

"Listen, I know what you're thinking. But it wasn't just *your budget*. All legal budgets across the board were cut by an upper echelon." I pressed her for a specific answer but only got vague notions of some overseer of all church legal matters.

"Nope. Can't do that. They can't treat my budget like the others. The church made a commitment to me. I made a deal with the church based on its commitment to me. I put my law license on the line. I kept my end of the bargain, and I insist that the church keep its end."

She tried to mollify me. I let her go on for a little bit then cut her off. "I'm not going to be handled on this, K.O. You have to go back to whoever cut my budget and tell them they can't cut this one."

"Merrell, listen to me. I tried. I already raised a stink. You have to listen. The church's legal budgets lately have been astronomical. I know. I see the money gushing out each month. It has become too much. And all of them got cut. Not just yours. Everyone is pissed off. Everybody has something that can't be cut."

"K.O., this is me. You're talking to *me*. You and I both know how important this legal action is. We are on the verge of cracking open the innermost secret files of the FBI on Scientology. Just ask Bill Walsh. (He was the church's FOIA attorney with whom I had been coordinating regarding FBI documents.) He'll tell you how important this discovery action is. This represents everything we've fought for since I joined the MAC Unit. The key document has been identified and is within our grasp. It's just one federal court order away. No one on our side of the fence would cut the budget for this. You explain that to the people you're dealing with. Not this budget. They can't cut this budget."

"Merrell," she said gently. "I can't change this."

As soon as I got off the phone with her, I phoned John Peterson. He wasn't in. I left a message. I did not receive a return call.

Angie & John at our house, circa 1999

John and I cross 10K finish line, 1988

Our family at Big Bear Lake, California, Dec. 1988

Family photo, including son-in-law, 2000

Angie, Kansas City, 1975, age 4

Angie, Auditor of the Year, Shrine Auditorium

Fran & Angie share a blissful wedding moment

Our family with bride & groom, Oct. 1991

Part 4

SEEDS OF REFORM

Chapter 30

EMERGENCE

Men in general judge more from appearances than from reality.
All men have eyes, but few have the gift of penetration.

– Niccolo Machiavelli

Judge Hanlon handed down his ruling in late November 1985, almost seven months after the conclusion of the trial. I was cleared of the charges of taking adverse actions against Cazares, but was found guilty on all the others, including Count I, Solicitation and Count VI, the State Attorney's Office conflict of interest charge.

As to punishment, the ruling stated: "Ordinarily, based on the nature of the charges on which guilt has been found, the undersigned would only recommend suspension for a limited period of time, especially in view of the Respondent's [character evidence] and the further fact that some punishment has already been inflicted on the Respondent because of the length of this proceeding.

"However, the undersigned is recommending disbarment because the record in this case fully supports the conclusion that the Respondent would place his Scientology commitment, allegiance and ethics... above the ethics on which the Florida Bar is founded and on which all members of the profession depend. He reapplied for a staff position with the church in September

1980[23] notwithstanding his prior ethical problems which are directly attributable to his commitments to the Church of Scientology.

"The 'Fair Game' policies of the Church of Scientology directed against those persons who do not embrace their tenets and are deemed to be enemies, are repugnant to all fair minded people.

"The Respondent fully participated in the 'Fair Game' policy once, and there is no showing that he will not do so in the future. The policies, tenets and doctrine as found by L. Ron Hubbard are binding and adhered to by all members of the church."

Testimony about the Fair Game policy came from Bar witness Nan McLean, a former Scientologist, litigant against the church, and client of Walter Logan's, the same attorney who represented Cazares and drafted the original bar complaint against me. McLean left the Toronto Church of Scientology in 1972, prior to my involvement in Scientology, but was allowed to testify that all Scientologists would know about the policy (which was officially canceled in 1968) and would be required to follow it and do whatever was asked of them.

Bad facts make bad law, as the saying goes. Plus, I did not testify in my own behalf, leaving a vacuum into which the mounds of hearsay evidence against me were sucked. I didn't blame Judge Hanlon. The book on him was that he was a fair judge. It actually comes through in his ruling, as I interpreted it. Had he only heard from me he would have given me a limited suspension, which would have been the fair result in my view.

But, he made errors of law. He enhanced a penalty based on religious affiliation and his ruling violated a U.S. Supreme Court case that held a lawyer cannot be disbarred solely on hearsay evidence.

Peter Young was standing by to file an appeal to the Florida Supreme Court.

* * *

In late January 1986, a news alert rippled through the Scientology community. All Scientologists were summoned to the Hollywood Palladium Theater on Sunset Boulevard in Hollywood for a monumental briefing. Rumors of the death of LRH swirled as the 4,000-seat theater filled to capacity. I made it inside. Many did not. External speakers were set up to accommodate those standing outside.

A diminutive man wearing a navy blue Sea Org uniform confidently strode to a lone wooden podium on the stage. He had a baby face and appeared to be about twenty years old, only a kid, really. "Hello," he said in a baritone voice. "My name is David Miscavige." I had never heard the name before. He spoke in a somber, measured tone, and soon came to the point: L. Ron Hubbard had died the preceding Friday. As Miscavige spoke, I felt an odd sensation, a kind of shiver, reverberate through me. Not because of the news of LRH's death; I had been hearing whispers for several years that he was in poor health. My attention was on the pretty boy face of the speaker. I saw in him a strong personality, an unconcealed ruthlessness, and the aura of a tyrant and a bully. I also sensed in him a tinge of triumph, as though his moment had finally arrived. He was the first person I had seen in all the years I had been searching that checked all the boxes for the source of the domination, the propaganda, the purge mentality, and the heavy-handed style of management that had infused church leadership through the likes of Bill Franks and Norman Starkey.

That's him, I said to myself. The more he spoke, and the more I felt the essence of the man behind the words, the more convinced I became.

Another speaker, attorney Earle Cooley, followed Miscavige to the podium. He stated that LRH's body had been cremated and its ashes spread at sea on Saturday pursuant to the wishes expressed in his last will and testament. And then yet another person spoke whose name I had never heard before: Pat Broeker. He and his wife Annie lived with LRH and were his personal aides and confidants. He spoke softly and carried himself in a gentle manner. He expressed his devotion to LRH and said how wonderful it had been to work for such a kind, caring man. He read from something LRH had written before his death appointing him and Annie as Loyal Officers of the Sea Org, a new title, which suggested, without stating it, that the baton for control over the Sea Org and Scientology had been transferred to them, and not to David Miscavige.

I left the memorial confused. LRH was a stickler for making explicit statements in writing. "If it isn't in writing, it isn't true," is one of the most quoted Scientology policies. The purpose of the policy was to stop what he called a "hidden, verbal data line." My burning question was, why hadn't he expressed the transfer of control in writing?

Miscavige was clearly the one who had orchestrated the event and appeared to be in charge. I hoped to hell it wasn't him or that my impression of him was wrong.

Chapter 31

OVER THE RAINBOW

Authoritarian power, held by breaking or perverting ARC [Affinity-Reality-Communication], ... brings to management certain destruction and brings to the group reduced efficiency or death.

— L. Ron Hubbard[24]

"The church is not going to support your appeal to the U.S. Supreme Court," Howie Gutfield informed me. He was part of the Office of Special Affairs (OSA), and about the fifth person to hold that position since the church began funding my Bar case two and a half years earlier. It was now December 1986. In November the Florida Supreme Court denied my appeal and upheld the disbarment. My last chance to save my Florida law license rested with the United States Supreme Court.

I reminded him that the church had agreed to provide me a full defense. "My defense isn't over until my appeals are exhausted." He said church attorneys had advised them that the legal issue in my case had little chance of success. I asked for the names of the attorneys and he gave me three: Paul Johnson and Larry Fuentes (two of the Florida attorneys), and Eric Lieberman. The opinions of Johnson and Fuentes did not concern me: they were not Constitutional lawyers. Lieberman's did. He was one of the country's foremost Constitutional experts and part of the highly respected New York law firm co-founded by the renowned civil libertarian, Leonard Boudin.

Eric Lieberman was also a colleague of Peter Young's. The two of them had worked with Leonard Boudin on the Pentagon Papers case. I gave Young the news over the phone. He said he didn't believe Gutfield. Nor did I. Church staffers have rarely been honest in their dealings with me. Young contacted Lieberman and called me back.

"Eric said he hadn't even read the Florida Supreme Court ruling and had no opinion to offer anyone." Young said he gave Lieberman a summary of the ruling and told him that our single issue for the U.S. Supreme Court was whether a lawyer can be disbarred based solely on hearsay evidence. I had been denied the ability to confront and cross-examine the true witnesses against me, in violation of a basic Constitutional right. The problem with hearsay evidence is that the person who has actual knowledge of what is being testified about is not present, and therefore the knowledge and credibility of the absent person cannot be challenged.

"Eric thought the issue was strong and that we should pursue it. He promised to call church staff and tell them exactly that." I told Young I had a feeling the church was still not going to fund me. "I've been down this road many times before," I said. I gave him my opinion that an order had been issued from high up within the church and that Gutfield was only a messenger.

Young told me not to worry, he would not abandon me in my time of need. If the church refused to continue funding the case, I should let him know about it and we would work out something I could afford. Sure enough, the Church refused.

* * *

"I know you are loyal to the church," Young said after we agreed on terms I could afford. We were in his apartment. "But the church does not deserve your loyalty." He was atypically angry. He had never spoken disparagingly of the church in my presence before. I didn't take up his comment. "The church is the only reason you're in this mess," he continued, "and they have treated you shoddily at almost every turn."

He didn't know the half of it. Only rarely had I informed him of my contentious interactions with church staff. I always refrained from blaming the church and didn't want to start now by expressing my agreement with his sentiments. Besides, I viewed the church as an organization made up of thousands of individuals, the vast majority of whom were well-intentioned and had no part in the decisions related to my legal case. My beef was limited to one or more mostly unseen hands at the top of the organization.

"Peter, I have my role in all of this."

"I don't care," he snapped back. "You never turn on another team member even if they make a mistake." I was startled by his reaction. He turned his attention to his desk, idly straightening some of the clutter. Without looking up, he added: "I used to respect the church. I don't anymore."

* * *

Review of the Florida Supreme Court ruling was not the only matter on his plate. Young was also helping me with my California Bar admission case which was set for trial in January. He wrote a fabulous motion to exclude the rulings of both Judge Hanlon and the Florida Supreme Court based on procedural irregularities in both those proceedings. Normally each state is required to respect the judicial decrees of other states under the U. S. Constitution's Full, Faith and Credit Clause. An exception exists however where it can be shown that the other state's proceedings were the result of violations of Constitutional due process.

My attorney for the California case was Dave Clare, but Young appeared for the limited purpose of arguing the motion. The hearing was before a panel of three California lawyers. One member of the panel set the tone of the hearing before Young got a word out. "Can anyone tell me," he said, looking from Young to Clare to Patrick Dixon, the lawyer representing the California Bar, "why a California lawyer must wait five years after a disbarment to apply for reinstatement but a lawyer disbarred in the State of Florida can apply for admission after only two months?"

His question made clear the need to either exclude the Florida decision or have it overturned by the U. S. Supreme Court. Young gave a good answer, starting with the fact that the conduct at the heart of the Florida case occurred ten years ago. He then segued into his argument why California should disregard the Florida rulings.

The panel thanked him for his appearance then denied the motion.

* * *

"If you file it you will put Scientology at risk," Howie Gutfield warned after I advised him by telephone that I planned to seek review of the Florida decision with the U.S. Supreme Court. "Putting Scientology at risk" is a high crime in Scientology ethics and justice codes, and grounds for expulsion. So he was threatening me.

"That's pure speculation, Howie. The Supreme Court has historically come to the rescue of minority groups, even in the midst of strong public sentiment against them." I named a few examples: Jehovah Witnesses, the NAACP, and the Communist Party among them. I threw in the fact that the church's own Constitutional lawyer, Eric Lieberman, told Young that he thinks we should proceed.

Gutfield held his ground. Naturally. What else could he do? He had his orders. "I'm willing to discuss this with the source of your order," I said. "Otherwise I'm filing."

"You should consider the matter fully," Gutfield said. "I can guarantee you that your Scientology career is on the line." He said he would personally do everything in his power to have me *declared* and that "others" will act similarly.

"Howie," I said pointedly, "I don't respond to threats. I told you I would talk to the source of the order. This conversation is over." I hung up.

Over the next few days a string of staff members called me and represented that they were the ones who made the decision. All but one, at a maximum, was lying. Every conversation started and ended with a threat of a Declare. My choice of words was not always repeatable. John Peterson, church in-house counsel, finally returned one of my messages asking for his assistance in obtaining a meeting with the decision-maker.

He told me that K.O. was the source of the order. "She's number eight," I said.

"What do you mean?"

"She's the eighth source of the order." I let my bitterness show. He said he was sorry to hear that and would do his best to arrange the meeting.

* * *

I met K.O. in George's restaurant on Fountain Avenue. She was the source of the order. Really, she said. She gave me the same reasons Gutfield gave me for not pursuing my appeal. The main difference between her and the others was that she was respectful and non-threatening; I could converse with her.

"K.O., let me talk to you about my life. Last December I was offered seventeen percent ownership of the independent insurance adjusting company I worked for. The owner made the offer based on my production record and contribution to the expansion of his company from a four-man firm to a statewide company. I turned him down. Why? Because I was confident that the Florida Supreme Court would rule in my favor and I would get licensed in California.

"I've already started a law firm with Norman Taylor." K.O. knew Taylor. He used to work in the church's legal department and went to law school after he left the staff. "We plan to specialize in the Lemon Law," a law that entitles purchasers of new vehicles to a refund or a replacement vehicle if their car proves defective, a 'lemon.'

"This law is on the books but I discovered that not one single automobile manufacturer is in compliance with it. No one at any of these companies is trained in handling this type of claim nor is there a person authorized to either refund or replace a vehicle. I'm excited about it. We can help a lot of people who don't know about the law or how to utilize it.

"My wife is pregnant. She is due at the end of May. Saving my Florida license and obtaining my California license means everything to me and my family.

"I have done so much for the church. I appeased the wishes of upper management at the risk of losing my license, and I kept my end of the agreement. You know the church did not keep its end. Yet I have been accused of being selfish and only looking after my own interests. I have been given orders all along the way and threatened with Declares if I didn't automatically comply with them."

K.O. said she was truly sorry I had been treated that way and agreed that I deserved better.

"It's more than that, K.O. What has our church become if people in management positions can order parishioners to do things in their private and professional lives without them even knowing who issued the order? Who would want to join a church like that? Treating members as though you own and control them really does put Scientology at risk, and is the hallmark of a cult. I mean, where the hell is that idea coming from? There's no policy basis for issuing orders to non-staff Scientologists."

K.O. said she understood and regretted that some church staff members get carried away, but pointed out the incredible demands and stress put on a limited number of people who are handling crises of great magnitude.

"There's no justification for issuing orders to me or to any public Scientologist. The practice should stop. Talk to them. Reason with them, yes, definitely. But the church shouldn't order them about. No one can plan their lives and be subject to out-of-the-blue orders issued by people who know nothing about their plans and personal situations. No one in their right mind would subject themselves to that."

She said my relationship with the church was a unique exception, and the church, existing in an imperfect world, was not perfect, and then went into my petition to the U. S. Supreme Court. She felt it could potentially harm the church's interests, and therefore I should voluntarily refrain from filing it.

"I got that. People are entitled to their opinions. I have a different one. And I'm prepared to accept responsibility for my actions. If my request for Supreme Court review actually harms the church, I will stand accountable. Until then, it's just your opinion versus mine – and Peter Young's and Eric Lieberman's, both of whom are far more qualified to render an opinion than either you or me."

She maintained her position and the longer we spoke the more convinced I became that she was not the source of the order. We eventually agreed that our meeting had run its course.

"So, what do you plan to do?" she asked. I told her I planned to appeal. The disappointment showed on her face, but to her credit she did not resort to threats of a Declare. "Okay," is all she said.

She never threatened me, but more "sources" of the order did. One was even put in writing. In a letter dated February 19, 1987, Warren McShane, the "Legal Affairs Manager" of RTC (Religious Technology Center) wrote, "[Y]our continuation of the appeal process would be a Suppressive Act not only to all Scientologists but to all American citizens. I can assure you that the Church shall treat any such Suppressive act in accordance with policy." He meant I would be *declared*.

I kept moving forward. When Young finished the brief, I reviewed it and sent it to the printer. Briefs filed with the U. S.

313

Supreme Court must be professionally typeset and printed. It isn't cheap.

* * *

Three days before the filing deadline, I was contacted by Mike Sutter, a name I had never heard before. He said he was the supervisor over OSA Int (Office of Special Affairs International). OSA replaced the G.O. as the entity responsible for handling external affairs. OSA Int was the equivalent of the former Guardian's Office Worldwide, but instead of being headquartered in England, its offices were in Hollywood.

"Over the rainbow," I said into the phone, more as a question than a statement. The term referred to the upper most strata of international management, the location of which was ultra secret but was rumored to be in the vicinity of Palm Springs, California.

"Yeah, I'm over the rainbow. Actually, I alternate between being supervisor of OSA Int and commanding officer of OSA Int with Kurt Weiland." (Another new name for me.) "Kurt and I rotate every six months."

He asked if we could meet to go over his order that I not file my petition to the U.S. Supreme Court. "You're now the thirteenth person to claim responsibility for the order," I said, wanting to hear how he reacted to me speaking directly.

"Yeah, that sucks. There's really no excuse for it, either." He went on to say that he hoped he could have a chance to get to know me and make up for all the screw-ups. I agreed and we scheduled a meeting for 8:30 that evening.

We met alone in an office at the Scientology complex on Sunset Boulevard. Dressed in a navy blue Sea Org uniform, he offered his hand and said he was glad to meet me, and again apologized for the way I had been hassled by lower level staff. He asked me to take a seat in front of his large desk.

He began to take up my Supreme Court petition, but I stopped him and said I would prefer to start by clearing the air.

"Sure," he said. I gave him highlights of my journey, starting with the deal I had made with the church. I hesitated on that one. "Were you aware and agreeable to that deal?" He nodded and said yes.

I went over the large numbers of staffers I had to interact with, probably twenty different people in all, some of whom I had never met before. "That's been one of the issues," I said. "No single terminal. John Peterson would have been the perfect one, since he and I are both lawyers, but he was rarely available." Sutter took it all in, bobbing his head along the way, throwing in an occasional apology.

"Another major problem is that low-level staff members who deal with me are issued orders and expected to carry them out. They can't reason with me or alter their orders based on facts I provide them. I'm a party in litigation, a co-party with the church in the civil cases. I'm in a decision-making position, yet I don't have contact with decision-makers in the church. Because you're at the top of the organization, and you issue orders down the chain of command, you might not realize what lower level staffers do with those orders."

Sutter scrunched his face as though considering for the first time the viewpoint of parishioners at the other end of orders into OSA from upper management and was intrigued by it.

For an example, I told him an of experience I encountered while preparing my opening brief to the Florida Supreme Court. Greg Shulman, who was an OSA staffer, gave me an order to rewrite the introduction to the brief. "He told me Eric Lieberman said it was only adequate, not good. Well, I thought it was great, so I called Eric, and he said he had not even read the brief or commented at all about it. "When I called Greg back and confronted him with Eric's statement, he said, and I quote, 'Oh, I wonder why he said that,' and then went on to something else."

Sutter shook his head and said, "Amazing."

"Another example is this order for me not to file my U. S. Supreme Court petition. As I told you, twelve other people claimed to be the source of the order. Only one of them did not get heavy-handed with me. Only one of them did not threaten me with a Declare. And that was Kathy O'Gorman."

Sutter struck a puzzled look. "You thought K.O. was the source of the order?" His question threw me since I had just finished saying so. "K.O. is not even in Legal."

That was news to me. "She isn't?"

"No. She's in finance."

I was shocked. I felt like a little kid who just learned there was no Santa Claus. "Well, all the more reason I shouldn't have to deal with low-level staff."

"I agree." He snatched a pen, scribbled something on a notepad, and handed me a note. "Here's my phone number. From now on I'm your terminal. If you run into any problems with OSA staff in the future, call me and I will take care of it."

I took the note, smiling. "Gee, thanks. I appreciate this."

"No problem," he said with a wave of his hand, as though we were buds to the end. "And that goes for *anything*, not just your legal cases."

"Wow. Cool." The air cleared. "Okay, I'm done. Thanks for hearing me out."

Sutter took over. "Let me give you some information to enable you to better understand why I prefer you not to file your appeal." He went over the church cases that were either currently before or on their way to the U.S. Supreme Court.

He said the case that concerned the church most was Wollersheim. One year earlier, a Los Angeles County jury had awarded former member Larry Wollersheim $5 million in compensatory damages and $25 million in punitive damages for what jurors found constituted intentional and negligent infliction of emotional distress.

This was the same case in which Carl Kohlweck had negotiated a $250,000 pre-trial settlement and was promptly fired when he recommended it to the church. Sutter wasn't aware that I knew about the missed opportunity to avoid the horrendous Wollersheim verdict and save the church tens of millions of dollars in legal fees and costs and probably an equal amount in bad press. And now I was being asked to forego my right of petition in order to save the church from this colossal screw-up.[25] *That's rich. The perks of being a dictator.*

Sutter leaned forward in his high-back executive chair and pulled a small stack of press clippings from a folder. "This is the negative press your Florida Bar case has generated." He handed me a stack of articles. All Florida publications. I hadn't seen them before. They were nasty. I commented that I was surprised the story had not made national news. I really was. Sutter didn't take up my comment.

"Let me give you upper management's viewpoint." He launched into his spiel: The G.O. activities of the 1970s nearly destroyed the church. It was barely saved by the CMO (Commodore's Messenger Organization). A very bad image of the church was created by the G.O. Current management and staff have been working night and day for years to turn it around. "We don't want *any* mention of 1970s activities *anywhere*. The G.O. people involved in these activities are regarded *very* poorly. They're lucky to still be in good standing and receiving Scientology services. Any problems from them in regard to bad press will not be tolerated."

"People shouldn't lump me into that group," I said. "One of my major objections is the way I'm regarded by OSA staff. What you just said helps explain it. The fact is, however, I actually helped clean up G.O. activities once I got on staff, which was before the appearance of CMO."

"I agree. We regard you differently since you were only a G.O. volunteer back when G.O. crimes were being committed."

"How do you regard me? I asked. "Honestly."

Sutter leaned back in his chair and smiled. "You want to know how we honestly feel about you? Okay I'll tell you, and this is the absolute truth. We think you have the balls of an elephant." He laughed. "That's the honest truth. No one can believe the balls you've got. We actually say that about you: 'Man, this guy has the balls of an elephant.'"

I smiled politely, but I wasn't in the same groove. First, I didn't feel that way about myself. I was thinking I'd been rather wimpy. Had it been any other organization, and had it not been for my desire to practice Scientology, the religion of my choice, I would not have taken the slightest bullshit off these guys, yet I had taken truckloads of it. Second, there was something revolting about the underlying attitude his comment revealed. Why should a Scientologist need balls of any size to navigate the red tape of OSA? It was like a totalitarian dictator admiring an individual citizen who dares to speak freely, and more evidence of the personality behind the rule by force and domination that I first saw and detested after the takeover of the G.O.

"We don't lump you into the G.O. crimes category," he continued. "Honestly. The two things the G.O. did that are killing the church today are: one, they committed crimes and then kept all the documents of their crimes in file cabinets that could be raided; and two, they sabotaged the handling of the civil cases. You weren't involved in either one of those. In fact, you're as much a victim of those things as the church is."

He propped his elbows on the desk. "One thing we isolated is that any legal case in which the seized documents get into evidence, either before a judge or a jury, we lose. Every single case. That happened to you, too.

"So we said, 'Fuck this shit. Get rid of any case that has seized documents as part of the record. Those documents are toxic. They're the kiss of death.' If you go forward with your appeal, you'll lose, because seized documents are part of the record in your case. It always happens that way. You will lose and the seized documents will poison the minds of the Supreme Court justices and then the church will lose its cases, too."

His argument made sense. It was plausible and rational. I also got the idea that he was not the source of the order. He kept speaking in the third person: *we* this, and *we* that. But I believed he was right up there with the big dogs.

"Let me ask you this," he said while I was thinking things over. "If you go forward and we lose Wollersheim, how would you feel about that?"

"Not good because I hope the church prevails. But without more information I would not connect the loss with the filing of my request for review."

Sutter sat erect and stared into my eyes. "You know, like it or not, the cold hard truth of the matter is that we're running things today, and we control the use of the technology."

I was astounded. I thought Scientology belonged to anyone and everyone who desired to study and pursue it. I always felt the subject was free in that sense. Sure, the courses and auditing cost money, but money is needed to keep the doors open. And that's the way it used to be. Sutter's pronouncement made it clear that the authority of OSA and upper management for issuing orders to parishioners came not from a written policy or Scientology tenets, but by fiat. They can do and order anything they want merely because they are in charge. It was a scary thought. Yet it totally explained what I had been up against. I wondered to whom this oppressive idea traced, and I had a good idea, but that was for another day.

"Are you saying I'll be *declared* if I proceed with my petition."

He calmly and confidently nodded his head, "Yes."

"Okay. So I have a lot to think about over the next couple of days. If I decide not to file the brief, will you compensate me for my current costs and expenses? I have about $10,000 into this."

"No."

"Will you at least cover my printing costs, which are a little over $1,500?"

Same answer.

"The church promised me a full defense of my Florida Bar case and I was assessed court costs by the Florida Bar in the approximate amount of $6,000. I would like that paid."

"Submit a written request. I can't promise you it will get approved, but that one seems reasonable to pay." (I did submit a request and it was denied.)

* * *

That evening I told Fran about my talk with Sutter. The conversation went very much like the one we had three years earlier concerning my decision whether to cooperate with authorities or make a deal with the church. We considered our Scientologist friends, Angie, her school and her friends, and our desire to remain eligible for Scientology services. We felt like we were over a barrel and hated being in that position.

Fran eventually asked the key question: what was the chance of success? The U.S. Supreme Court accepts one out of fifty applications for writs, I told her. "That's a two percent chance that they even issue a writ. And that doesn't include how they'll rule on our petition. I could still win or lose on that."

My answer more or less ended the conversation. The odds were too long.

* * *

In March the California Bar admission panel ruled that I had failed to meet my burden of proof to demonstrate I had the requisite moral character to become a member of the California bar. I appealed the decision to the Committee of Bar Examiners. A hearing was scheduled for the middle of May.

In the meantime I was contacted by an OSA staff member and told not to appeal my admissions case, to just drop the matter. I called the phone number Mike Sutter gave me. A woman answered. I left a message. Sutter did not return my call. I left two or three more messages before I gave up.

I was financially tapped out and could not afford to pay a lawyer to appear on my behalf at the hearing before the Committee of Bar Examiners, so I presented my own appeal. When I finished one of the committee members took over. He summarized for the other members the case in Florida against me, then tore into me with a blistering cross-examination while the other members looked on with unsympathetic eyes.

"You were subpoenaed to appear as a witness before a Pinellas-Pasco grand jury, but did not appear, did you?" "You challenged the subpoenas, in fact. Why?" He took up each civil suit deposition in which I took the Fifth rather than answer the questions. I responded to each salvo as politely as I could, which was difficult given the fact that I was talking mostly to lawyers who have read and studied the U. S. Constitution, some of whom had probably even advised a client or two to take the same steps I took. He asked about my membership in and affiliation with the Church of Scientology, and I told the Committee that they should not make assumptions about the extent of my knowledge or agreement with church policies and practices, and cited California and U. S. Supreme Court decisions declaring such assumptions are constitutionally impermissible.

"The point I'm making," he finally said, "is that you covered up the misdeeds of the church by your failure to testify in Florida."

So that's what it came down to in both Florida and California. Testify if you want to practice law. Pay the price if you don't. I responded to the Committee but saw the effect my words were having on them and knew they were falling on deaf ears.

* * *

Ten days after the hearing my son John was born, on May 26. Two days later I received notice from the Committee that my appeal had been denied.

That was a tough night and I couldn't sleep. I went into my home office, sat at my desk, hung my head and cried. I felt as though the whole world was against me. The two groups I had joined, the church and the legal profession, both hated me. At least the powers that be in each group did. At my lowest point, I heard a stir in the crib near my desk. My newborn son had awakened. The moment I looked over the crib rail he grinned. I saw the unconditional love in his face. *He* didn't hate me. He didn't care that I didn't have a law license. True, he didn't know what the hell one was, but that was the point: I was his dad, and nothing else mattered. I picked him up and hugged him, and began to realize what all I did have. I had him. I had Angie. I had Fran. And that mattered most. I would somehow make do with everything else.

Chapter 32

LEAVING THE NEST

Watching your daughter being collected by her date feels like handing over a million-dollar Stradivarius to a gorilla.

– Jim Bishop
American journalist/author

"Have you thought about what you want to do after graduation?" I asked Angie, sitting at the kitchen table with Fran. She was the equivalent of a senior in public high school at Delphi Academy, a private school in La Cañada. She said she was interested in training to be an auditor. We knew she had that interest, we just didn't know how strong the interest was. "Are you interested in going to college?" I asked. She had no definite interest at the time. "Maybe later."

"Here's what mom and I talked about: We will support you in whatever decision you make but if you're interested in training to be an auditor we want to make a deal with you." I offered that we would pay for her Scientology training through a certain level, including the internship and all the materials, and an E-meter, too. At the time, that training package cost $10,000.

"On one condition. Promise that you will finish the entire program before you decide to join staff or the Sea Org or go to college." Joining staff meant signing a contract for up to five years in a Scientology organization as I had done twice, once in

St. Louis and again for the G.O. The Sea Org was a lifetime commitment on the order of joining the priesthood.

Angie broke into a broad grin and gave a robust, "Agreed."

"I want to make sure we have a solid agreement, because you can always join staff now and get the training for free, and the cost of the training package is a lot of money for us." She said she understood.

I explained that I had taken that same training package during a break in law school and it remained the best decision I had made in my life and I wished I had known about it and taken it before college or making any major decisions about the rest of my life. She said she appreciated the advice, which fit with her thinking; she actually wanted to learn to be an auditor before she decided about her future.

Just to make sure we had a clear agreement, I added: "Angie, when you get on course you will be recruited.".

She said she already had. Sea Org recruiters had come by Delphi Academy. That was news to me. "Oh?" I stole a glance at Fran, who also seemed surprised. "What did you tell them?"

"That I wasn't interested at the time."

"Okay, but recruitment will become more intense after you get out of high school and on course at CC." I knew she planned to do her training at Celebrity Centre because she and some of her friends had already taken introductory courses there and she was, after all, a minor celebrity in her own right. She acted and modeled as a child, and still did a gig or two, although her current age group was a dead zone for all but the top-name talents. CC was a Sea Org organization, meaning that all staffers were members of the Sea Org, and Sea Org recruiters could be persistent – and persuasive.

She said she knew that. "Dad, I want to do this." The excitement in her face convinced us of her resolve. She sealed the deal with a big hug.

* * *

Two years later: "Dad, I want to join the Sea Org." She was on her internship, just shy of completing the entire training package. "Mom said it was okay with her if it was okay with you."

"Angie, we had an agreement." She knew, and planned to honor it if I held her to it. "What are we talking about? Three, four weeks?" She agreed but said she had been promised she could complete the internship upon joining the Sea Org.

I held my ground.

A few days later she said, "Dad, I really want to join now."

Again, I held my ground.

The following evening she called during a course break and asked me if I would meet with her Sea Org recruiters. "Just a second, Angie." I cupped the phone. "She wants me to meet with her recruiters." Fran shrugged, as if to say, *so do it.*

"She knows my position. Why is she doing this?" I had the answer as soon as the question passed my lips. Fran gave it. "Because they're putting pressure on her and she won't go against her father's wishes. You should go in and take the pressure off her."

I groaned. "Big help, you are." She laughed.

"Okay," I said to Angie. "I'll be there in half an hour." She gave me a hearty thanks and I said, "Yeah, yeah. You're welcome."

I was greeted by two young men dressed in Sea Org uniforms in the lobby of Celebrity Centre. They were kids, really, perhaps twenty. "Are you Angie's dad?" one of them asked. I nodded and he offered his hand. "Greg LaClaire." He introduced his partner, too. I've forgotten his name.

They led me to a desk and Greg asked what it would take for me to let Angie join the Sea Org. "I don't mind if she joins the Sea Org," I said. Greg cocked his head and grinned at his partner. "Oh. She said she had to wait until she finished the internship."

"She's talking about a promise she made to her parents in return for us buying her the training package."

"So she can't join the Sea Org now because of that agreement?" Greg said.

"If she wants to keep her agreement with me, yes, she can't join the Sea Org, or staff, or go to college, until she completes the internship."

"So you're blocking her from joining the Sea Org now."

"No. She's nineteen. I can't block her from joining the Sea Org. She can join whenever she wants." Greg and the other guy shared puzzled, skeptical looks.

"But she won't do that because of her promise to you," the other guy said.

"That's what I understand. We raised her to honor her agreements and it looks like we've done a good job on that."

Greg said that Angie had been accepted into the Tech Training Unit, which meant that she would go straight into training and be trained through the highest level, which was required for Celebrity Centre staff auditors and is the equivalent in time and hours to a master's degree program in college. He added that Angie would be allowed to complete her internship prior to being placed on the EPF, a sort of boot camp for Sea Org recruits.

I said that Angie told me the same thing.

"Then why not let her join now?" the other guy said.

"Why don't you let her honor her agreement with her parents and take her off your product board for a few weeks? See? It works both ways, but you want to turn it on me and I really shouldn't be part of the equation."

Greg's demeanor shifted. He became serious, and with it, his uniform became more prominent. He said he wanted me to release her from the agreement.

"In all due respect to you and your position in the Sea Org, you need to butt out of my relationship with my daughter. What takes place between her and me is a private matter and none of your business."

Greg reminded me that he was a recruiter for the Sea Org and that Angie was ready and willing to join, and that I was preventing that from happening. His face grew stern as he spoke. His buddy looked like he was ready to pounce on me.

"Hey guys. Don't get heavy with me. I came all the way from La Crescenta to meet with you. Please recognize that. I mean, come on, you want her to join the Sea Org, right?" They nodded. "You want her to sign a billion year contract, and you can't wait three weeks?"

Greg accused me of being "out-ethics," a Scientology term that means unethical. He then went into a sermon about the altruistic aims of the Sea Org, saving the planet and so on.

I took his response as a "no" to my question. I got up to go, and they jumped to their feet. I turned to leave and Greg's pal jumped in front of me. "Is this going to get physical?" I said. His stature slackened and I passed by him.

Two days later I got something in the mail from Greg. It was a copy of a KR he had written on me. A KR is a Knowledge Report. In the Navy, we called it a chit, a report of wrongdoing, a violation of the rules, etc. I was outraged. "That asshole KR'ed me," I said to Fran. "Look. He sent copies of the damn thing everywhere." I flashed the paper so she could see the top of it, which designates the job titles of all the recipients of the report. Greg's KR said I was "counter-intention to the Sea Org," opposed to its aims, in other words, and presented his version of our meeting in support of his charge.

"I knew I shouldn't have gone in there. Now I have to take time to correct this piece of shit KR." Which I did after I calmed down. I sent copies to all the recipients of the KR and its author.

Angie finished her internship a few weeks later and joined the Sea Org.

* * *

"Someone proposed to me," Angie announced to Fran and me a few months later. She asked for our permission to marry. Fran was ecstatic, and gave her a big hug.

"Gee," I said. "Who's the lucky guy? Anybody I know?"

She paused and gave me an uneasy look. "Well, actually you do know him. Greg LaClaire."

"Oh, no. Don't tell me it's him. That won't work for me, Angie. Come on, you can do better than that." Angie kept her cool as Fran broke out laughing. "What are you doing? This isn't funny." She cupped her mouth but couldn't suppress her laugh. "I'm sorry," she managed to say through the laughter.

Then something struck me. "Wait a minute, Fran. This could be worse than I thought. Angie, did he have an interest in you during your recruitment?"

She admitted he did. "See, Fran? This guy had an ulterior motive and KR'ed my ass without disclosing any of it. I'm sorry, Angie, but this is not okay with me. I have some outstanding issues with OSA Int. (One of the recipients of the KR.) I haven't gone into it with you, and I won't now, because it's my personal problem and I'm working to sort it out, but a KR accusing me of blocking the recruitment of a Sea Org member goes on top of my other issues, and hurts me. I know Greg didn't know any of this, but his conduct is reckless and an abuse of his power as a Sea Org member. It's just a really, really bad sign and I don't want anything to do with him. I don't approve of you marrying him."

Angie said she was sorry about the trouble his KR caused and that she would not marry him without my blessing. "He knows he was wrong about the way he treated you and he plans to withdraw the KR and write you an apology letter."

"Yeah, well, it better be a damned good one."

After Angie left I said to Fran, "I can't believe this is happening. Of all the guys in the world she picks this one."

Fran took me by the arm. "But honey, she loves him." I rolled my eyes. She reminded me that I gave her an engagement ring knowing her mother wanted her to attend business school in Des Moines before we got engaged.

"But I didn't KR her," I said, joking. She laughed, and I added: "I'm glad you can see the difference."

The next time Angie visited she asked if I had received Greg's letter. I told her I had. "What did you think about it?" I told her I appreciated the letter and was also pleased he had withdrawn the KR. "But, to be honest, I still have a bad feeling about him."

I was reluctant to go any further with my candor, which would have meant explaining that I didn't like the direction in which the Sea Org and the church were headed. The domination and control bothered me. At first it was limited to the top management echelon, but it was gradually trickling down from the hierarchy, through the staff, and onto regular church members. If the church had been like that when I first became interested in Scientology I would have run the other way. And if I felt that way, Scientologists and even the general public must perceive it, too, and shy away and never learn about or receive the benefits of the technology. It was a troubling trend and I thought Greg was riding the wrong wave. He was a neophyte; not nearly as bad as, say, Norman Starkey and Bill Franks, but I saw in him an impressionable zealot who could become that way. He reminded me of the character Rolfe in *The Sound of Music*, the telegram boy who was in love with "Sixteen Going on Seventeen" Liesl, but later blew the whistle on Liesl and her family during their escape from the Nazis. Greg even bore a resemblance to Rolfe. But I didn't say any of that.

Angie nodded respectfully and didn't push it.

Months went by. Angie, who lived in a Sea Org dorm, visited often but didn't bring up Greg. After one of her visits I asked Fran if she was still interested in marrying him. "Of course. She's in love." I asked her if Angie was upset with me for not blessing her marriage. "No. She loves you, too. She'll wait as long as she has to wait."

"Do you think I'm being ridiculous?" I asked. She said I was being true to my own feelings about Greg, which was my right and duty as her father.

The next time Angie visited, I motioned her aside and asked if she still wanted to marry Greg. She said she did and added that she thought that I would like him, too, if I got to know him under different circumstances.

"Well then, I guess I misjudged him. If he's good enough for you, he's good enough for me. You have my approval to marry him."

Angie was bursting with glee. She gave me a big hug and a kiss. Fran ran into the room and Angie lunged for her with open arms. "He said I could marry Greg." After they hugged, Fran came to me. "Thank you. See how happy you've made her." She then gave me a kiss. One big happy family. Or rather, one small happy family.

* * *

Angie went on to complete her higher level training and became the top auditor at Celebrity Centre, and later its Senior Case Supervisor, meaning that she oversaw the case progress of all CC parishioners and the auditing standards of all staff auditors. She was widely loved and admired, as I was constantly reminded by people when they learned she was my daughter.

The rules prohibited Angie from telling us which celebrities she counseled, but we heard plenty from others who could share the information. For example, Fran and I became friends with John Haigney and his wife Lee Ann, the sister of Tom Cruise. We met John and Lee Ann when we picked up our son at day care. Their son, Sean, was one of our son John's best friends. When Lee Ann learned that we had a daughter on staff at Celebrity Centre, and that it was Angie, she reacted excitedly. "Angie LaClaire is your daughter! She audited my sister, Cass. Tom loves Angie for the job she did for Cass."

We became close friends and eventually met everyone in her family not named Tom. Lee Ann kept us updated on Angie's activities that involved her family. So when Angie would tell us that she was going out of town to New Jersey (where Tom's family resided at the time) or to Telluride, Colorado (one of

Tom's residences), we knew the purpose of the trip from Lee Ann.

One day I dropped by Celebrity Centre and ran into the Rev. Alfreddie Johnson, a Baptist minister from inner-city Los Angeles. He ran a community outreach program where I had assisted him on most Saturdays over a period of five years. He said he always wanted to help steer inner city youth away from drugs and gangs and toward productive lives, but nothing really worked until he discovered Scientology's Study Technology. "Finally I had some tools that worked," he said. He put the word out for persons trained in the Technology to volunteer as tutors, and I responded.

"What are you doing here?" Alfreddie asked. "Is this your church?" I told him I had just come by to see my daughter. "Who's that?" he asked, and I gave Angie's name.

"Angie is your daughter?" he said with a surprised reaction much like Lee Ann's. "She's Isaac's auditor. He loves Angie." He meant Isaac Hayes. I had seen him promote Scientology and perform at Scientology events. I assumed that he had received Scientology services. Alfreddie's comment confirmed it.

"Really?" I said. "I didn't know that."

"Yeah. Isaac can't say enough good things about her." He stared at me in amazement. "Man, I didn't know Angie was your daughter."

Chapter 33

TRUTH REVEALED

Power tends to corrupt and absolute power corrupts absolutely.

– Lord Acton
English Catholic historian/politician/writer

"Hey," I said into the phone. "Marty Rathbun and Mike Rinder just went public." Rathbun had been the right hand man of David Miscavige for twenty-some years and Rinder was the former Commanding Officer of OSA Int and the spokesman for the church. "No shit?" the voice at the other end of the line said.

"No shit," I said. "I just e-mailed you two links. One is to a *St. Petersburg Times* article.[26] The other is to a video series[27] of an in-depth interview with Marty. "Check them out and call me back."

I was speaking to a person I would later dub Letterhead.[28] In the article dated June 21, 2009, and in related videos, Rinder, Rathbun and two other former high-ranking international executives, and further alleged that David Miscavige tightly controlled all of Scientology in a maniacal, sadistic manner that included unprovoked physical violence against international Scientology executives alleged that Miscavige "commands such power that managers follow his orders, however bizarre, with lemming-like obedience."

Rinder, who claimed he was physically attacked by Miscavige more than 50 times, said, "The issue wasn't the physical pain of it. The issue was the humiliation and the domination. It's the fact that the domination you're getting – hit in the face, kicked – and you can't do anything about it. If you tried, you'd be attacking COB," meaning Chairman of the Board of Religious Technology Center, Miscavige's official position.

Rathbun said Miscavige's "mistreatment of staff has driven away managers and paralyzed those who stay. It's becoming chaos because there's no form of organization. Nobody's respected because he's constantly denigrating and beating on people."

When asked by the interviewer how Miscavige gets away with it, Rathbun said, in the video clip entitled "Command and Control," that Miscavige instills such a level of control and fear that people don't defy him. "He's so vengeful that you can be persona non grata for the next twelve years if you ever do anything that indicates that you have any intention that is even slightly different than any of his intentions. You could be head of the (highly respected Watchdog Committee, an administrative body comprised of international executives) and if you even sneezed wrong he could have you busting rocks for the next twelve years. So there was that fear factor.

"Also he has managed to convince Scientologists that he is the anointed one, appointed by L. Ron Hubbard to carry forward (his) legacy. It's a complete and utter, one hundred percent bald faced lie. But he successfully orchestrated it and they believe it. And when they believe that, they're willing to do almost anything."

In the video clip entitled "Core Beliefs," Rathbun explained that there is a 180-degree dichotomy of approach between Founder L. Ron Hubbard and Miscavige; that the purpose of Scientology is to make a person more himself, but Miscavige uses Scientology to mold behavioral patterns. Rathbun also said that the policy of disconnection, which was canceled in 1968, was intended by Hubbard to be a common sense thing: if you're with somebody who is dragging you down, it's your right not to listen to them. But that Miscavige manipulated reports to Hubbard that induced him to reinstate the policy, and Miscavige has turned it into a dictate to control members' communications and loyalties.

Hubbard used Scientology to free people; Miscavige uses the technology to dominate and control them.

Consequently, Rathbun said in the clip entitled "Scientology in Decline?" the key delivery statistics (auditing and training) have been in a twenty-year decline dating back to about three years after Hubbard's death in 1986, when Miscavige obtained full control.

An hour or so later, Letterhead called me back. "That explains everything, doesn't it?" Letterhead had his own run-ins with OSA Int. and was the only person with whom I had shared some of my stories. From our individual experiences we both knew there was something rotten at the top so we compared notes in an effort to isolate the source, which I strongly suspected was Miscavige.

"Everything," I agreed.

"What are we going to do about it?"

"I don't know. I think we need to see it play out a little."

It played out like this: Rathbun revealed more information on his blog, and encouraged members to withdraw their support for the church and publicly announce their independence. Many did. Meanwhile the church, which we now understood was really Miscavige and persons acting under his complete control, counterattacked, calling the former high-ranking Sea Org members liars and flatly denying their charges. The media jumped in, and there were hints of law enforcement investigations and calls for revocation of the church's tax-exempt status.

"I don't want to leave the church," Letterhead said. "It's my church. I want that son-of-a-bitch (Miscavige) to leave."

I agreed and said, "I'm glad they spilled the beans but I want to reform the church, not destroy it," adding that the solution to charges of corporate corruption is an independent internal investigation conducted by persons not accused of wrongdoing. Neither of us knew how to influence that result. We decided to discreetly reach out to other professionals while we continued to monitor the situation.

* * *

Letterhead introduced me to "Chris" on a conference call. While getting acquainted he asked about my work under the False Claims Act.[29] I worked on behalf of the government in a dozen of such cases, including what was once the biggest health care fraud case in the country, not as an attorney but as an investigator/paralegal. "Fifty FBI agents with an 18-wheeler truck raided the billing company's offices."

We talked about Chris's legal experience and then turned our attention to the purpose of the call. "The way the church is handling this is a complete disaster," Chris said, in reference to Rathbun and Rinder having gone public. "It needs to conduct internal investigations and stop attacking ex-Scientologists who speak out." We were witnessing a clash between two titans, Rathbun and Miscavige, and that it had become intensely personal, a fight to the death, and that neither seemed to care about the interests of the church and the repute of Scientology.

"How can the three of us inject some sanity to change that?" I asked.

Chris suggested we write a letter to the church's lead counsel, Monique Yingling, a Washington power attorney, and remind her of her fiduciary duties to her client, the Church of Scientology International (CSI), as opposed to Miscavige who was an individual and chairman of the board of Religious Technology Center (RTC), a separate corporation that supposedly had no management authority over CSI. "Write the letter as a lawyer and concerned Scientologist, and request that internal investigations be conducted by the appropriate corporate officials, independent of Miscavige or anyone else implicated in charges of wrongdoing."

"Great idea," I said. "Any volunteers?" They laughed, after which I offered to write the letter but said it needed to go on an attorney's letterhead and there were only two people on the line who qualified.

We discussed hiring an attorney, but then Letterhead volunteered – and in so doing, earned his alias. Chris and I praised him for his valor and promised to attend his funeral. We later made a pact to go public and publish the letter if he got declared for presenting it. Chris said, "Isn't it sad when lawyers who care about their church are afraid to speak out and defend it? This is what our church has become under Miscavige."

The letter was sent to Yingling on February 3, 2010. Copies were sent to a number of other in-house church lawyers and to the corporate and tax staffer at OSA Int, which is a department within CSI according to the church's corporate structure.

The letter read in part:

> "One of the main thrusts of Rathbun's public statements has been allegations of [Miscavige's] "takeover" of the Church, the annihilation of his potential rivals, the destruction of checks and balances put in place by LRH (namely, the Watch Dog Committee and the Int Exec Strata), and the alleged lavish lifestyle he enjoys.

> "These claims strike to the heart of the core qualifications for tax-exempt status. No one person may single-handedly govern a nonprofit organization. Private benefit by one person, called inurement, is unlawful and grounds for revocation of tax-exempt status."

The letter called for "an internal investigation, independent of all employees and officers allegedly engaged in the wrongful acts and then reform the underlying administrative and ethical situations and publicly announce the reforms/results," and asked for Miscavige to "step down while it is conducted."

A week later, Letterhead was still standing, but there was no response to the letter. We regrouped. I told them that I had been investigating the corporate structure of Scientology and had made an eye-opening discovery about the Church of Spiritual Technology, (CST). Neither of them knew much about CST, other than its role in preserving Scientology technology on platinum plates by burying them in nuclear-safe bunkers, or some such thing.

CST is a senior echelon to both the other two religious corporate entities, Religious Technology Center (RTC), of which Miscavige was Chairman, and Church of Scientology International (CSI). "CST has the power to eliminate both RTC and CSI and re-license another organization to take its place."

Chris and Letterhead were surprised. "It's true," I said. "LRH created CST as a fail-safe in the event RTC went off the rails. CST has an option to purchase the rights owned by RTC for a mere two hundred dollars." Those rights were the trademarks and upper level technology of Scientology, the only power held by RTC.

"It gets better," I added. "CST has a Board of Special Directors, in addition to boards of trustees and general directors. The special directors are non-Scientologist California lawyers whose express duties are to obtain and maintain tax-exempt status." I told them I was currently preparing a memorandum that laid all this out, but thought that we should send another letter addressed to the special directors.

Chris asked who the trustees and general directors were, and said, "They have standing." That meant they had the right to file a legal action to enforce religious corporation law and ensure that the boards of CST were independent and able to exercise their legal duties, including the obligation to investigate potential wrongdoing.

"I don't know who they are yet," I said. "I'm working on that. In the meantime, we can lean on the special directors and ask them to conduct an investigation."

We sent our second letter on March 10, 2010 to Sherman Lenske, Stephen Lenske, and Lawrence Heller, whom we learned were the three special directors of CST, with copies to various church lawyers and legal staff, as well as to Miscavige. Our six-page letter quoted from the bylaws of CST, which Hubbard himself wrote and oversaw.

The letter read in part:

> "In establishing CST," the letter stated in part, "LRH set up three separate boards, with internal checks and balances," and named the boards: the Board of Trustees; the Board of General Directors; and the Board of Special Directors. "The special directors are named in the original bylaws, but the general directors and trustees are not. Nowhere in Church publications or on its website have I seen a list of names of the general directors and trustees."
>
> . . .
>
> "I have directed this letter to the special directors in the hope that they will cause an investigation of RTC/CSI leadership since the matter falls directly within their fiduciary duties, which are, as expressed by LRH: [enumerated duties omitted]."
>
> . . .
>
> "The tax exempt status is potentially in jeopardy. Not only do allegations being bandied about on the Internet and reported in the media raise disqualifying issues, but some media are calling for a re-consideration."
>
> . . .
>
> "We can overcome the abuse claims only by using standard LRH policies and the protocol adopted by Corporate America. Otherwise we put the Church at risk of ever-increasing negative PR, governmental intervention, and loss of tax-exempt status."
>
> . . .

This time Jim Morrow, the Corporate & Tax Director at OSA Int, contacted Letterhead and asked him – respectfully, according to Letterhead – to stop sending letters to church attorneys. By then I had uncovered new information and relayed it to our group. "Terri Gamboa is one of the original trustees of CST."

Letterhead knew her, Chris didn't. We filled him in. Terri was one of the original "Watch Messengers," physically present with LRH eight hours a day, from the age of 12 onward. LRH and Mary Sue Hubbard were her legal guardians. LRH appointed her executive director of Author Services, Inc. (ASI), the copyright owner of both his fiction and Scientology publications. ASI ran the church after the takeover of the G.O. while LRH was in hiding and isolated. LRH held Terri in higher esteem than Miscavige, as evidenced by her ASI appointment and also by her lifetime appointment as a trustee of CST, which gave her legal power over RTC and Miscavige. I knew Terri from years earlier when I worked in the Mission All Clear Unit. She was one of the sane ones in power and we got along. I didn't know whether she might be interested in helping in a reform effort.

"She blew from Int Base back in the early nineties," I said. A "blow," in Scientology terms, is an unauthorized departure. Int Base is the International Base in the California desert outside Hemet. "Marty [Rathbun] talks about her in one of the video clips. "The one entitled, *What happened in Nashville.*"[30]

"So, what happened in Nashville?" Chris asked.

"When Terri left the Int Base, she drove to Nashville. Miscavige went nuts and had private investigators track her down. Miscavige suspected that she had taken some critical document from his safe. Someone remembered that Terri had a briefcase with her when she left, so Miscavige ordered Rathbun to find her and get into that briefcase at all costs. Rathbun knew a private investigator who was good at opening locked briefcases without a trace, so a bunch of them went to Nashville to distract Terri while the investigator broke into her briefcase.

"But the document wasn't in there. Miscavige didn't reveal what the document was or what secret it contained."

The three of us considered contacting her. "She's toxic," I said. "Not only has she been *declared* but Miscavige has had her under surveillance for years. Now I know why. With a lifetime appointment as a CST trustee and an LRH favorite, she's a real threat to his usurpation of the checks and balances LRH created and ordered implemented."

"She's the reason I got ordered to sec checks in 1993," Letterhead said. Her father, Peter Gillham, had complained to Letterhead about the church's disconnection policy. "He was distraught that the church had ordered him to not contact either Terri or his other two children who had also left the Sea Org. Peter later confessed to the church that he had spilled his heart out to me. Then OSA Int called me in and asked me why I had not written a Knowledge Report on Peter Gillham."

"That's where I reconnected with Merrell," Letterhead recalled. We were both in line getting sec checks at OSA Int."

Chris asked why I was getting sec checks. "General principles," I joked, not wanting to get into it then. "They noticed that I was still kicking, so they zapped me one more time. But that was the last time. I walked out of that one and told them I was done being punished."

"You walked out of a sec check and didn't get declared?" Chris said incredulously.

"True," I said. "The sec checker asked me if I knew the consequences of walking out of one. I told her I did, and that I also knew the consequence of continuing. I was losing my dignity and integrity, and that was worse. So I told her to tell the church to do what it had to do because I was doing what I had to do."

"Good for you," Chris said.

* * *

"Terri, this is Merrell Vannier. Do you remember me?"

She did and asked whether I was still a member of the church. I told her I was, and that I was investigating the corporate power structure of the church on behalf of a small band of Scientology lawyers who wanted reform. I asked if she was interested in meeting with me and told her I was willing to travel to Las Vegas, where she lived and worked as a real estate broker.

She asked me exactly what was I investigating. "You were a trustee of CST (Church of Spiritual Technology) right?" She said she was. "Did you resign your position?" She said she hadn't but that Miscavige kept an undated, signed resignation letter in a safe over which he had sole control. (It later occurred to me that perhaps it was this document that Miscavige hoped to retrieve in Nashville.) "Doesn't matter. That's unlawful. The courts won't uphold it."

"Really?" she said in a tone that told me I had piqued her interest.

"You had a lifetime appointment."

"I did?"

"You didn't know that?" She said she didn't.

"Did you know that CST has options to buy back the Scientology trademarks and trade secrets from RTC (Religious Technology Center), and thereby eliminate RTC?" She didn't know that, either. I went on, "And because RTC licensed CSI (Church of Scientology International, "The Mother Church") to use those marks and trade secrets, RTC has a senior relationship with CSI, which means that CST is a senior entity to both RTC and CSI and has a statutory power of investigation over both?" She said she didn't know any of that, and asked how I knew it. I told her that I had found and collected copies of all of LRH's testamentary documents as well as copies of the articles and bylaws of all three religious corporations.

"Okay," she said quickly. "Let's meet."

Chapter 34

THE DIE IS CAST

Optimism is the faith that leads to achievement. Nothing can be done without hope and confidence.

– Helen Keller
American author

Over dinner, I asked Terri Gamboa why she left the Sea Org. She said conditions and the treatment of staffers had become so gruesome, and Miscavige treated people so viciously, that she couldn't take it anymore. "That wasn't what we signed up for."

The event that triggered her departure occurred when Miscavige hauled a bunch of Int staff to watch another staffer be security checked in front of them. As the victim disclosed various transgressions and secrets, Miscavige at first derided him. Then he ordered the onlookers to spit in the confessor's face, and they did, one-by-one. Terri was the only one who refused to do it. Miscavige glared at her, then walked out of the room. "I knew he would be gunning for me next. No one defies Miscavige."

Soon afterward, Miscavige assigned her to manual labor at the Int Base out by Hemet, and ordered her to undergo security checks. One day, her overseer ordered her to move a large pile of heavy rocks in the hot desert sun, which she did. As she finished, she noticed the enforcer glance up at one of the office buildings on the base, and then he ordered her to move the rocks back to their original location. She looked at the building and saw Miscavige in a window watching her sadistically.

She moved the rocks, but said "I knew then that I was done." She added that she and her husband snuck out a window one night shortly afterward and fled. "He was too evil and had no compassion toward other human beings; it was all about power and the glory for him."

I asked her if she had seen the video testimonies of Rathbun, Rinder and the other former Sea Org members describing alleged abuses inflicted on them by Miscavige, and if she believed them based on her knowledge of the people and the conditions at Int Base. "They're all telling the truth. After Miscavige took over it got bad and kept getting worse," she said.

I expressed surprise that people put up with such abuse. "Miscavige is incredibly clever, and manipulative," she said. "By the time he came after someone, that person was no longer able to stand up to him."

She said she had seen this side of Miscavige early on, but that it grew worse as he gained more power. "But they all knew it," she said, speaking about executives close to Miscavige. She said she had spoken to several of them who were sent by Miscavige to try to coax her to come back. She laid out her reasons for leaving and told them that Miscavige was "running the place as a dictator and that LRH would never have tolerated that. He intended it to be run by boards he established prior to his death."

"In Nashville I told Marty Rathbun and another high official that Miscavige was insane and was destroying the place, and that many of the Int execs were unhappy with how he was running things. I suggested they should join together to reorganize and restore order with the good people still there. Marty agreed with most of what I said, but at the same time he said that Miscavige made him what he was, that he was a nobody before he met Miscavige, and that Miscavige made him somebody. That was really the last chance we had."

"We might have one glimmer of a chance left," I said.

I gave her copies of the CST bylaws and directed her attention to specific provisions. "We didn't do any of this," she insisted. "We didn't have board meetings."

I asked her how it worked. She said: "Miscavige dictated the minutes and the OSA Int legal staff prepared them and took them around for signatures. Nobody read them. There was no time to. We were just told to sign them, that they were just legal formalities. Miscavige was working with the attorneys and knew what needed to be done, and we trusted him."

I handed her copies of California law for nonprofit religious corporations and pointed out the requirement that such corporations be controlled by their boards of directors. She said she didn't know about that but Miscavige would not have allowed it, anyway.

"Attorneys Lenske, Lenske & Heller are the three special directors of CST. Did you know them?"

"I was one of the people who hired them," she said. LRH sent her out as part of a team to interview lawyers to represent him. Norman Starkey was the other member of the team overseen by Miscavige.

"Didn't they go over the bylaws and duties for you and the other trustees?"

She said they didn't. "Miscaive had the duty to implement the entire revised corporate structure that LRH devised and approved for the future of the church, but it didn't happen. He must have hidden everything as part of his goal to take all the power for himself. As the overseer of the mission, he was in the perfect position to do that."

She explained that Miscavige was a quick learner and took the initiative to dive in and learn the law about how to run corporations legally. "He eventually took over dealing directly with Lenske, Lenske & Heller, and started briefing us. The lawyers told Miscavige how to set up the corporations and he orchestrated the whole thing. LRH was off the lines and in hiding and couldn't see what Miscavige was doing."

"So that's how he did it," I said. Miscavige became the sole person working with the attorneys and isolated them from the trustees of the various corporations so he could commandeer their powers over him.

I wanted to compile a list of CST general directors appointed by the trustees during her tenure. "I take it that you didn't appoint any." She confirmed my suspicion. Miscavige handpicked the directors and ousted anyone who exercised any independence.

"That's the main function of the trustees," I said, "to appoint directors annually. They serve at the pleasure of the trustees."

"They served at the pleasure of Miscavige," she said.

I showed Terri a document from a legal proceeding involving the tax exempt status of CST. Dated 1993, it listed her as one of the three trustees. She looked it over, her eyes grew wide as she read. "Oh, my god, now I get it."

"Get what?"

"I was out of the country during the application process for the tax-exempt status process." (The IRS granted all churches of Scientology tax exempt status in 1993.) A dream job had fallen from the sky and landed in her lap. She and her husband were approached by a wealthy Hong Kong businessman to run a horse ranch in Australia." Terri is Australian and an avid equestrian. She owns horses and rides twice each week with her sister. Her specialties as a real estate broker are properties where raising and keeping horses is allowed and luxury homes on ranch acreage.

"We were suspicious at the time and wondered if it was real or not," she said. It turned out that the horse ranch and the handsome compensation were real but she later found out that Miscavige had engineered the whole operation and spent a ton of money funding it. "We wondered why he did that. That is why – to get us out of the country."

She was listed as a lifetime trustee of CST in documents the church submitted to the IRS as part of the application for the church's tax-exempt status. Had she been interviewed, she could have revealed that the corporate boards were a sham, and that the fail-safe provisions that LRH had installed when he created his estate plan and the bylaws of CST (the ability to eliminate RTC by exercising the options to purchase the rights bequeathed to it by LRH) were, in fact, controlled by Miscavige. The fox was guarding the hen house, in other words. Alternatively, had Terri learned about her trustee powers, and the lifetime appointment, she could have claimed her position as a CST trustee and, with the power of that position, implemented LRH's plan for checks and balances spread among seven boards of trustees and directors among the three religious corporations.

This evidence was dynamite.

* * *

"Guys," I said to our group of Scientology lawyers, "it's worse than I thought. There are zero checks and balances now. The boards of trustees and general directors of all the corporations are captive boards. Miscavige worked alone with Lenske, Lenske & Heller and kept Terri in the dark while he usurped for himself all the corporate powers that LRH intended to be shared among his trusted aides. The churches of Scientology are mere alter egos of Miscavige. It's a total betrayal of the last will and wishes of LRH."

We discussed our options and decided to retain a nationally renowned practitioner in religious corporate law while I continued my investigation. We also decided to write another letter to the CST special directors and church attorneys.

We wrote a total of six letters over a span of three months. Our legal strategy to enforce remedial actions would take time and resources to develop. I am not at liberty to discuss that strategy or its status because it is ongoing.

I created the website at www.savescientology.com, which went live on January 1, 2011. I reported the bulk of my findings there.

Within a week or two, I received a tip from a reliable source inside OSA Int. "Miscavige is livid. He knows you're behind both the letters and the website. He ordered us to get the evidence and *declare* you." I thanked the tipster, and tightened my personal and website security even more.

* * *

"Did you get a copy of Debbie Cook's e-mail?" a supporter of my website excitedly asked me on New Year's Day 2012. Debbie Cook was in the Sea Org for 29 years and for 17 of them she served as the Commanding Officer of the Flag Land Base in Clearwater, which is regarded as the Mecca of Scientology technology. She was widely known and loved. "She sent an e-mail blast to Scientologists. Her message parallels the website. I'll forward it to you."

Cook's e-mail warned Scientologists about the lack of checks and balances at the very highest levels of the organizations of Scientology and drew a distinction between the religion (i.e., technology) of Scientology and the churches of Scientology. Before I received the e-mail, another supporter called with the same news. "She must be a fan of your website," he said.

If two different people thought Cook's e-mail was aligned with the content of my web site, then Miscavige might make the same connection.

There comes a point when the powers that be decide to act, with or without evidence and proper procedure, as I learned in my Florida Bar case. Apparently that point had been reached by Miscavige. He blew a gasket and demanded of OSA Int:

"Bring me his fucking head!"

At least that was the tip I received.

Chapter 35

THE HAMMER DROPS

In a time of universal deceit – telling the truth is a revolutionary act.

– George Orwell

When the elevator doors opened on the third floor of the historic Braley Building in Pasadena, California, now known as the Church of Scientology of Pasadena, I knew right away that the hammer was about to drop.

I was taking a course consisting of seventy-six hour long taped lectures by L. Ron Hubbard, given in Philadelphia in 1952, that covered his research into the potentials of the spirit of man (as opposed to the body) and the anatomy of matter, energy, space and time, the components of the material universe. Every student in Scientology has a schedule. Mine was Tuesdays and Thursdays from 1:00 to 3:30 p.m. This day was a Tuesday, January 24, 2012 to be precise.

Standing outside the elevator door to greet me that day were Kirsten Caetano and Julian Schwartz, both dressed in Sea Org uniforms. Kirsten was the Security Chief for OSA Int (Office of Special Affairs, International). Julian was the Ethics Officer for a Los Angeles church.

The purpose of Julian's presence may have been explained by his size. He was huge, perhaps six-foot-five and 250 pounds, or more on both counts. Kirsten was petite, thirtyish, with a steely face and an Arctic vibe. I had one previous encounter with her, at Celebrity Centre more than a decade earlier, when I was doing a program known as the Purification Rundown, or "Purif" in Scientology jargon.

* * *

"You need to report to the Ethics Officer," my Purif supervisor said to me upon my arrival there one day. I asked why. She said she didn't know.

The Purification Rundown is a program designed to clear the body and mind of toxins and drugs. In theory, toxins build up in the fatty tissues of the body, and can be cleansed by doing this program which involves exercise, vitamins, minerals, and hours in a sauna to sweat out impurities. I had done the Purif in 1980 when it was first released, and was doing it a second time in 2001 because I'd had an appendectomy under general anesthesia two years earlier. I also wanted to rid my body and mind of all the smog and junk I had accumulated from the environment as a long-distance runner and bicyclist over the prior fifteen years. During that period I ran a dozen marathons and hundreds of other running and bicycle races and triathlons, and trained for them.

I had never done a Scientology service at Celebrity Centre before, and chose it this time, mainly because it had great facilities: two nice, large saunas; comfortable resting areas; and a small gym with high-quality exercise equipment.

I entered the Ethics office and a young woman behind the desk told me to sit down. Her attitude was on the hostile side, and her face was taut, so it came across more like an order than an invitation. The fact that she wore a Sea Org uniform further chilled the atmosphere. I took a seat in a wooden chair in front of her desk. She wanted to go over a report she had received from OSA Int.

It didn't occur to me at the time that she was not part of Celebrity Centre (CC) staff, though it should have been obvious. CC staff wore business-dress uniforms, kind of like jazzed up airline stewards, as opposed to the military-like uniforms of most Sea Org members. The woman was in the CC Ethics office, so I just assumed she was part of CC staff. I later learned that she was the OSA Int Security Chief.

"What's your name?" I asked, wanting to break the ice.

"Kirsten," she said. She started to talk about the report when I interrupted. "My name is Merrell."

"I know." The ice didn't break, not even a hairline fracture. In fact I achieved the opposite result. She was clearly annoyed by my social banter. "The report says that you upset Bill Walsh." I happened to run into the high-powered Washington attorney in the sauna the previous day and we chatted for a bit.

"Upset him? I did no such thing. We used to work on church legal cases together and we haven't seen or worked with each other in fifteen years."

"That's not the report I've got. I want you to change your Purif schedule so that you don't run into him anymore." Her look was uncompromising, which meant that she was carrying out an order and needed to report back my compliance.

"I'd like to see a copy of the report," I said, falling back on Scientology policy rather than blowing my stack. Numerous basic policies applied: (1) *If it isn't in writing, it isn't true*; (2) an Ethics Officer cannot act on unverified reports; and, (3) a person charged with wrongdoing must be confronted with the evidence against him.

"I don't have it in writing."

I threw up my hands. "Well then, I guess we're done."

"Don't go back to the Purif. That's an order."

"Listen, Kirsten. I don't follow illegal orders."

"I was told you might be a problem. Why can't you be part of the team?

"What team is that?" I asked.

She went ballistic, and screamed at me. "Why can't you just change your fucking schedule?" I stared at her in disbelief. She glowered back. I had an answer for her question but didn't feel like giving it to her under the circumstances. I searched for another way to break the impasse.

An idea struck me. "I know how to solve this." She perked up. "Bill is in the Purif facilities now. Why don't you call him up here and go over the report with the two of us?"

She sneered. "That's not gonna happen. I need you to change your schedule."

"I picked my time slot because it works for me," I said. "I just finished editing a feature-length film and need some time in the mornings and late afternoons to oversee the rest of post-production."[31]

"Why don't you do the Purif in the evening?"

"Because I coach my son's baseball team and spend time with my wife in the evening. She has a job and that's our only time together."

She groaned and scooted her chair back. "I'll try to round up a written report. It might take me a few minutes." I got up as well. "Where are you going?" she asked.

"While you're doing that I'm going to the RTC Reports desk in the lobby to write a report." An RTC reports desk is situated in a prominent place in every Scientology church. Its purpose is to protect the purity of Scientology technology and policy.

She gave me a leery, subdued look, then resigned herself to my prerogative to write a report. "Just don't go to the Purif without me clearing it."

Before I was done writing, Tommy Davis tapped me on the shoulder. "Hey, Merrell. You don't need to finish that. I got it worked out." The son of actress Anne Archer, Tommy worked in the CC President's Office. We were on friendly terms. Tommy's wife, Nadine, was Angie's best friend, and Greg (Angie's husband) worked for Tommy. Fran and I had dined with the four of them and occasionally ran into them together when we visited Angie. Tommy asked me to step outside with him.

He told me that nobody said I had upset Bill Walsh. It was a false report. He said that OSA Int. (Office of Special Affairs, International) was monitoring Bill's progress closely and reading his Daily Reports because he was the first major church attorney to ever take a Scientology service. (Each person on the program must turn in a report at the end of the day and note any reactions that occurred while in the sauna; how they were doing; etc.)

They wanted everything to go perfectly, Tommy said. "Bill reported that he had run into you... but in a good way. He said that he was pleasantly surprised to run into someone he knew and had worked with before. Someone at OSA was concerned about you being with him."

"Who was that?" I asked.

"Oh I don't know. I didn't ask. But it's bullshit, and you were mishandled because of it, and that's getting sorted out. I apologize for it. It was wrong to ask you to change your schedule. You can have whatever schedule you want."

I thanked him for that, but asked him to please find out for me who the person was. "This isn't the first time I've run into this kind of problem coming from OSA, and I'd like to get to the bottom of it."

He assured me that he would look into it, then asked me if there was anything else he could do for me. "Yeah, as a matter of fact there is. Would you tell Kirsten to lighten up?"

* * *

As I stepped off the elevator in the Pasadena church, Kirsten stepped in front of me, her left arm extended to my right. "May I have a word with you."

"Sure." I followed her lead. The towering Julian fell in behind me.

Kirsten led me to a door. "Let's go in here so we can have some privacy." Inside was a large empty course room, with chairs on either side of four or five ten-foot long tables. The chairs were for students. A file folder and other materials were neatly stacked on one of the middle tables.

Kirsten walked to a chair next to the stack when the door opened. In walked Mike Sutter. Julian Schwartz was nowhere in sight. I don't know where Sutter came from or when Julian had left us. Sutter must have been stationed in a stairwell waiting for us to pass by. Obviously, the whole event was planned and orchestrated.

Dressed in a short-sleeved, crisp white Sea Org uniform, Sutter took the chair in front of the materials and asked me to take the seat opposite him. Kirsten and Sutter were between me and the door. I noticed something strange about Sutter's appearance compared to the one and only time I had seen him previously. He was strikingly thin. Most people fill out as they age; men often develop a paunch. His skin was off-color, a pale orange, not a healthy tan. I had read reports on the Internet that he had been banished to what is known as "The Hole" at Scientology's International Base. So notorious and degraded are the conditions and treatment of people in The Hole, based on multiple accounts from defectors, that it has its own Wikipedia page.[32] Perhaps the reports were true. That would explain his appearance.

The whole thing caught me off guard and I was a little unnerved. They were prepared. I wasn't. I wanted to feel comfortable and a little prepared for what was about to happen. "Hey guys, before we get started I'd like to use the restroom. Is that okay?" They both nodded their agreement.

Julian was standing guard outside the door. "Potty break," I said as I walked by.

Sutter was rumored to be part of a small team of top-level aides who were authorized to go on the Internet to read the claims of defectors and whistleblowers and meet with them in an attempt to either orally *declare* them or handle them, by which is meant: get them to see the error of their ways, recant, spill the beans on others, and come back into the fold. I wondered if they would try to handle me.

As I washed my hands in the Pasadena church's restroom, I recalled my previous encounter with Sutter in which he gave me his private number and falsely promised to fix any future issues I had with OSA staff. I decided to start off the meeting by busting his balls with that.

Back in the chair, I felt composed and confident. "Hey, Mike. Our paths crossed once before. Do you remember that?" He looked skyward, his face twisted in thought. After a few seconds he lowered and shook his head. "No. No I don't. Sorry."

His reaction staggered me. I remembered every detail, every word spoken. Of course, it concerned my professional status and livelihood. But that was precisely the point. He was carrying out a Miscavige order – as I now knew – that affected the rest of a man's life, his career, and his family. To Sutter, it was probably just one of thousands of orders he had carried out since then, from the important to the mundane. I would have busted his balls anyway by reminding him of our encounter but I felt as though I had seen inside his soul as he looked inward, and it was dark and hollow. Nobody home. It was pathetic. I knew then that the stories about him were true. He had been punished, degraded and humiliated into nothing but a lap dog for his master, Miscavige. I pitied him. He might be ready to *declare* me but I still had my integrity. Give me that over membership any day. I was the more fortunate of the two. So I let it go.

Sutter opened the folder in front of him to reveal Goldenrod. That meant I was officially being declared. Goldenrod is named after the color of the paper Declare orders are written on. Normally members can only be declared following a Committee of Evidence (with written charges and evidence presented to the accused prior to a formal hearing conducted by a panel of three fellow members). But these were not normal times for the church. Now, members were being *declared* verbally with no regard for church ethics and justice policies and procedures.

Some were even being *declared* in absentia and notified by letter of the declaration as a *fait accompli.*

Reading from the Goldenrod, Sutter declared me to be a suppressive person and expelled me from the Church of Scientology. He rattled off a number of charges: engaged in suppressive acts, connected to people who were engaged in suppressive acts, and one or two more. I faded out. I hated vague charges like those. They can cover anything. What constitutes a violation is, like beauty, in the eye of the beholder. I reacted to these charges the same way I react when I read about charges against citizens in other countries run by dictators, charges like *disseminating provocative rumors* or *actions that violate public order or the tranquility of citizens.* But I was reeling a bit.

"What's all that mean?" I asked.

"You know."

"Actually, I don't. Can you give me something specific?"

Again he said, "You know." I glanced at Kirsten. She was silent, but if looks could kill. Behind her hateful glare I even sensed a hint of enjoyment.

I let out a chuckle. "This is Kafkaesque, not Scientology." Sutter said he didn't know that word. I told him that Franz Kafka was a writer from Prague in the last century who wrote about situations that a person had no chance of resolving. Kirsten scoffed and Sutter continued reading.

"Your only (person of contact) is the International Justice Chief in the event that you come to your senses." That meant I was prohibited from speaking with other Scientologists, they were prohibited from speaking to me, and the church's policy of disconnection would kick in. Other Scientologists, including Fran, Angie and John were required to disconnect from me. In the case of my wife and son, they would have to move out of the house, or kick me out.

I knew Angie would have to comply with the policy. That hurt a lot. As a Sea Org member married to another Sea Org member whose family was very actively involved in Scientology, she was in a difficult position. She would risk losing her husband, her in-laws and longtime friends if she disobeyed the rule, in addition to being *declared* herself and expelled from the Sea Org. I doubted that Fran would disconnect after forty-two years of marriage, but I was unsure what John would do. He was not actively involved in Scientology and might not agree with or even know about the policy. Besides, he still lived at home as a part-time college student and couldn't afford to move out. Since 1985, Fran had worked as an executive for a company owned by Scientologists. I didn't think the owners were shortsighted enough to fire her if she refused to disconnect from me, but one never knows; pressure could be brought to bear on them from above.

I asked Sutter if he had any written reports or evidence to support the charges against me. When he said he didn't, I reminded him that a Declare is not valid unless a person is first confronted with evidence and allowed to respond.

"I'm not going to debate you," he said.

"I'm not trying to debate you. I want Scientology justice policy to be applied." I knew they were carrying out a Miscavige order and had no independent judgment in the matter. I wasn't trying to avoid what I knew was set in stone. I wanted to draw out as many policy violations as possible so I could write a report and challenge it as a "false Declare." This would entitle me to a hearing, which I also knew would not be granted. But it made a record. Someday, sanity might be restored, reforms put in place, and arbitrary orders and actions emanating from Miscavige's maniacal regime set aside.

Sutter answered my request by rereading the vague charges. I rose to leave. "I can't work with this. Do what you will." He accused me of "blowing," the term for an unauthorized departure. I kept walking. Sutter followed after me.

As I reached for the doorknob, he blurted out: "Mike Rinder."

I stopped and turned. "What about him?"

"You know."

I laughed. "This is a joke."

357

As I stepped out of the room, Julian stirred. He silently escorted me down the stairwell that emptied outside the building.

* * *

Telling Fran was the hardest part. I waited until she got home from work. She took the news like a haymaker to the head. She was visibly shaken, trembling. The first words out of her mouth were, "Angie. She'll have to disconnect." I did my best to comfort her, and she finally came to grips with it. Sort of. After I thought she was on top of it, she started crying again. She and Angie were of course very close. One of my greatest enjoyments of fatherhood was witnessing their relationship, mother and daughter. It really tore me up to see Fran suffer like this.

Finally, I said to her, "Listen, Fran. Maybe it would be best if I moved out."

She snapped out of it. "Don't be ridiculous. I'm not going to disconnect from you." She said she would be okay, that it would just take time, and added: "Hopefully she will at least call me."

But Angie didn't call. We've never heard from her since.

We waited a few days to tell John. By then Fran was doing much better.

"Have you heard from your sister?" she asked.

"No. That's weird, too, because I even texted her and she didn't text back like she normally does." Fran and I glanced at each other. John picked up on it. "Why, what's going on?" I told him I had been declared a suppressive person and expelled from the church. He was dumbfounded, and said, "That's crazy. You're not a suppressive person. Why did they do that?"

I told him I suspected it may be due to reform activities I had undertaken. I explained how I had teamed up with some other Scientologist lawyers and written letters to other church lawyers and executives calling for internal investigations into charges of abuse of office, and re-instituting a system of checks and balances as intended by L. Ron Hubbard. "We also asked them to cancel the policy of disconnection."

To my surprise, John said he was proud of me.

He asked if Angie knew what I was telling him. I said she didn't. He asked whether she had even called either one of us. When I gave the same answer, he got upset and said, "Well then I don't care to talk to her, anyway" and stormed away.

I called him back. "John, please don't be mad at her. She will have been told a lot of bad things about me and ..." I was going to mention the pressures on her from her marriage, but John didn't want to hear it.

"She should at least call and find out your side of the story," he said.

Chapter 36

SHUNNED

In the End, we will remember not the words of our enemies, but the silence of our friends.

— Martin Luther King, Jr.

"I heard you were *declared*. Is that true?" said the caller, a Scientologist and dear friend I had met soon after I arrived in Los Angeles in October 1979.

"That's the same rumor I heard," I said, partly in jest. "Don't believe it until you see something in writing." He said he would look into it but in the meantime he thought it best not to talk to me.

A few days later he contacted me and said an ethics officer at a local church told him I had indeed been *declared* but was not authorized to show him the Declaration. But he called his son who, as a Sea Org member, was allowed to view it and he confirmed that I had been *declared* in writing.

"Well, I haven't seen the issue and ..." I was going to explain the circumstances, but he interrupted me.

"You know the rules," he said, and hung up.

At least he contacted me to verify that I had been *declared*.

Because the Declaration was secret (for reasons unknown to me), I was amazed how quickly word of it spread throughout the Scientology community. Barely a week after my friend hung up on me, I was leaving the Pasadena Courthouse when I saw another long-time friend walking toward me on the wide sidewalk by the courthouse. I wondered if she knew, and figured I was about to find out. I planned to greet her warmly as I normally would, and exchange how-do-you-dos.

When she got to within twenty-five feet of me she took a sudden interest in the drab architecture of the government edifice. I followed her eyes and saw nothing worthy of her attention. No signs, no ornate fixtures, no one standing on the ledge of the roof about to jump off. Nothing. Yet her attention remained fixated on that ugly, boring wall as she walked all the way past me. I would've said "Hi," anyway, but obviously it would have been too much for her to bear.

Letterhead called me a day or two later and said that a mutual friend of ours called him and asked if he had received word of my *declare*. This person was a very prominent businessman and Scientologist. I knew then how my situation was being handled by the Office of Special Affairs: they were using stalwart loyalists to make calls to the Scientologists they knew I was connected to–a whispering campaign to enforce the declaration.

"What'd you tell him?" I asked.

"I told him I hadn't seen anything in writing and reminded him, 'if it isn't in writing, it isn't true.'"

"Good for you. Try to get your hands on the Declaration and burn me a copy. I want to find out what's being said about me to Angie and to my friends."

Not everyone had gotten the word, even a year later. I ran into one friend at Trader Joe's, a grocery store. She greeted me cheerily and asked what I was up to. I told her I was writing another book. She didn't ask what it was about, and I wouldn't have told her anyway, but it was this book. I asked how she was doing, and she said she had just finished a certain Scientology service and, while beaming radiantly, shared her satisfaction with the service and told me how much she had benefited from it.

"Good for you," I said. "Congratulations."

I meant it, too. As a matter of personal policy I do not impose my religious and political beliefs on someone who doesn't ask for or welcome them. That's what is so silly about the disconnection policy and proves that Miscavige uses it to control his flock and lacks any compassion regarding the harm it causes families and relationships, or the damage it does to the image of Scientology. If my daughter doesn't want to hear about my reform activities, all she has to do is say she isn't interested. We can talk about and do other things. Hubbard's words in the original policy actually read: "Handle or disconnect." If someone in your circle insists on trashing you for your affiliation with Scientology, or anything else, deal with them if you can. Simply asking someone to please not bring that up may suffice to defuse any actual conflict.

The wildest example so far occurred recently in my chiropractor's office. I had just finished receiving treatment and went to the receptionist desk to pay for it when I spotted John Taussig sitting in the waiting area. He's the guy who, in October 1979, showed me the Paulette Cooper legal files that I had volunteered to organize. We became good friends and maintained contact with each other over the years, even after he left the G.O. staff to practice law in Pasadena. In fact, he introduced me to the chiropractor when I sustained a running injury.

The moment he saw me, he hastily buried his head in a magazine. I noticed a couple of other people in the area raise a questioning brow. It was that obvious, and too much for me to let pass. "Hi, John," I said with the same enthusiasm I was accustomed to showing him.

He raised his head, meekly returned my hello, and dropped it down again. I doubt that he realized the spectacle he was causing. All three of the people in the room watched in obvious discomfort over his uncivil behavior.

I hadn't seen John since I was *declared*. We were both avid baseball fans. He's a Red Sox fan; I'm a Cardinals fan. I missed sharing our thrills over our teams' successes and would have normally talked to him about the 2013 World Series, if we had not watched one or more of the games together. I spoke from my heart:

"You won another World Series. Congratulations. That must have been fun."

He looked at me with a nervous smile as I spoke, nodded slightly, then quickly returned to his magazine. Obviously, he wanted to be anyplace in the world other than in that waiting area in my presence.

About that time his wife, Judy, appeared from a treatment room behind me and walked briskly past me. She's the person I once worked with in the Mission All Clear Unit and who later ordered me to accept disbarment. After she left the church staff we rekindled our relationship. She even presided over my son John's naming ceremony.

"Hi, Judy," I said.

She walked right out the door as John rose from his seat and joined her, and did not give me the slightest attention. The witnesses turned their bewildered faces to me.

"Weird, huh?" I said to the woman nearest me.

"Very weird," she replied. "What was that all about?"

I told her it was complicated.

Many Scientologists remain in contact with me, and, ironically, I now have more Scientologist friends than I did before as a result of my reform activities. Most of them know me as "Admin," the anonymous (until now) administrator of www.savescientology.com. I have a huge number of supporters. By my estimate seventy-five percent of all Scientologists want to see a change in Scientology leadership. They keep a very low profile, though, many of them waiting for the right moment to spring into action. A new term has emerged in the Scientology community to describe their status: "under the radar."

I still miss my other friends. So does Fran. We don't socialize with others nearly as much as we once did, because all our long-time friends have cut us off. We are both closer to our families, and to each other, as a result.

We miss Angie most of all, of course. Every Christmas and her birthdays are especially tough on us. We have developed secret ways of learning what and how she is doing. Obviously I can't go into that more. At least that's something.

The only tension related to Angie that has developed between Fran and me is whether I should write and publish this book. Fran was especially stressed when I first announced my intention to do it.

"If you publish it, I will never see Angie again," she said, almost in tears.

"We haven't heard from her in almost two years," I said. "What makes you think that will change if I remain silent?"

There was still hope, she said.

"You go on hoping," I said. "I'm going to *do* something."

That's as bad as it got between us. I quelled that argument by promising not to publish what I write without her permission.

In the months it took me to write the book, I have reasoned with her. I pointed out two trends that give me hope that Scientology can be reformed, Miscavige removed, and the disconnection policy canceled: (1) an ever-increasing public awareness of Miscavige and his abuses, and (2) more and more Scientologists are becoming informed of the situation and want reform.

I have repeatedly told Fran that I was still willing to separate so she could be reunited with Angie. She keeps slamming the door on that option. Recently, I wondered out loud what would happen if I were to die. "Do you think Angie would be allowed to contact you, then?"

"Absolutely," she said. "You're the only reason she had to disconnect."

I felt bad about that. "Yeah, I've got kind of a feisty way about me, don't I?"

"Kind of?" she said.

"Well, I didn't use to be that way. I just don't like being pushed around by a bully, and I don't like seeing my friends bullied into submission, and made shadows of their former selves."

On reflection, she touched on a trait in me that was too much a part of my essence to change. "I bet you wish you hadn't married an activist," I said.

Her reaction surprised me. She didn't say anything – which made me think she really felt that way. I couldn't blame her if she did. Look what she was going through. And all because of me. I'm the one who was attracted to Scientology. She followed me into that world.

"If you had it to do over again, knowing what you know now, would you have married me?" I asked her one day.

She thought about it for a moment, then said, "If I had it to do over again, I would not have gotten involved with Scientology. Not if I knew I could lose my daughter."

I offered, once again, to separate.

She was emphatic: "No, I don't want to do that. I just want my daughter back."

I told her I'd do what I could to arrange that – short of submission, of course.

* * *

One story encapsulates the transformation of management styles from the benevolent dictatorship of Hubbard, in which he strove to empower Scientologists, treat them fairly, and make Scientology fun, to the iron-fisted control of Miscavige, who like many despots, doesn't show the slightest compassion about the havoc and harm his policies and practices wreak. He bullied one of my dearest friends into submission.

That story begins in 1971, my first day of law school.

I brought home another beginning student to meet Fran. His name was Roger Nevins.[33] We made an odd pairing. Roger was dressed in bib overalls, wore sandals, and had long hair and a beard. Fran was looking out the picture window of our three-bedroom, rented ranch house in Raytown, a suburb of Kansas City.

She later said to me, "When I saw him get out of the car, I thought, 'My God, what has Merrell dragged home?'"

"Get past your initial reaction," I told her, "and just get to know him. He's actually a good guy." For some strange reason, Roger and I immediately hit it off. Since he lived nearby, we could car pool and study together. Plus, he was married and had a son not much older than Angie.

Roger and I became study partners and our families began to socialize. I drew the line when it came to drugs, though. He did them, I didn't. He once invited me to a party. "There will be LSD there in case you want to try it." I declined.

He visited a friend of his in Berkeley the next summer, and when he returned he was talking excitedly about Scientology. He raved about a course he took, saying it increased his ability to communicate and that I should look into it.

I told him I didn't have a problem communicating. "If I have something to say, I'll say it, and if I don't, I won't."

But it was much more than that, he said, adding that he did some drills, one-on-one with another person, sitting three feet apart, and learned to face that person without blinking for two straight hours. Clearly, he considered that to be a wondrous accomplishment.

"I don't care if I blink when I look at people." I said.

He said I was missing the point, and he tried other ways to share his newfound enthusiasm for the subject with me, but nothing he said appealed to me. *Some hippie thing,* I thought.

Then one day I stopped by his house. It was my turn to drive. As usual, he was late. So I went inside to get him. I heard the shower running. He said he'd be done shortly and to have a seat and turn on his stereo or something. He had a kick-ass record collection, a lot of great rock music that wasn't played on the AM radio stations I listened to.

I turned it on and took a seat. I saw a book next to the chair: *"Dianetics: The Modern Science of Mental Health,"* by L. Ron

Hubbard. The title intrigued me. I began reading the Introduction, and was immediately captivated.

"Where did you get this book?" I said when he came out of the bathroom, still toweling off. "This is amazing!"

"In California," he said. "I tried to tell you about it but you weren't interested."

"You didn't tell me about this. You were talking about being able to not blink in front of someone."

"I said there was more to it than that."

"Jesus, Roger. This is what you should have told me." I flashed the opening pages of the book at him. "I want to read the whole thing."

He said I could when he finished it. I looked at the page he had dog-eared. He was barely a quarter of the way through it and he'd been back from California for more than a month.

"Let me borrow it. I'll have it back to you within a week."

* * *

Roger and I became close friends. After law school, our paths separated for a few years. I moved to Florida, of course. He clerked for a judge in Kansas City, went into private practice for a year or so, then took a job with a title insurance company. He climbed the corporate ladder and became a highly-sought-after title insurance executive, which brought him to California in the early 1980s, and we resumed our relationship. We talked about anything and everything, and he became my best and most trusted friend. Hardly a weekend went by that our families didn't get together. We celebrated Christmases together, went on weekend camping trips together, and so on. His career continued to soar. He became the president of a title insurance company and, later, of the California Land Title Association.

He began to drift apart from me in the early to mid-90s. It coincided with and paralleled the shift in the direction Scientology took after Miscavige gained full control. Whereas Hubbard placed an emphasis on Scientology training and auditing, and on obtaining results from the application of Scientology, Miscavige emphasized status and behavior. The more a person contributed to a Scientology fund, the higher status one received. "Patron" was initially the highest status. It required a donation of $40,000.

That amount was too rich for my blood. Besides, I was against the concept of statuses. I was also opposed to having my behavior modified to suit the whims of a controlling leader. But Roger and his wife became Patrons.

One day Roger and I were talking about the demands being made on Scientologists and when he remarked, "You know, Merrell, I just don't hang with people who aren't actively involved and in good standing with upper management."

I was a little stunned, and didn't say anything for a while. I thought back to the Roger I knew in law school, the nonconformist, anti-establishment Roger, and here he was conforming to this new controlling style of management. I also thought his comment helped explain our weakening relationship. He must have picked up on that. It seemed like he wished he had not spoken so candidly and could take it back.

Over the next ten years, our relationship cooled further. We still got together occasionally, usually as part of a larger gathering of mutual friends, but the chumminess had all but dissipated. Then I discovered that he had resigned from his corporate job and left the title industry altogether, and was looking for a job in an entirely different field, ideally with a Scientologist-owned company.

When I asked why he had done that, he said that some of the industry practices bothered him and that it had come up in his auditing. Most likely something had come up in a security check, the frequent use of which Miscavige required of parishioners at Roger's high level of Scientology auditing attainment.

* * *

Soon after my conversation with Roger, which occurred in 2005, a Scientologist who owned two water damage restoration franchises retained me as a business consultant. His once highly profitable businesses were dying. I quickly identified one problem: his industry had evolved. In its early days, buying a yellow page ad was all it took to make money. But when other people saw how easy it was to set up shop and make a profit, the business became highly competitive. Profit margins were forced down, and really good management skills were increasingly necessary to survive.

Fortunately, I knew an excellent administrator who was looking for a job. I recommended Roger. The franchise owner hired him to a deal that paid Roger a healthy six-figure income.

Roger and I spent more time together because of our business connection. I tried to repair our personal relationship during that period, proceeding gingerly. Eventually, I made a breakthrough.

He confided that he had gotten into a lot of trouble for testifying as a character witness in my second application to join the California Bar in 1991 (which also failed). OSA Int., the Office of Special Affairs, International, had ordered me, under threat of *declare*, to withdraw the application after I took and passed a second bar exam. I ignored the order, and told them to *declare* me and be done with it and to stop threatening to do it.

Roger said he went through hell when he tried to get accepted onto a very high auditing level in Scientology. Admission to the level required a thorough "eligibility check." What constitutes eligibility? Here are Roger's words:

"I had three RTC representatives leaning over me and grilling me about my testimony in your Bar application case." (RTC refers to Religious Technology Center – Miscavige's official title is Chairman of the Board of RTC)

"Why?" I asked. "What was wrong with you doing that?"

"Because you were ordered not to apply," he replied.

"But you didn't know that."

"I told them that. They didn't care. It went against *command intention.*"

"Command intention" is a Miscavige term. The first time I heard it was in the early 90s. The definition I was given by an OSA Int staffer, when I was called on the carpet for violating it, was convoluted and confusing. I learned the true definition by trial and error. It means to do whatever Miscavige wants done, which he sometimes doesn't know until after someone does something he doesn't like, but if you are truly a good Scientologist you should discern it well in advance and never displease him. After what Roger said next, I refined the definition even more.

"So they raked you over the coals?" I said.

He shook his head and sighed heavily. "It was gruesome. I decided on one thing then and there: I'm *never* going to go through that again."

I knew the solution he arrived at by his behavior from that time forward: he decided to toe the line. There was another way that could have enabled him to "*never* go through that again." When I was in similar situations I took that other route. The result was that Roger was allowed to take the high level services but I was not.

My revised definition of "command intention" can be stated in one word: submit. Or, two words, really: submit fully.

This definition brings greater clarity to the words of Mike Sutter – the thirteenth person to claim responsibility for ordering me not to appeal the Florida Supreme Court's ruling disbarring me. In February 1987, he said, "... like it or not, the cold hard truth of the matter is that we're running things today, and we control the use of the technology."

In a subsequent conversation with Roger, I spoke about some of my troubles with OSA Int, all of which revolved around my not following orders. I thought OSA had no authority to issue such an order in the first place, and they were also arbitrary and harmful, I told him.

Roger said I should probably take a look at the way I approach OSA.

"So what would you do," I asked, "if you were given an order that impacted negatively on your life or profession, and you thought it was baseless and without authority?"

He said he would try and reason with the OSA staffer.

"Okay," I said. "Let's say you try that and get nowhere, and in the process learn that the person you're talking to doesn't have the authority to reason, and you become convinced that the order is completely arbitrary. What would you do then?"

"I'd comply," he said.

"Even if the order harmed you or your family?"

"Yes," he said.

"What if you also thought the order was fpotentially harmful to the church, that whoever issued the order had their head up their ass, or whatever?"

"Well," he said, "You might think I have a yellow stripe up my spine, but ..."

I wasn't thinking that. I wasn't being judgmental at all. I was astonished by his remarks, and was simply trying to reconcile this Roger with the Roger I once knew, the independent-minded, anti-establishment guy. But now that he mentioned it, yes, a yellow stripe up his spine would fit with what I was hearing.

He continued "... My attitude is that these guys joined the Sea Org and are taking responsibility for Scientology. I'm going to back them no matter what. I would defer to their judgments."

And there it was. I had my answer. The difference between him, then and now, and between him and me, was that he had fully submitted, and I had not. In fact, one of the most valuable abilities I gained from Scientology, in my estimation, was the ability to hold my ground and maintain my integrity, even in the face of tremendous peer pressure and formidable opposing forces.

I haven't heard from Roger or his family since my *declare*. I don't fault or blame him for his attitude. I still love and miss him – and his entire family.

The problem is Miscavige, the lack of internal checks and balances, and the control mechanisms he uses to maintain his absolute power over the churches of Scientology and its members, chiefly among them:

The oppressive and inhumane policy and practice of forced disconnection, of shunning disfavored members by all who remain with the church.

Chapter 37

DON ALVERZO

*One hen; two ducks; three squawking geese; four Limerick oysters;
five corpulent porpoises; six pairs of Don Alverzo's tweezers . . .*

– An old radio announcer's test

"I'm pretty sure I know you. I think I audited you in 1981," Tom Martiniano wrote in an e-mail sent to info@savescientology.com in June 2013. Like many others, Tom occasionally communicated with me, the website's anonymous administrator, about articles posted on the site's blog. As Tom did in this e-mail, many also put out feelers to learn the identity of the person who ran the site. For security purposes, and as a matter of policy, I didn't bite. I ignored this portion of his e-mail but replied to the remainder.

"I did the rollback missions back in 1981," he later wrote.

A "rollback" is an internal security measure designed to trace illegal or destructive actions and harmful statements (which are also known as an "enemy lines") to their source. An auditor trained in the rollback procedure asks each person with knowledge of a particular destructive or criminal action, "Who ordered _____ (the act)?" and asks each person who heard an enemy line, "Who said _____ (enemy line)? Reading an E-meter, the auditor rolls back the line of questioning to the source of the action or enemy line to whomever started or instigated it, in other words. Once a source is found, a thorough investigation is then conducted of that individual. Often, an outside intelligence agency is discovered to be running that person.

Martiniano's e-mail went on to state that Mary Sue Hubbard sent him a letter during his rollback missions after she stepped down from her position as controller and overseer of the Guardian's Office, but before she went to prison in early 1983. She told him that he should focus his attention on David Miscavige and Norman Starkey, both of whom she was sure were government plants.

His statement piqued my interest. I wanted to know more. But I was not ready to confirm my identity. I wrote back: "I came to a similar conclusion separately, on my own, well, not really a conclusion, but... this conversation will have to go on a back burner for another time. Would love to sit down with you for a few hours some day."

Martiniano took the conversation to another level with his next e-mail:

Paul Klopper "was a real plant and worked for Paulette Cooper who, along with Paul's dad, a big time attorney in LA, worked in conjunction with the FBI on making all legal cases of the church go south. He was my first customer on the rollback mission at U.S.G.O. Paul freely admitted it."

As mentioned earlier, Paul Klopper was the Director of the U.S.G.O. Legal Bureau and the person who appeared at the Lawyer's Conference, alongside Ann Mulligan, Mary Sue's top aide for Legal.

I replied to his e-mail: "If there were any plants in the G.O. who were sabotaging legal cases, Suspect No. 1 for me is Ann Mulligan. (Her husband, Jimmy, could also have been a plant.) But then, she was also totally incompetent.

"One last thing, and this is probably best suited for in-person comm, but I want to tie up a loose end. Some straight talk, here. I remember getting plant checked by you. No offense, but that really fucked me up."

As mentioned in the postscript to Chapter 24, Martiniano revealed to me that he was ordered to get me to confess to being implanted. Here is the text of his e-mail:

"So you know - I was ordered to do that. Not to justify, but you were delivered to me and I was told you were in deep doo-doo for the CW (Clearwater) thing and that it was vital to prove you were implanted by the FBI in order to save the Church embarrassment and possible legal trouble. Norman and Steve Marlow (the IG) were on my ass hard. They pulled me in a room and told me I had to prove the implant thing to 'save the Church.' I am horribly sorry for that and I still do think about it from time to time. It was really horrible."

Steve Marlow was the Inspector General, the then-head of Religious Technology Center (RTC) and direct subordinate of David Miscavige. I didn't know Marlow and never had any dealings with him.

"Obviously," Martiniano later added, "Miscavige was the person who issued the order. He ran Starkey and Marlow."

Martiniano's e-mail continued: "Klopper was a different story altogether. He refused to pick up the cans with me and I asked him why. He said 'If I start talking, you will end up *declaring* me.' I (repeated my request) and got him to pick up the cans. He just started talking. Told me the whole thing. I didn't have to do anything."

Martiniano went on to state that, after obtaining Klopper's full confession, he asked him to report to the Ethics office rather than escort him there. "He ran like a rabbit," and Martiniano reached him by telephone at Klopper's home in Long Beach. "He told me he was packing. I said, 'Please, what about LRH?' He laughed and said 'I'm not a Scientologist, I'm a reborn Christian' and hung up. He was gone."

Martiniano said the evidence indicated Jimmy Mulligan had knowledge of the criminal acts but did not show that he personally ordered or instigated them, which Martiniano found confusing. So he re-interviewed one of Mulligan's subordinates and uncovered his method. At staff product conferences –

where future actions and tasks are decided upon and assigned to individual staffers – Mulligan would demand solutions for obtaining desired intelligence. When one of the staff members suggested a potential solution like, "Well, we could do a B & E to get it," Mulligan would perk up as though he liked the idea, but he would never come out and tell them to do it. Instead he would say something like, "Well, you guys figure it out and get it done."

Martiniano said he went to Johnny, the person in charge of his mission, and said, "I know how Jimmy is doing it. I'm going to put him on this sec check," and handed Johnny a list of questions he wanted to ask Mulligan on the E-meter. He asked Johnny to prepare the auditing folder while he grabbed a quick bite to eat. Martiniano explained what happened next in his e-mail:

"I took the folder and went to the eighth floor (of Lebanon Hall). (Mulligan's office) door was locked and when I tried (to open it) his secretary said he wasn't there. Said he left in a hurry ten minutes ago. Said it was odd because he took personal belongings with him. I kicked the door open and there, right in the middle of his desk, on a legal pad, in long hand, was the following (I memorized it):

"'Dear Tom, I know you're coming to get me but I can't allow that. I don't want to go to jail. I want you to know that I love Scientology more than anything but I had to do this - they (the FBI) made me do it. Don't look for us in Texas, we won't be there. Yours truly, Jimmy.'

"I was stunned," Martiniano added. "I went down to Johnny's office and pulled him out on the street. I told him his office was bugged. We got the (Private Investigator) down there and he found three bugs in Johnny's office and one in each auditing room. Said they were military grade. We had him sweep all around but never found the receivers. We figured (the listening posts) were in vans on the street."

Martiniano said he presumed that Ann Mulligan, who fled with Jimmy, was also a plant, working for the FBI. He continued in his e-mail:

"That's what you were up against. The U.S.G.O. was rife with not only plants, but idiots. And I always say "Poor (Mary Sue), she was set up for the fall by (Miscavige). She was the (one positive) in the whole area and was made to take the fall."[34]

His e-mail concluded with a bare statement that struck near and dear to my heart. "Don Alverzo was another plant."

I wanted to know more.

* * *

"Tell me why you think Don Alverzo was a plant?" I said to Martiniano in my home when we met in June 2013 for the first time since early 1982.

He explained that he had been on two rollback missions. The first one was inside U.S.G.O. in Los Angeles. He had learned that Paul Klopper and Jimmy Mulligan were FBI plants, and presumably Ann as well. The second rollback mission went inside the G.O.'s worldwide headquarters in England.

"We kept index cards and made a chart with arrows connecting criminal acts and enemy lines to individuals." (An enemy line is a false and harmful statement spread internally with the purpose of having it accepted as fact.) "We interviewed G.O. staff or read their write-ups."

His statement reminded me of the process U.S.G.O. staff underwent after the takeover, as described in Chapter 22. Everyone had to provide detailed write-ups of their activities for the G.O. that were illegal or potentially harmful to the church.

"All arrows pointed to Don Alverzo," Martiniano said. "I pulled him in for a security check. He kept giving me different names." One of the questions on a standard security check asks whether the person under investigation goes by an alias. If the E-meter "reads," the auditor is trained to get the alias and all the details associated with its use until the needle freely and smoothly moves from side to side. The operator rechecks the question to make sure the needle no longer reacts. If it does still react, the operator asks for another alias. Martiniano said the E-meter kept reacting and he kept pulling more aliases out of Alverzo.

"The very first time I asked the question, I got a long read," Martiniano said. He gave me a different name and I cleared the needle. I rechecked the question. Same read. At first, Don said no, he didn't use another name, but then he gave me one, which cleared the needle. I went back to recheck the question. It reads again. I told him to come clean, and he said there were no more names."

I asked Martiniano if he remembered either of the names Alverzo gave him, and he said he didn't. "Was Jerry Levin one of them?" I asked. He said the name rang a bell but he couldn't say for sure.

"After the third name he gave up didn't clear the needle, I leaned on him. Don, or whatever his name was, was steadfast, a cool cucumber. He insisted he was telling the truth. I then thought back to his cover story, a helicopter pilot in Vietnam. I called bullshit on his Vietnam history. I told him that I fought in Vietnam and didn't believe his history.[35] Don stood by it."

Martiniano began to recite his conversation with Don. "Okay, what did you do there? 'Flew Huey 1Ds,' he said. Out of what bases? He named several bases, including Phu Cat. I had not been to any of them, but I had ridden in plenty of Huey 1Ds. So I asked Don what the takeoff rpm of the Huey 1D was, and he said, '33,000.'

"'No, it isn't,' I said to him. For the first time Don took on a forlorn, worried look, like a deer in the headlights."

"What is the takeoff rpm of a Huey 1D?" I asked.

"Hell, I didn't know," he replied. "But I knew it wasn't 33,000."[36]

"So what happened next?"

"I told him to pick up the cans and come clean with me. He motioned for me to go outside and I went along, wondering what he was up to. We walked a little bit and then he said that we were being monitored and watched. I asked where, and he pointed all around. I wasn't buying any of it. I said, 'Listen, you need to come clean with me.'

At first he said that he and his wife would go to jail if he talked. But then he more or less admitted that he was working for someone and they had threatened him. He said, 'They will kill my family if I talk.' He tended to talk in alarming terms.

"I took the Sea Org insignia off my shoulders and told Don that he was going to talk or I was going to beat it out of him. He calmly said that beating him up wouldn't work, it would only get me in trouble. I knew he was right. All I could do was write it all up, which is what I did. I let him go and wrote it up."

"Why didn't the church *declare* him?"

"Probably based on my report. I warned that he was dangerous and should not be allowed back into the United States. All our arrows pointed to Alverzo for the 'enemy line' that LRH was the source of G.O. crimes, and he kept dropping LRH's name as the authority for his criminal actions, which I took as a subtle threat that he would say the same thing to authorities if I or the church went too far with him."

Martiniano said he never got any feedback from his report, and assumed that everyone thought Don was too hot of a potato to mess with, although Martiniano later told me, after learning more about my background, that he wished he had been given an expert in FBI COINTELPRO, intelligence and the law like me to work with. "I was just a mild-mannered auditor when I was pulled in to do the rollback missions. I really didn't know what to do with a guy like Don Alverzo."

"Who did Alverzo work for?" I asked.

"He didn't say. I guess Interpol, because he once said that if I leaned on him too much that he would melt into Europe. Who talks like that? Ordinary people can't 'melt into Europe' by themselves. Also because of something that happened a few days later.

"I was standing on the edge of a street [in England] waiting for a bus. A female Sea Org member who was part of my mission was with me. A fancy Mercedes with gold trim pulled up to the curb and the driver stepped out, a guy with red hair wearing a tightly fitted leather jacket, a kind of reddish brown with matching pants, and a gold wristwatch.

"He walked up to me and asked me in English with a German accent, 'Are you Tom Martiniano?' I told him I was. The man raised his hand in the shape of a handgun, with his forefinger pointed in my face, and said, 'Bang, you're a dead man.' I was staring at him in disbelief when the guy repeated the exercise, expressions and all. 'Bang, you're a dead man.' He then turned and got back into his car and drove off.

"As he pulled away, the girl next to me said, 'Who the fuck was that?'

"Interpol, I told her." Martiniano said he interpreted the episode as a warning to leave Alverzo alone or he would be killed, meaning that Alverzo had reported him to his handlers."

Martiniano asked, "You worked with him. What did you think? Was he a plant?"

"I gotta tell you, Tom. I loved the guy. He was a kick to work with and be around. I also loved Molly. Fran and I really enjoyed them both. So, my heart says no. And I am rarely wrong about people – and I have *never* been *this* wrong about someone. I mean, if he was sent in as a plant, I blew this one completely."

The word duped came to mind, which made me think of John Fernandez, the Bar prosecutor telling my lawyer, Bennie Lazzara, that he thought I had been duped. And I remembered protesting his opinion, insisting that I had not been. Of course, Fernandez meant that I had been duped by the church, or at least by the G.O. I'm sure he didn't want to hear about me, the church and the G.O. all being duped by an FBI agent provocateur.

"On the other hand," I said. "Personal feelings aside, the facts present a compelling case that he was a plant from the get-go. His skills in intelligence and clandestine know-how were par excellence. I have never read in any spy novel, or seen in any spy movie, a character more adept at his craft. You don't learn skills like that flying a helicopter in Vietnam or by reading a book."

I disclosed that my emotional feelings toward Don, and Fran's and my feelings for him and Molly, had not been reciprocated. "I mean, if our roles were reversed, I would have contacted him years ago, bought him a beer, thrown an arm around his shoulder, and said whatever it took to convey my sympathy for him getting run over by a bus that I had set in motion.

"He didn't do that or anything I consider remotely close to that."

Martiniano reiterated his one hundred percent conviction that Alverzo was a spy, sent into the G.O. to bring about its downfall, put LRH on the run, and allow someone like Miscavige, who was also a plant, to take control. He asked for my opinion on the overall scene from an intelligence perspective.

I began by saying, "Wes Swearingen, former Special Agent in Charge of the Los Angeles Field Office of the FBI, once said to me regarding COINTELPRO: 'If you can imagine it, it probably happened.'"

Then I gave him my intelligence analysis, which I cautioned was not a finding of fact based on admissible evidence, but rather was an estimate of probabilities based on all known facts and the expertise of the analyst. An intelligence analysis is dynamic, meant to be updated with new information and greater insight, which went something like this:

Don Alverzo was a well trained intelligence agent embedded into the G.O. with instructions to instigate criminal activities. I doubt he was Interpol. He was likely FBI, possibly CIA. Both agencies are highly skilled in clandestine arts such as black bag jobs. They usually stay off each other's turf. The FBI is domestic, CIA is foreign. His mission was to sabotage the G.O., instigate criminal acts into the culture of the G.O. and get them endorsed by Jane Kember, Mary Sue, and even by LRH, if he could, and if he couldn't bring LRH into the criminal activity, to at least create that impression by spreading the idea. The one name Alverzo refused to give up to you in his security check was his code name. FBI documents are indexed by names. If someone goes after his FBI informant file pursuant to the Freedom of Information Act, they will need his code name, as you do with CIA or other intelligence agencies.

Sometime before or soon after the FBI raided the G.O. offices in Los Angeles and Washington, the feds put on a full court press to turn high-ranking G.O. members into informants. They turned Paul Klopper by going through his father, a top Los Angeles lawyer, which is also how their communication channel ran: Paul reported to his father, who reported to the FBI, and vice versa, thereby providing a buffer and cloaking their communications with the attorney-client privilege.

The FBI turned Jimmy and Ann Mulligan some time after Jimmy became exposed to criminal liability, which occurred as early as 1972. Next to Alverzo, Jimmy Mulligan was most responsible for G.O. criminal activity. G.O. executives above and below him in the chain of command went to jail. Neither of the two most culpable persons were indicted or served time. This fact alone is a gigantic red flag.

Miscavige was a cunning opportunist with a lust for power. He volunteered to head the fact-finding mission into the G.O. that LRH ordered after the raids occurred. Miscavige is a quick learner and was devious enough to see a golden opportunity. LRH was aging, in poor health, isolated, under threat of criminal indictment, and subject to being subpoenaed for depositions in the lawsuits. G.O. leadership was weak and vulnerable as a result of the culture of criminal conduct instigated by Alverzo. Miscavige found plenty of evidence to support his damning reports to LRH, and he painted the worst picture imaginable in order to obtain LRH's endorsement of the G.O.'s takeover – five months *after* it occurred, according to a later statement by Miscavige.[37] He subverted the checks and balances LRH implemented and then eliminated his potential rivals after LRH's death. He kept LRH isolated, with severely limited access to church staff by making sure the legal cases involving him were not resolved until after his death, then Miscavige settled them within months, proving that he knew all along how to resolve them quickly.

The FBI and intelligence community desperately wanted to shatter the G.O.'s intelligence network and remove LRH and Mary Sue from power – two persons who could not be controlled or compromised.

A 1965 comment from L. Ron Hubbard is interesting. He said the efforts of the United States government since 1955, which stepped up in 1963, were directed at taking control of Scientology rather than forbidding or stopping it.[38]

Miscavige, with Starkey by his side, contacted the FBI and cut a deal. Leave LRH alone and they, Miscavige and Starkey, would take down the G.O. and cover up the FBI's role in both the takeover and all previous counterintelligence operations against the church. Starkey's motive was that he loved and was deeply loyal to LRH. He was not that bright, however, and he was totally under the thumb of Miscavige. Terri Gamboa told me that Miscavige demeaned and disciplined Starkey more than any other staff member. She said he had been a decent, compassionate guy, and that I just saw a clone of Miscavige that had been hammered into Starkey to ensure that his orders were carried out.

"I think it is telling that Miscavige ordered you, through Starkey, to obtain a false admission from me that I was a plant, and not just any plant but an FBI plant, right after my notes suspecting *them* of being FBI plants were discovered and confiscated."

Take my assessment of probabilities for what it is. Everything that happened can also be explained by incompetence, stupidity or in other lesser malignant ways. Heinlein's Razor[39] may apply: *'Never attribute to malice that which is adequately explained by incompetence, but don't rule out malice.'*

Besides, I don't think it matters that much how we got to this point. The situation with which we are confronted is the same, regardless of how it came to be. Corporate checks and balances designed by LRH need to be reinstated, transparency instituted and the church reformed. Disconnection, security checks and the Fair Game policies need to be forever abolished. The technology, or religion, of Scientology is what matters. The churches of Scientology are institutions. LRH's view, as expressed in his estate plan, was that the churches are valuable only so long as, and to the degree that further the aims of the religion. The church in its current form – CST, RTC and CSI – is clearly not aligned with that purpose. Today, it is merely a corporate alter ego of David Miscavige. Miscavige doing business as CST, RTC and CSI. It is being used by him to mold and control the behavior of its members to keep them from thinking for themselves in order to protect his kingdom.

It can be fixed. The trustees and directors of CST should be educated and counseled about their legal duties and how to carry them out; the attorney generals of the states in which Scientology organizations operate, especially California, should enforce the laws requiring independent boards, and reconstitute them; and the IRS should mandate the implementation of checks and balances and the independent boards through its power to impose "Intermediate Sanctions" on tax-exempt organizations.

We're working on it. Stay tuned to the Save Scientology website and help make it happen, if you're interested.

Fran's senior prom, May 1968

Our wedding, June 1969

Easter, 1969

At Angie's wedding, 1991

EPILOGUE

In 1985 I ran into Alverzo. A mutual friend told me he was in Los Angeles and wanted to get together with old friends and had named me as one. We met in a reserved room in the back of a pizzeria. Alverzo sat across a broad table from me with about ten others present. We barely spoke one-on-one. I understood. Litigation was ongoing.

"Sorry about your legal troubles," he said. I nodded and said, "Some day I would like to talk." He nodded to that.

The problem was, I didn't know his real name or address; he controlled my access to him. All my communications went through the mutual friend, from whom I once asked for Alverzo's address so I could correspond with him. "I'll run it by Don," he said and later told me that Alverzo preferred that I communicate through him. "Put it in a sealed envelope and give it to me. I'll pass it on without opening it."

I guessed that Alverzo didn't want me to know his real name, but didn't say that to the friend because I didn't want to reveal that I knew Don went by an alias. I settled for exchanging occasional hellos through the intermediary, and in time even those faded away.

After I began in earnest to write this book, which rekindled old memories and lingering questions, I resolved to discover his real name and address and contact him directly. Not that I expected him to talk. Since he knew how to reach me and hadn't over the many years when it was legally safe to do so it appeared that he didn't want to. If Alverzo was indeed an agent provocateur he may have been under orders and therefore had a professional obligation not to reveal his real name or get personal with me. In fact, I thought his reaction to a contact from me might establish whether or not he was an agent since, on a purely personal basis, he owed me the courtesy of a reply at a minimum.

A private investigator assisted me. We spun our wheels for many hours and days. Finally, I came across a picture of Molly, Fran's handler in Clearwater. "We should be hunting for Molly, not Don," I said. "They married in the fall of 1976 when they worked in Clearwater." I floated Molly's picture and asked people from that era for a last name. I also did an internet search to find the names for which Molly was a nickname, and came up with Margaret and Mary.

The last name *Harlow* came back from a person who saw the picture.

The investigator ran those first and last names through the Pinellas County marriage license records. His search came back empty. Back to the drawing board. As I was nearing my wits' end, my phone rang. "Check your e-mail," the investigator said. I noticed an undertone of triumph in his words. I hung up and hurriedly opened my inbox.

Attached to his e-mail was a Hillsborough County marriage license. Mary Harrison Harlow and Jeffrey Kim Marino, wed on November 16, 1976, witnessed by three people I knew to be former Flag G.O. staff members. Bingo!

The investigator ran the name Jeffrey Marino through data bases and provided me with Jeff Marino's business and work addresses, phone numbers and a wealth of other information. Marino was the president of his family business. I checked the company's website – and sure enough – there was a picture of the person I knew as Don Alverzo. I was thrilled. Finally, after all these years, I had a real name and contact information.

I called Tom Martiniano. "Was Jeff Marino one of the names Alverzo gave you?"

"Yes, I believe it was," he said with a spark in his voice.

"That's his real name," I said. "Man, the guy has led the life of Riley. Several nice residences, president of his family business which has more than one location on Long Island, and what really stuck out: he has a clean, I mean super clean, Google search page. Compared to mine, and those of others he touched, it doesn't seem right."

The next day, I placed a call to one of two business numbers. As I waited for someone to pick up, I was jittery. Thirty-seven years of pent-up questions and emotions swirled through me. I reminded myself to keep it simple, to move one step at a time. The serious subjects would have to be discussed in person. A male voice came on the line. I asked for Jeff Marino. Man, hearing that name come out of my mouth for him felt weird.

"Jeff works at the other yard. Plus, he doesn't come in until the afternoon." I felt the arrow plunge deeper into my back. Dude was semi-retired.

It was still morning in New York, so I called one of the residence numbers listed with his name. A default voice recording asked me to leave a message. It did not give a name. I hung up and called one of the cell phone numbers I had for him. I reached the recording of a younger man's voice who gave his name (last name Marino). I assumed it was Jeff and Molly's son. I left a detailed message, giving my name and number and said I was an old friend trying to reach Jeff and Molly, and asked that my message be passed on to them.

By the time I called the other yard, it was closed for the day. I tried the residence number again, and got the recording. This time I left a detailed message.

The following Monday, after hearing nothing back, I called the "other yard" early in the afternoon New York time. A man answered and said that Jeff was not available but that he could page him. I gave him my phone number, then asked to speak with Molly, who managed the company's finances according to my information. She was also not available but could be paged. I asked when Jeff might return. "I don't know," he said. "He's the boss." He offered to put my messages on the bulletin board. "That way, they will definitely see them." I told him to do that.

Neither Jeff nor Molly returned any of my messages. I assume it was because of professional obligations, nothing personal.

END NOTES

1. The length of the contract is symbolic of the commitment to accomplish the aims of Scientology – the spiritual salvation of all persons – no matter how long it takes, and should not be taken literally.

2. Richard (Murphy) did not play football in high school. That summer he was injured in an accident involving farm machinery and one of his legs had to be amputated just below the knee.

3. Food and Drug Administration.

4. *Founding Church of Scientology of Washington, D. C. v. U.S.* (1969) 409 F2d. 1161.

5. Both Sam Miller and Murphy are aliases. Real names not recalled.

6. An alias. Real name not recalled.

7. Dr. James Springer is an alias – for privacy reasons, and also to protect his daughter who assisted me in my research for this chapter. Rex Banks is also an alias – I don't recall his real name, and there would be privacy considerations if I did.

8. In 1977 Anita Bryant was singing about Florida orange juice and leading anti-gay crusades. Today, the patronizing of gay bars is a recognized right and an impermissible subject for cross-examination. Indeed, as of January 6, 2015, same-sex marriage is legal in Florida.

9. Rita Flemming is an alias, as is the name of her organization, neither of which I recall or was able to discover through research.

10. Logan later became a circuit court judge in Florida's Sixth Judicial Circuit, which serves Pinellas and Pasco Counties. He retired in 2015.

11. Not from an actual transcript, which I could not locate.

12. For these two, and 130 other Scientology assists that anyone can learn to perform, see the Assists Processing Handbook by L. Ron Hubbard.

13. French for "inciting agent."

14. Burton also was a contributor to *The Age of Surveillance* by Frank J. Donner.

15. U.S. Drug Enforcement Agency.

16. Hubbard, The Journal of Scientology, Issue 3-G, Sept 1952, "Danger: Black Dianetics!"

17. http://counsellingresource.com/features/2011/11/08/gaslighting/

18. The word "declare" is italicized whenever used as a verb with this Scientology meaning.

19. The word "Declare" is capitalized whenever it is used as a noun referring to the order itself.

20. This and all subsequent dialogue put in transcript form are based partly on memory, partly on transcripts in my possession, and partly from motions and appeal briefs that quoted from transcripts of the record.

21. *The Dangers of Dissent: The FBI and Civil Liberties Since 1965*, Lexington Books; Greenberg also authored: *Surveillance in America: Critical Analysis of the FBI, 1920 to the Present*.

22. In 1986 a jury awarded Wollersheim $31 million. The church appealed and continued to litigate the case until it finally agreed to settle. It paid $8.7 million on May 9, 2002.

23. September 1980 was the (wrong) date given on my G.O. application that was obtained from the church by civil litigants who gave it to the Florida Bar. I signed my G.O. contract in March 1980.

24. .From *An Essay on Management*.

25. After over 20 years of litigation, the church paid $8.7 million to settle the Wollersheim case in 2002.

26. (Since the publication of the article, the *St. Petersburg Times* became the *Tampa Bay Times*.)
http://www.tampabay.com/news/scientology-the-truth-rundown-part-1-of-3-in-a-special-report-on-the/1012148

27. http://www.tampabay.com/specials/2009/reports/project/rathbun.shtml

28. Letterhead is obviously an alias. So is Chris. I do not have permission to use their real names. Obviously, Letterhead's real name is known to the recipients of his letters, but his role in sending the letters has not been publicly revealed as of this writing.

29. The False Claims Act is a federal law that imposes liability on persons and companies (typically federal contractors) who defraud governmental programs. It is the federal government's primary tool in combating fraud.

30. http://www.tampabay.com/specials/2009/reports/project/rathbun.shtml

31. *Haunted House* was the name of the film that was later distributed on DVD by The Asylum, but which is now out of print. For more information, see:
http://www.hauntedhousemovie.net/

32. http://en.wikipedia.org/wiki/The_Hole_%28Scientology%29

33.Roger Nevins is an alias for privacy reasons.

34. Mary Sue Hubbard served a year in prison beginning in January 1983 after exhausting her appeals against her conviction. She died of breast cancer in 2002.

35. Martiniano wrote a book entitled, *Vietnam: Teenage Wasteland*, about his experience in Vietnam. I loved the book and recommend it highly. It is available at Amazon Books.

36. According to Wikipedia, the takeoff rpm of the Huey 1D is 6,600.

37. "The Man Behind Scientology," Part 3, *St. Petersburg Times* (Oct 25, 1998 edition).

http://www.sptimes.com/TampaBay/102598/scientologypart3.html

38. Scientology Policy Letter 14 Jun 65 Issue III "Politics, Freedom from"

39. A razor, used in this sense, refers to the act of shaving away unnecessary assumptions to get to the simplest explanation. Heinlein is science fiction writer Robert A. Heinlein, who had one character say to another, in his 1941 novella, *Logic of Empire*, "You have attributed conditions to villainy that simply result from stupidity."